IMAGES
of America

MERRIMACK

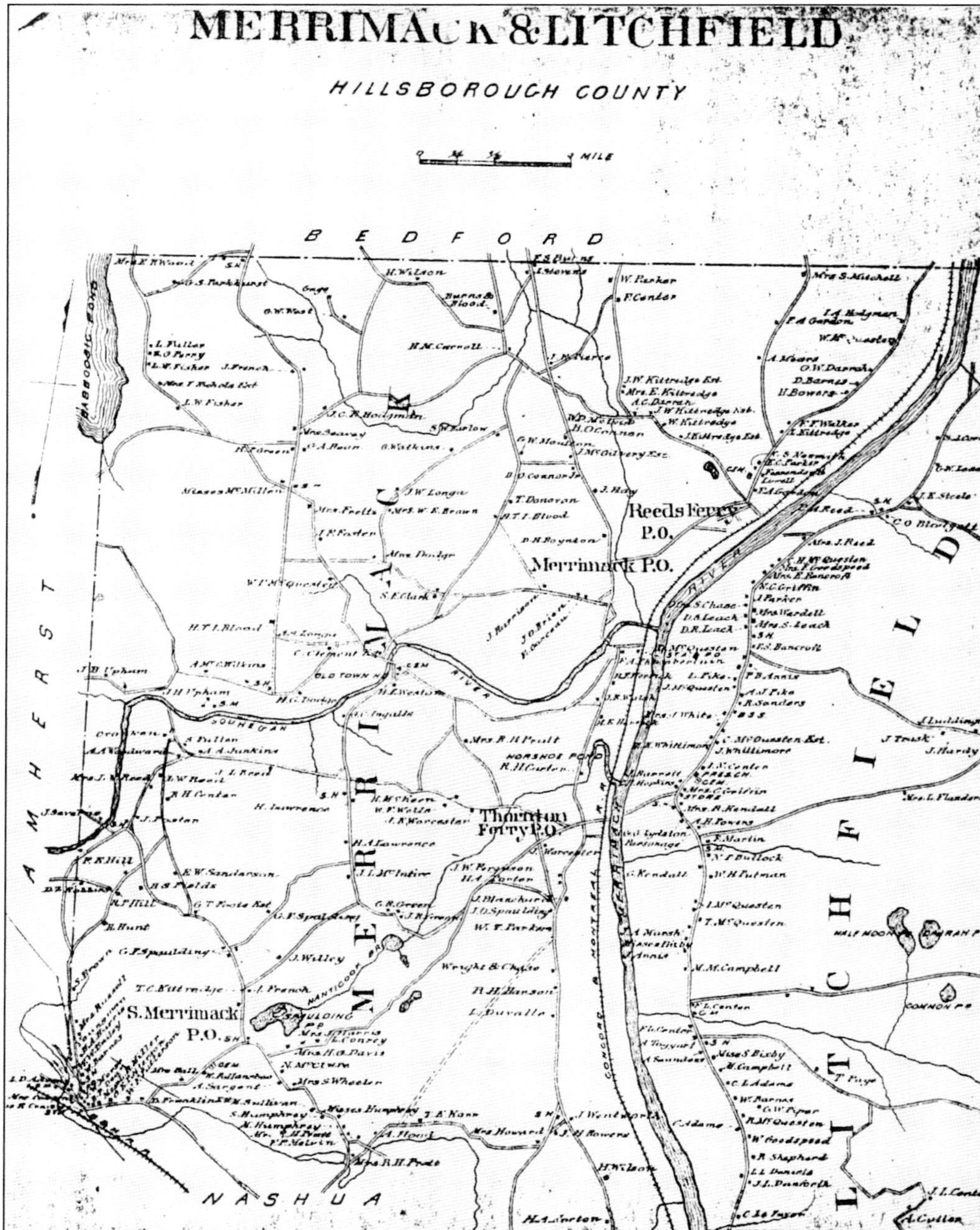
MERRIMACK & LITCHFIELD
HILLSBOROUGH COUNTY
MILE
BEDFORD
AMHERST
NASHUA
MERRIMACK
LITCHFIELD
Reeds Ferry P.O.
Merrimack P.O.
Thornton Ferry P.O.
S. Merrimack P.O.
SOUHEGAN RIVER
HORSHOE POND
HALF MOON P.
DARRAH P.
COMMON P.

IMAGES
of America

MERRIMACK

Merrimack Historic Committee
250th Anniversary Celebration

ARCADIA
PUBLISHING

ISBN 978-0-7385-8960-2

Published by Arcadia Publishing
Charleston, South Carolina

Printed in the United States of America

For all general information contact Arcadia Publishing at:
Telephone 843-853-2070
Fax 843-853-0044
E-mail sales@arcadiapublishing.com
For customer service and orders:
Toll-Free 1-888-313-2665

Visit us on the Internet at www.arcadiapublishing.com

Contents

Acknowledgments

This book was made possible by the efforts of many people. Rosemary Gagne brought the idea to the 250th Anniversary Committee with all the information needed to publish a book. A committee was quickly formed and work on the book started. The committee members are Joyce Bishop, Barbara Condon, Rosemary Gagne, and Ruth Liberty. Barbara Condon was appointed chairperson.

The pictures of Merrimack used in this book were obtained from many sources. We wish to thank the following people for the loan of their photographs: Kevin and Phyllis Annis, Helen Burghardt, Barbara Condon, Lorraine Cox, Dwight Damon, Patricia Daniels, Emma Dodge, Roland Doty, Stanley Drobysh, Isabelle Duxbury, Rosemary Gagne, Ann Giacapuzzi, Betty Getz, Doris Green, Charles and Elaine Hall, Frank Hall, Patsy Heywood, Andrea and Kevin Hieken, Donald R. Johnson, Detective Ronald Ketchie, Henry Kiestlinger, Gilda Kremer, John Lastowka Jr., Doris MacIntyre, Myrna Martelose, Dennis McGivern (Friends of Kids Kove), the Merrimack Chamber of Commerce, the Merrimack Conservation Commission (Linda Wilson), the Merrimack Parks and Recreation Department, Patricia Morrill, Elaine Paquin, Irene Peterson, Arlean Pike, Richard Price, Joseph Pynenburg Jr., Joseph Raycraft, Fay and Glenna Read, the Republican Women's Club (Yvonne Hinkley), Denise Roy, Marguerite Ryan, Donald Smith, Lynda Tomasian, Clayton and Laila Todd, the Town of Merrimack, Electa Thresher, Louis and Rachel Watkins, Otis Whittaker, Clarence and Josephine Worster, and Cecile Yanuzenski. We also extend our thanks to Brian Lawrence of Cameraland for making copies of many of the photographs, and all the friends, residents, former residents, and organizations of the town of Merrimack, who helped make this book possible.

Merrimack Historic Commission
250th Anniversary Celebration

Introduction

This year the town of Merrimack is 250 years old. This book was compiled in commemoration of that anniversary. It is not a history and was never intended to be one. It is merely a collection of pictures, depicting the life and times of Merrimack. We include the following only as background.

In 1746, when Merrimack was incorporated, less than fifty families lived here. Pawtucket, Nashuaway, and Penacook Indians camped along the banks of the Souhegan and Merrimack Rivers. The Penacooks were the greatest in number and their chief, Passaconaway, was the ruler of all the tribes in the Merrimack Valley.

The rivers were the main source of travel. Merrimack had two ferry landings on the Merrimack River: Reed's Ferry was at the northern end of town, while Thornton's Ferry was at the southern end. There were taverns near the ferries to accommodate travelers. The taverns were also used by the men of Merrimack for socializing and catching up on news.

There were few stores and no schools. Industry consisted of saw and grist mills; one or the other was located on every pond, stream, and waterway. Most of the residents were farmers. A site for a meetinghouse was determined, a cemetery fenced, and a minister chosen: life began in Merrimack.

The nineteenth century saw the town grow a great deal. It soon became apparent that the meetinghouse was too small and too far from the center of town, so as the church and government separated, two new churches were built in more convenient locations: one in South Merrimack and the other on Baboosic Lake Road. A new town hall was built to replace the meetinghouse. The need for schools was recognized and soon Merrimack had eight one or two-room schoolhouses. Later, the number increased to twelve, and each neighborhood had its own school, as there was no transportation for the children. School was taught in the summer and winter only; in the spring and fall children were needed to work on the farms, because very little labor was imported. Near the end of the century, a form of higher education appeared in Merrimack: the McGaw Normal Institute, a teachers' college, was opened in Reed's Ferry. It later became the high school, only to be torn down when the present high school was built on McElwain Street.

Industry changed to brickyards and bricks were floated on barges down the Merrimack River to be sold in Lowell, Massachusetts. In Reed's Ferry, a cooperage shop was built by the Fessenden and Lowell Company. The Old White Mill, on Main Street, saw many changes over the years.

Built as a woolen mill, it became a tannery, and then several small companies operated there. It is now a chemical company.

When the railroad came to town the trains stopped at four locations. Two of the depots still exist today. One is a business and the other is part of a private home.

Merrimack eventually split into four districts: Reed's Ferry, Souhegan Village, Thornton's Ferry, and South Merrimack. Each had its own post office, schools, stores, and social life.

The town flourished in the twentieth century as its population increased. The small neighborhood schools closed and three elementary schools, a middle school, and a high school were built. Farms were replaced with developments, apartments, and condominiums. Industry changed once again; modern facilities housed manufacturers of paper products, furniture, and electronics. A brewery and hamlet were opened, and the Clydesdales moved to Merrimack. Stores become shopping malls.

The onetime volunteer fire department grew to a full-time force with three fire stations. The police department got its own facilities. The Town Hall, the library, and the schools all had additions built.

Roads, which had once been mostly dirt and only one-car wide, were improved and paved. Highways were built and the small town disappeared forever. As we approach the twenty-first century, we are once again faced with growth problems and changes. Buildings are too small and schools are crowded. The population has continued to increase and travel has taken its toll on the roads. History repeats itself and life goes on as it has for 250 years.

As you look through this book, keep in mind it is not a history of Merrimack. It is simply a stroll down Memory Lane.

One

Buildings

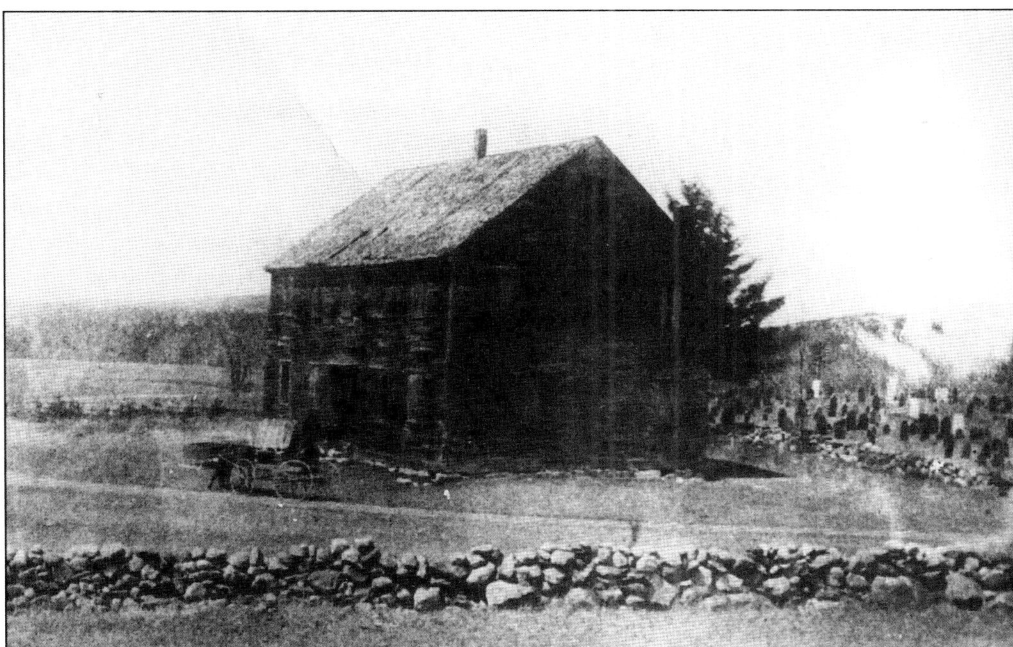

THE FIRST MEETINGHOUSE. In 1751 plans were made to build a meetinghouse at the exact center of town. The building stood at the corner of Turkey Hill Road and Meetinghouse Road until it burned to the ground in 1896. The granite step now marks the site.

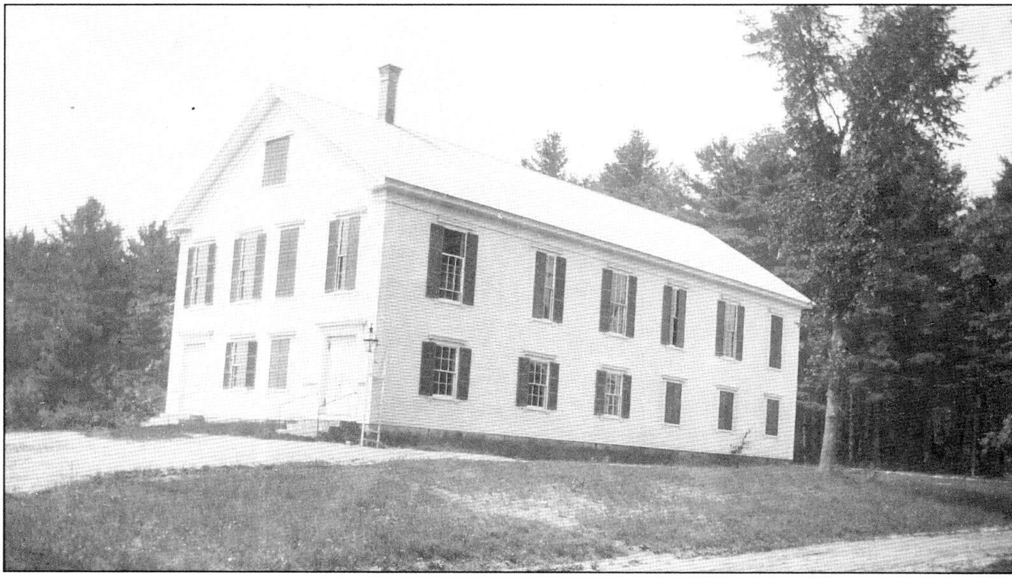

THE TOWN HALL—WEST WING. Merrimack's first municipal building was built on Baboosic Lake Road in 1872. Many remember town meetings held on the second floor with dinner served downstairs by the ladies of the town. The first floor consisted of a kitchen, dining room, and selectmen's office. The second floor featured a meeting room with a stage.

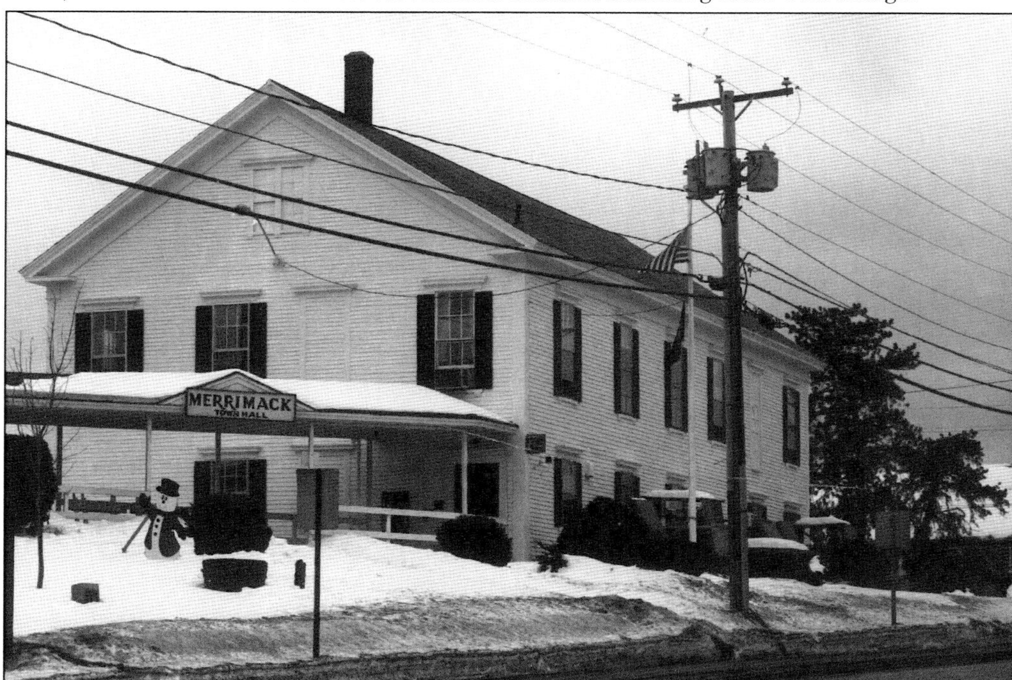

THE TOWN HALL ADDITION. The original Town Hall was added to in 1980 creating the current Town Hall complex. The town clerk/tax collector and selectmen's offices are housed in the east wing as well as the assessing, finance, and police departments. The planning, building, and code enforcement departments and the Merrimack District Court occupy the west wing.

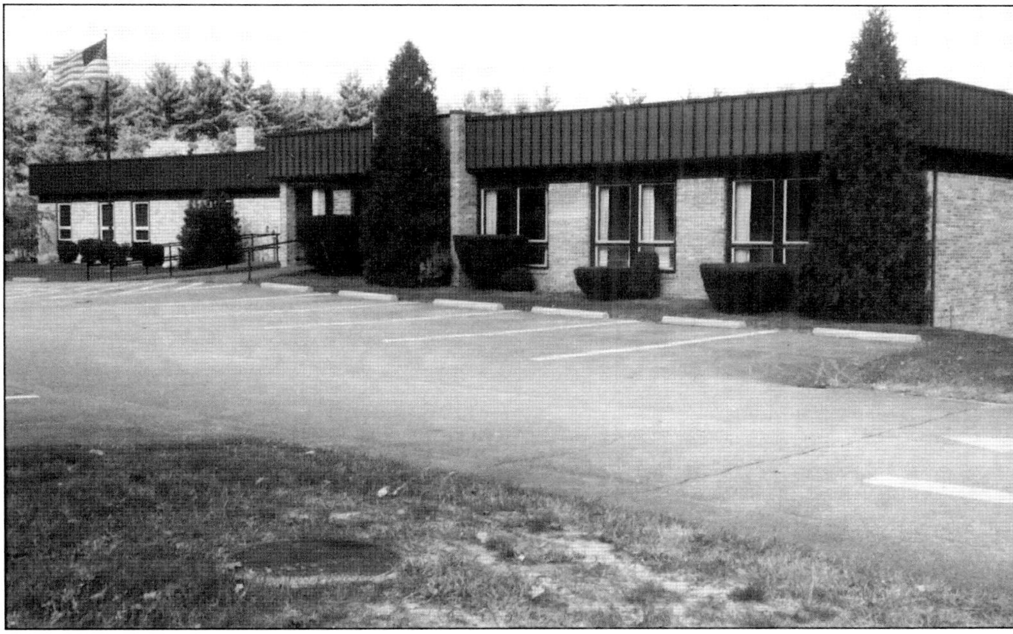

THE MERRIMACK MEDICAL CENTER. When the question arose of how to attract a resident physician, it was determined that Merrimack would have to build a medical center. The center on Baboosic Lake Road was built in 1960. At the 25th Anniversary Celebration, the buildings were dedicated to G. Donald Deveraux and Lillian Davis.

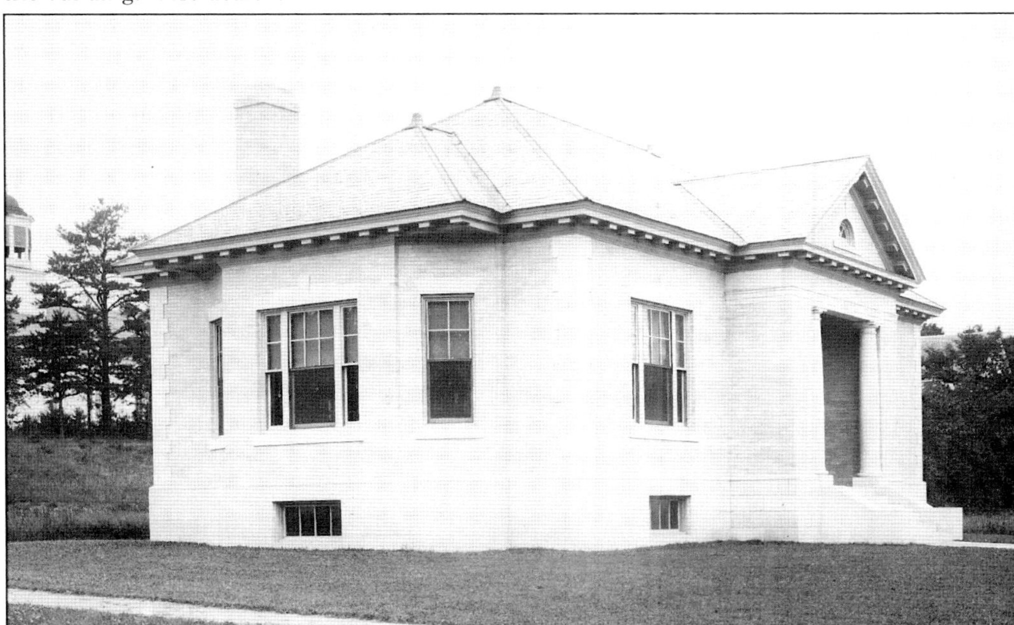

THE MERRIMACK PUBLIC LIBRARY. Merrimack's first public library was located in the home of Emma Cross on Loop Road. In 1925, the Lowell Memorial Library was built on Route 3. The addition was added in 1979. Some of the rooms in the library are dedicated in memory of local residents.

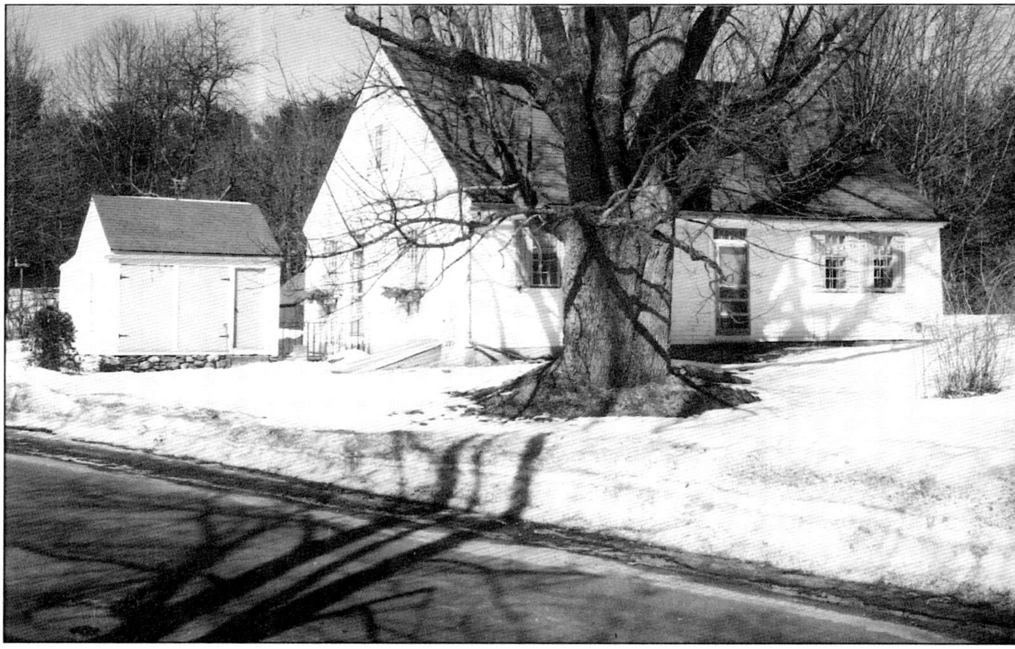

THE KENT HOMESTEAD. This Cape-style house was built on Peaslee Road in 1798 by Jonathan Wheeler. When he died, it passed to his daughter, then to her daughters. G. Harold Kent inherited the homestead from his father, who had married first one then the other daughter. This property, therefore, has always been owned by the family of Jonathan Wheeler.

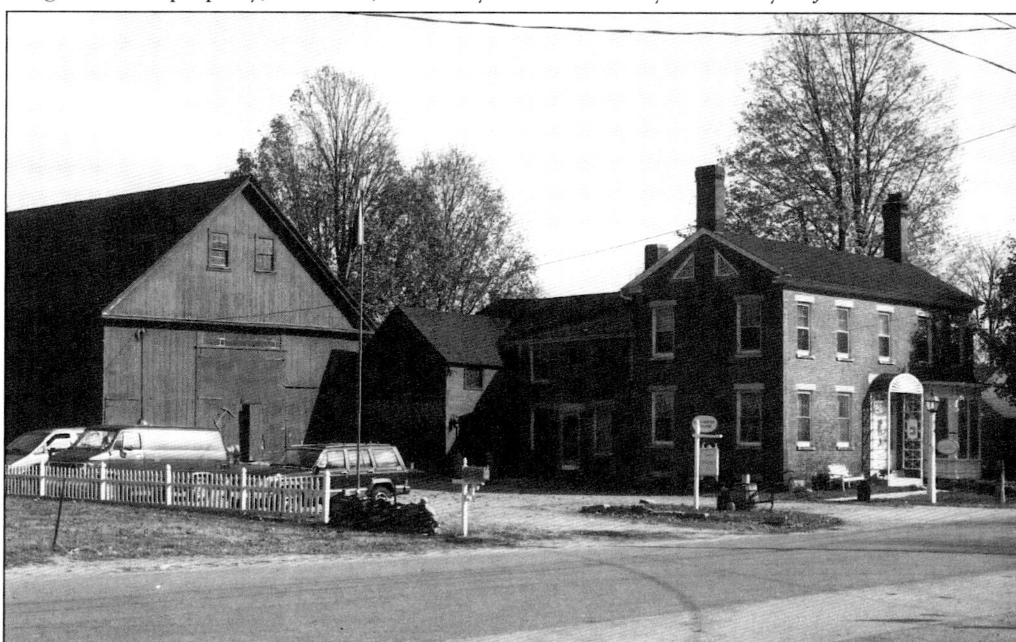

THE MOWER HOMESTEAD. The former home of Reverend Stephen Allen, this house on Depot Street is a fine example of the few remaining brick houses in Merrimack. Brick houses date back to the early 1800s. The ell constructed of wood was probably built at an earlier date.

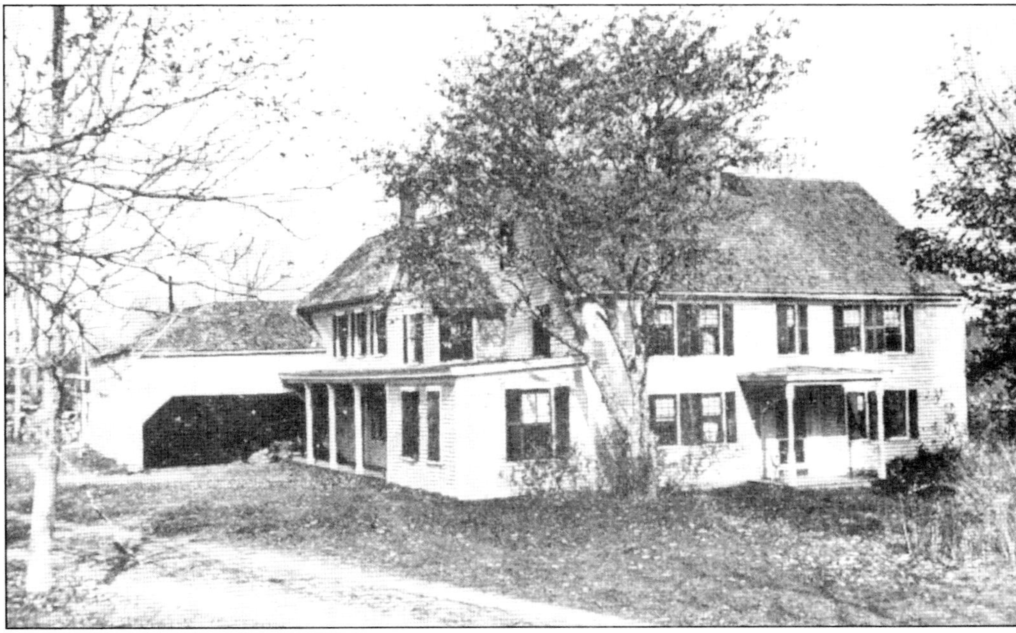

THE SPAULDING HOMESTEAD. The Spaulding family owned this house on Peaslee Road until the late 1950s. Reverend Charles S. Haynes, who married a Spaulding, lived here from 1901 until his death. The house originally had carved moldings depicting hearts over the interior doors. It is said this meant it was built for a bride. It was also known as Appledorn Farm.

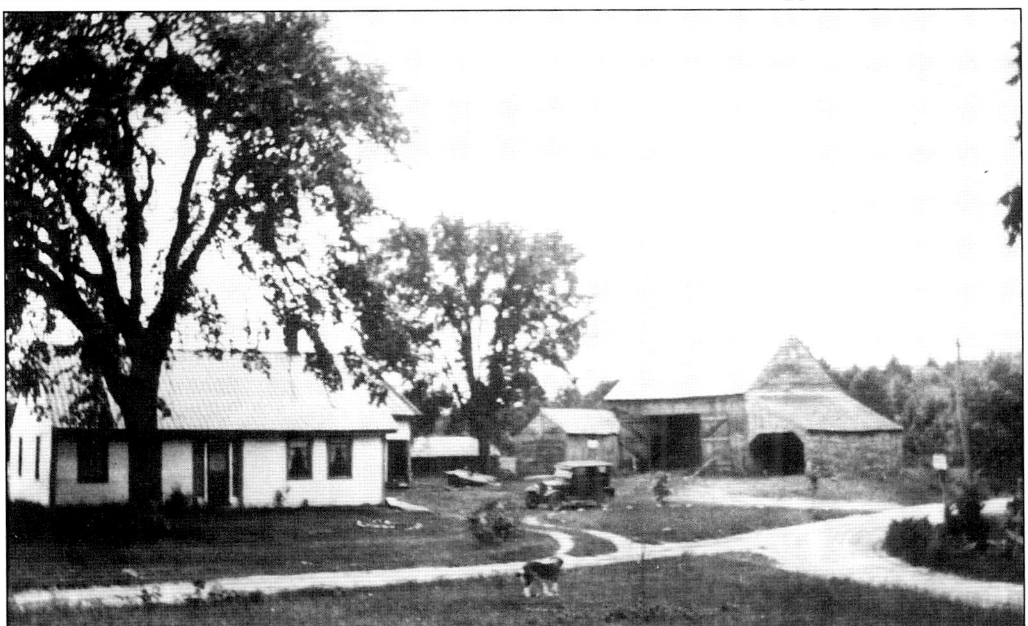

THE WESTON HOMESTEAD. The first home of Reverend Burnap was this farm located on Meetinghouse Road. The Reverend and his family lived here for twenty years before moving to a larger house on the other side of the river. The barn has been torn down and the interior of the house has seen many changes.

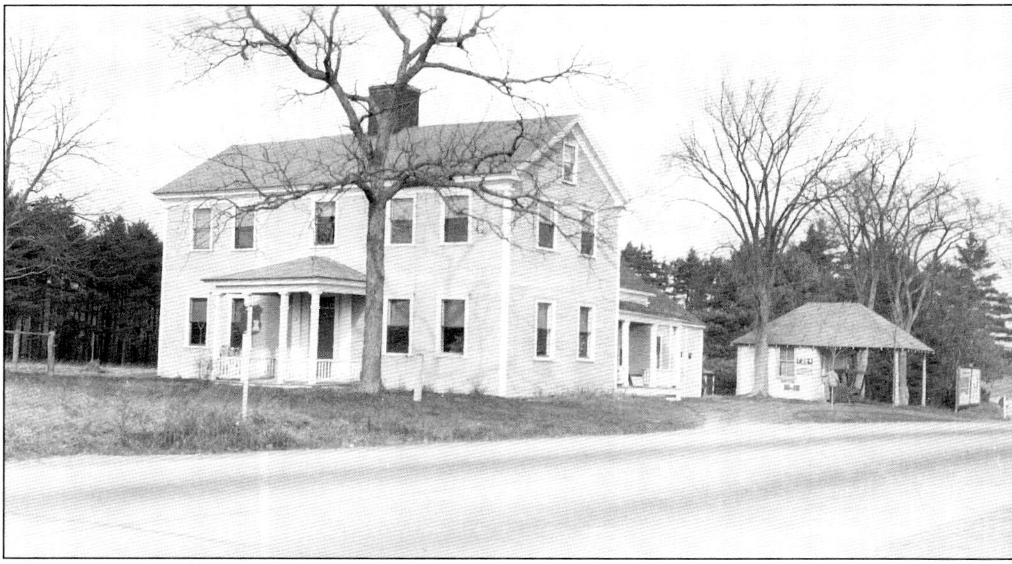

THE SMITH FARM. This house, on Daniel Webster Highway, was part of a large farm that spanned both sides of the road. Probably built in the late 1700s, it had fireplaces in every room and a massive beehive oven in the kitchen. It was taken down and reassembled in Maine. St. James Methodist Church now occupies the site.

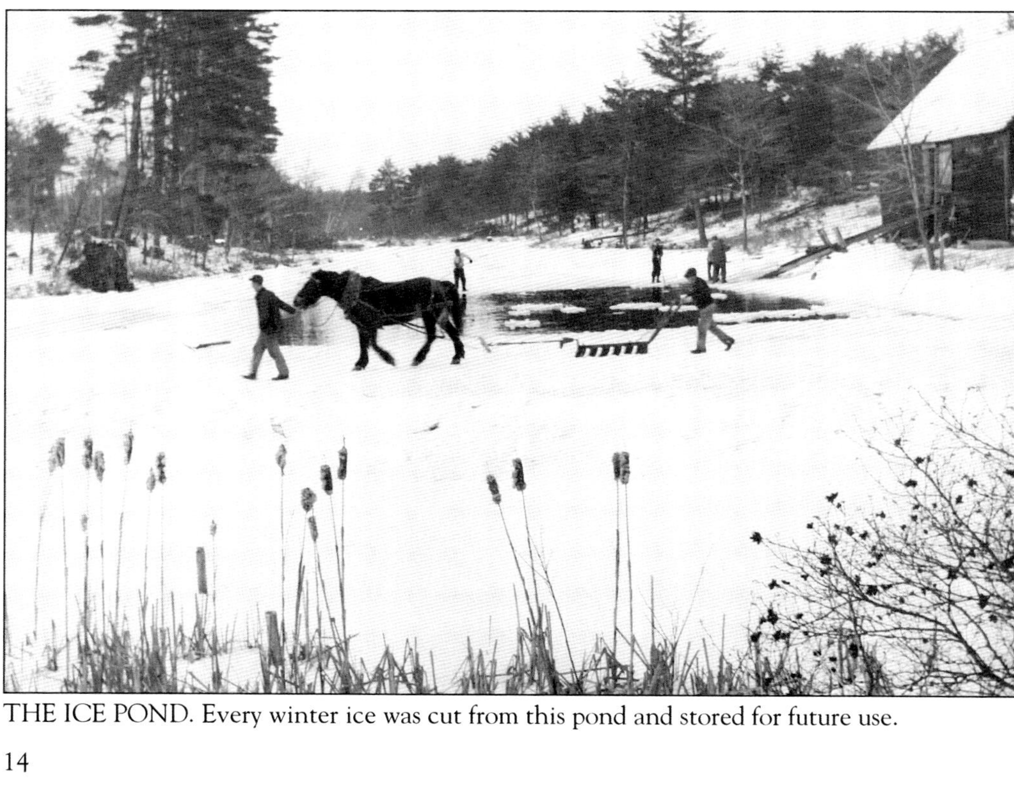

THE ICE POND. Every winter ice was cut from this pond and stored for future use.

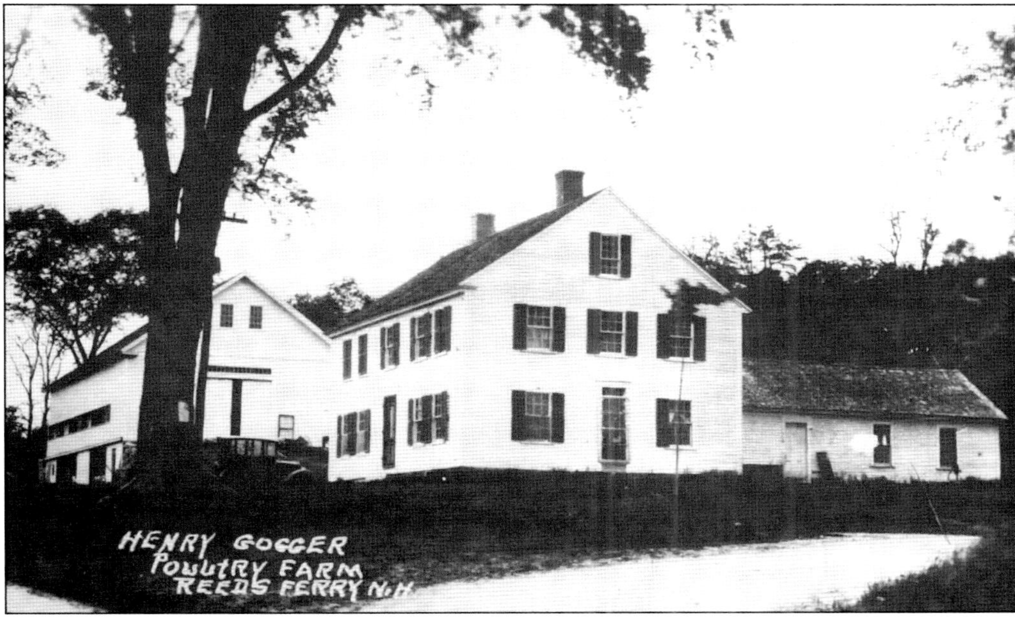

THE GEORGE HOMESTEAD. Overlooking the Souhegan River, this property was once one of Merrimack's largest farms. It was the second home of Reverend Jacob Burnap. Many of Merrimack's earlier homes are of this style: a small one-story building with a large addition added at a later date.

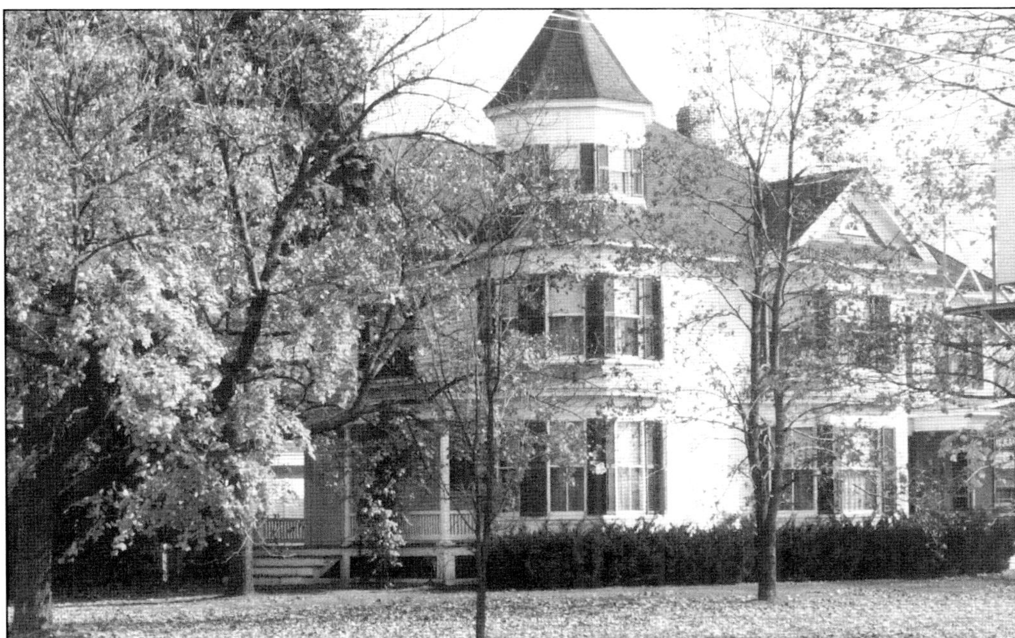

THE HASELTINE HOMESTEAD. This lovely Victorian home on Daniel Webster Highway was once owned by Mr. and Mrs. Arthur Gordon, who made the Lowell Memorial Library a reality. After many years as a private residence in the Reed's Ferry section of town, part of the building was converted to a restaurant.

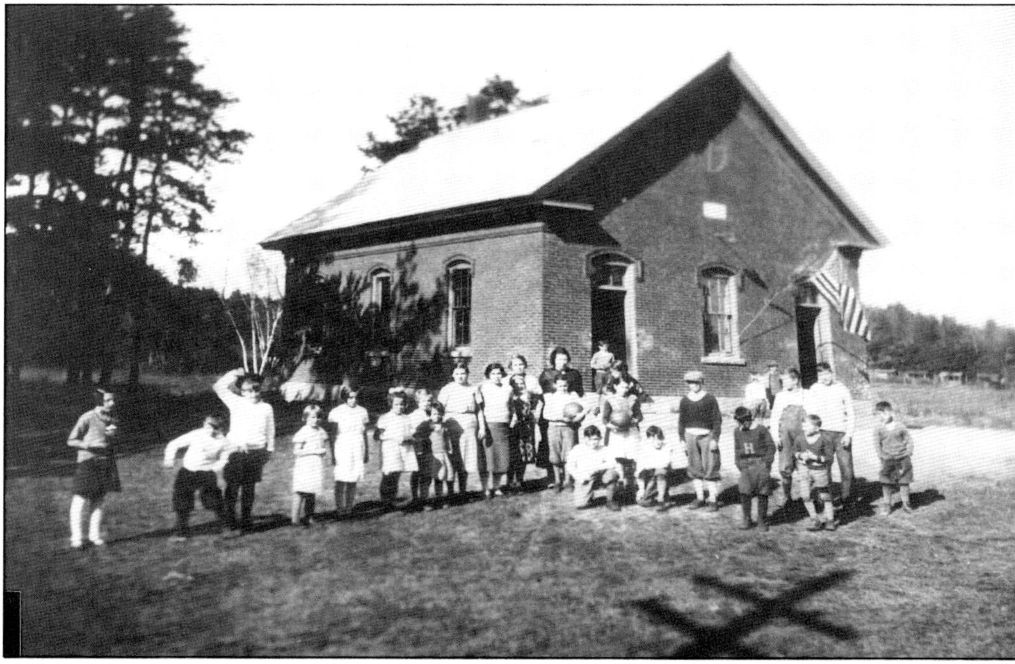

THE BRICK SCHOOLHOUSE. In the mid-1800s there were several brickyards in Merrimack. Bricks became plentiful and were used to build schools. By 1900 Merrimack had several two-room brick schools that held eight grades each. All have since been torn down.

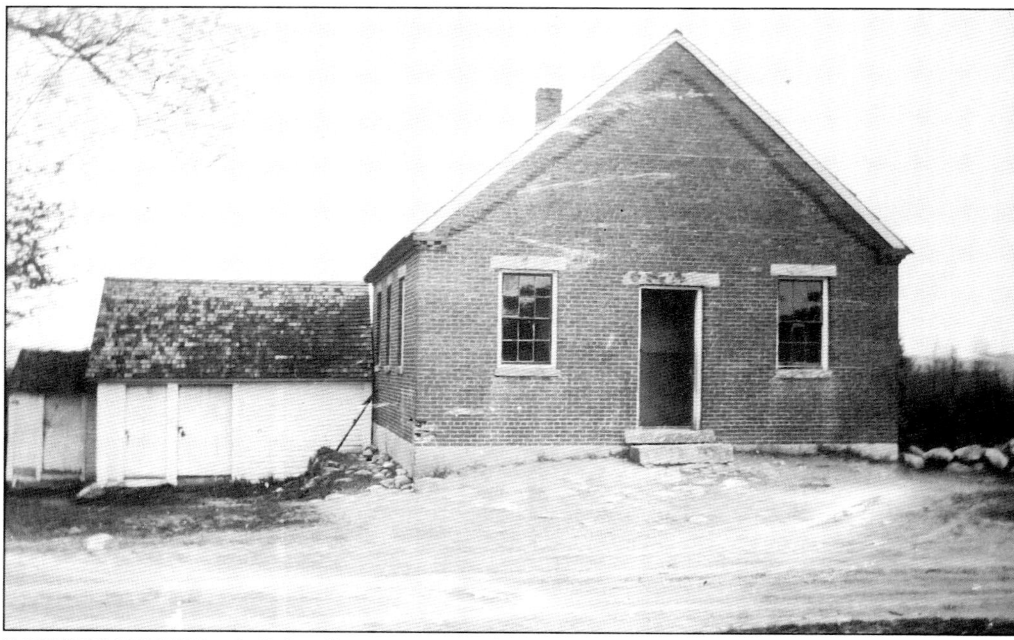

SCHOOLHOUSE #6. Schoolhouse #6 was located on Amherst Road at the intersection of Peaslee Road. School was taught here for many years until fewer schools were needed. The property was then sold and the building converted to a private residence that was later destroyed by a fire.

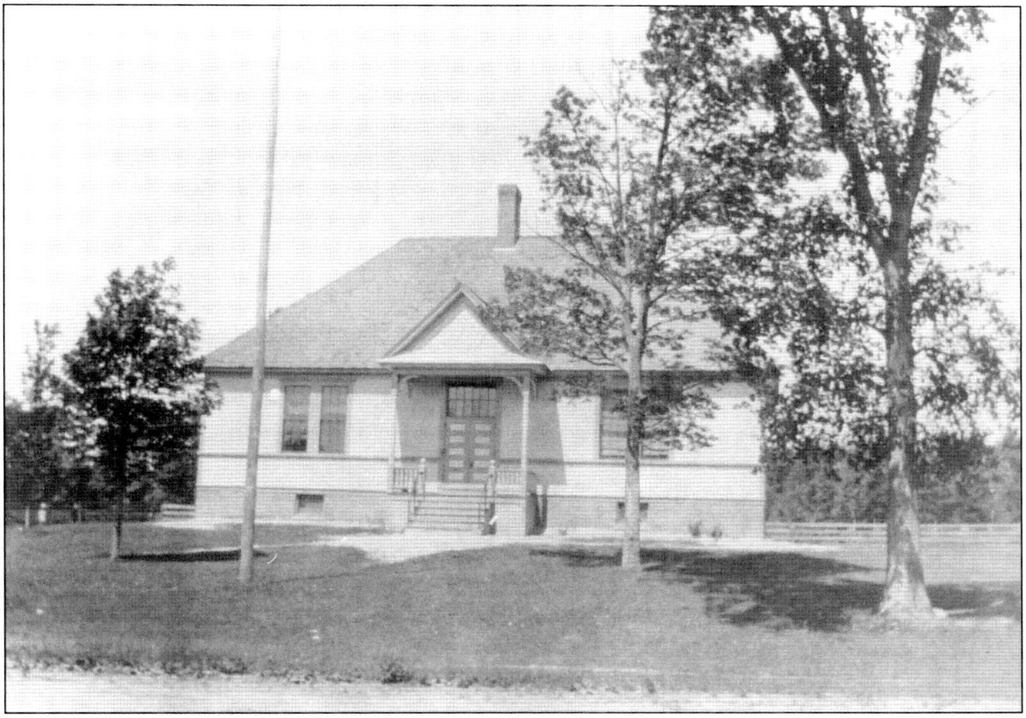

SCHOOLHOUSE #3. When the small one and two-room schoolhouses were closed, this one, on Daniel Webster Highway, become a private home. Many years and renovations later, after the McGaw Normal Institute was torn down, it was moved to the McGaw site on Depot Street and became a school once again.

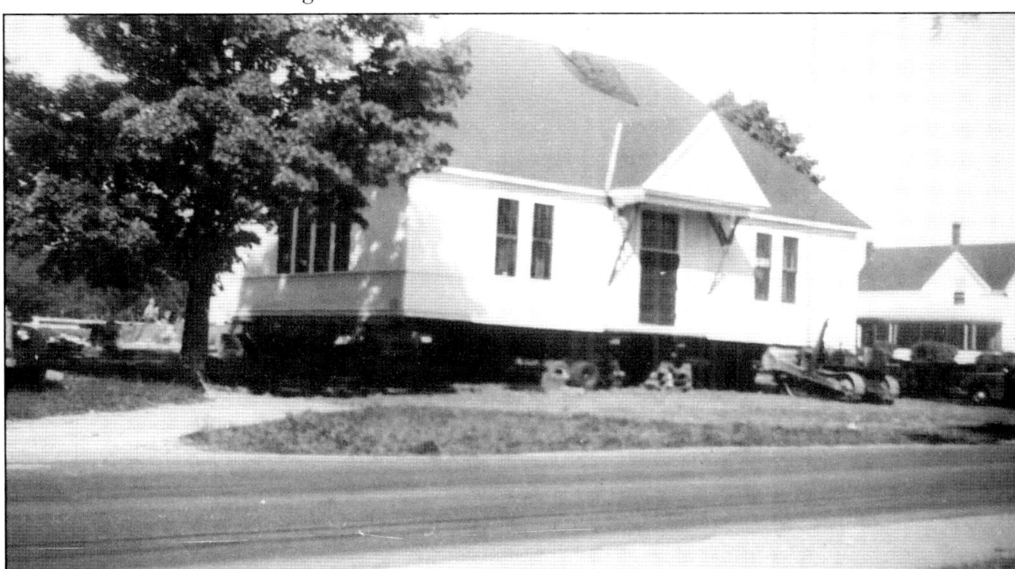

THE MERRIMACK PARENT TEACHERS ASSOCIATION KINDERGARTEN. Schoolhouse #3 was jacked up, placed on dollies, and towed down the road to Depot Street to become the PTA Kindergarten, Merrimack's first kindergarten.

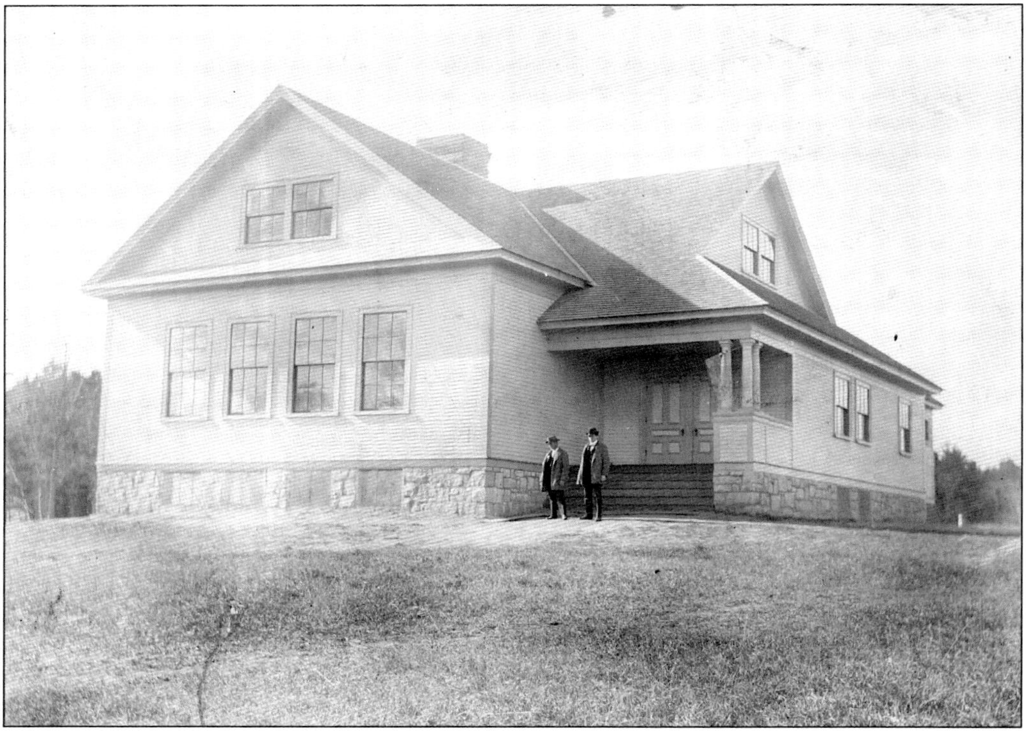

SCHOOLHOUSE #9. Built in the early 1900s, this was a two-room schoolhouse with eight grades, located on Church Street. By 1948, only the sixth grade was taught here. The school was closed when the new elementary schools were built and it later housed the police department. It is now the Merrimack Senior Center.

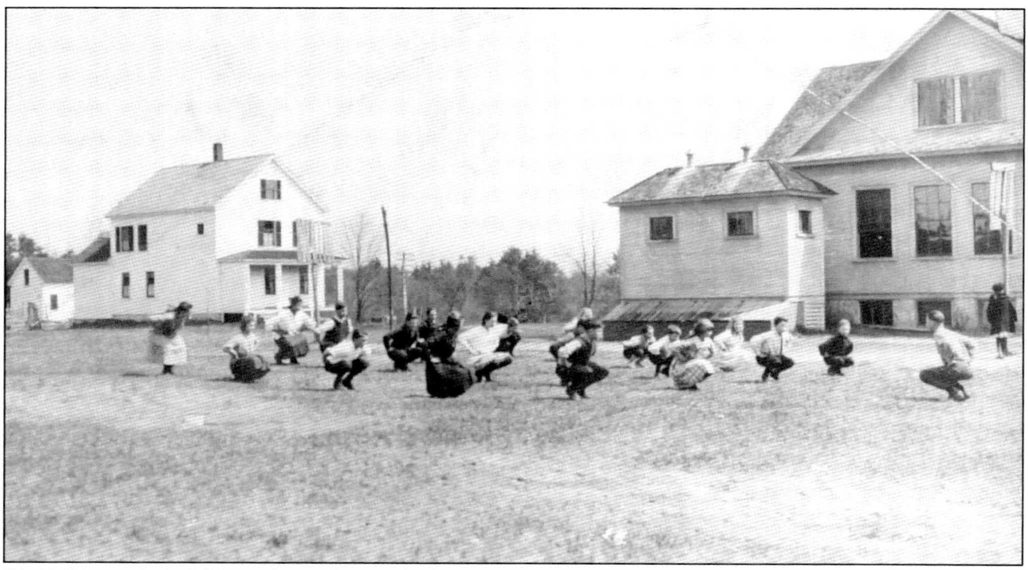

PHYSICAL EDUCATION. Physical education is not new to the Merrimack school system. It was taught at Schoolhouse #9 years before it became a required class. This is perhaps the start of aerobic exercises in the town.

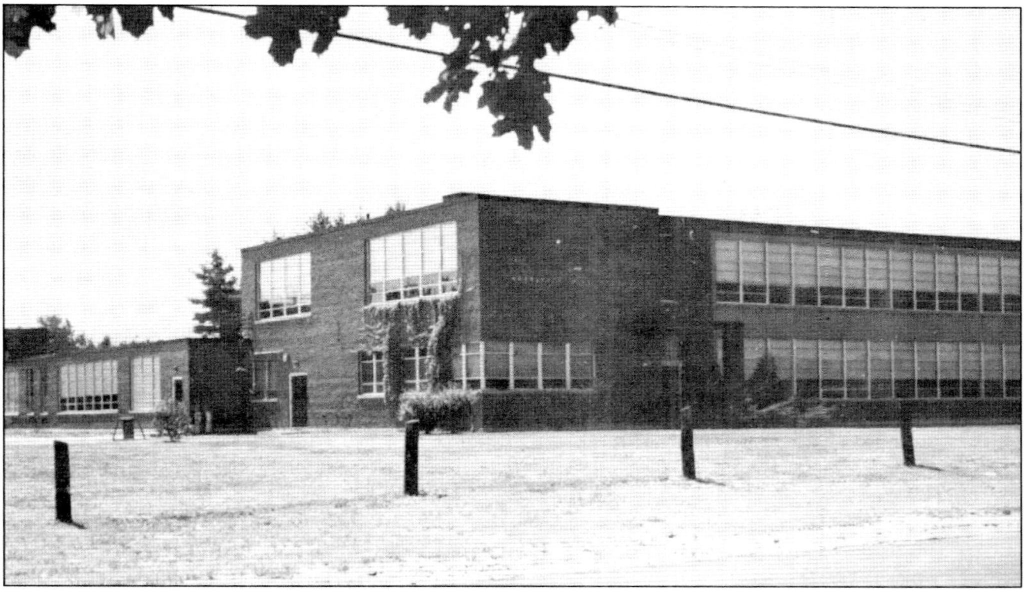

THE MASTRICOLA SCHOOL COMPLEX. In 1958, Merrimack was given the James Mastricola Farm on which to build a school. When it was decided the site was not an appropriate location for a school, it was sold, and the money used for an addition to the school on Baboosic Lake Road. The addition is Mastricola Elementary and the existing school is the Middle School.

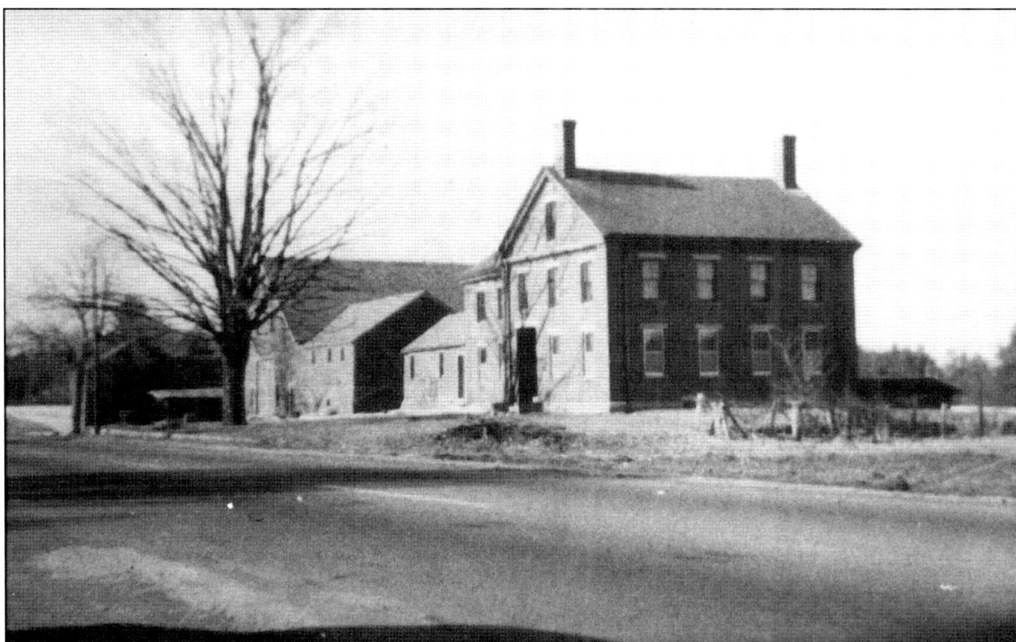

THE MASTRICOLA HOMESTEAD. This outstanding brick farmhouse, with an attached barn and sheds, stood on Daniel Webster Highway near the Nashua city line. It was torn down after James Mastricola died and a paper manufacturing firm now occupies the site.

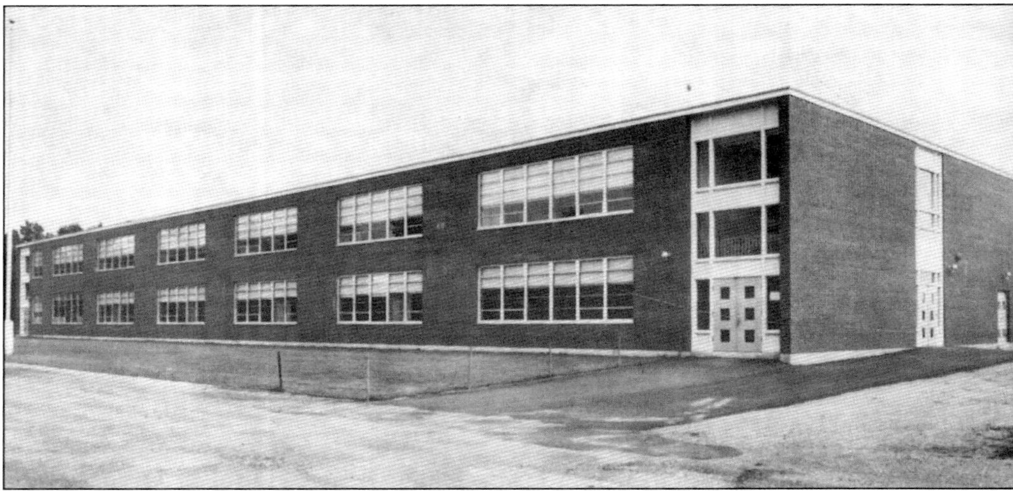

THE MERRIMACK HIGH SCHOOL. The first high school classes were held at the McGaw Normal Institute and then moved to what is now the Middle School. This building was soon outgrown and an addition had to be built.

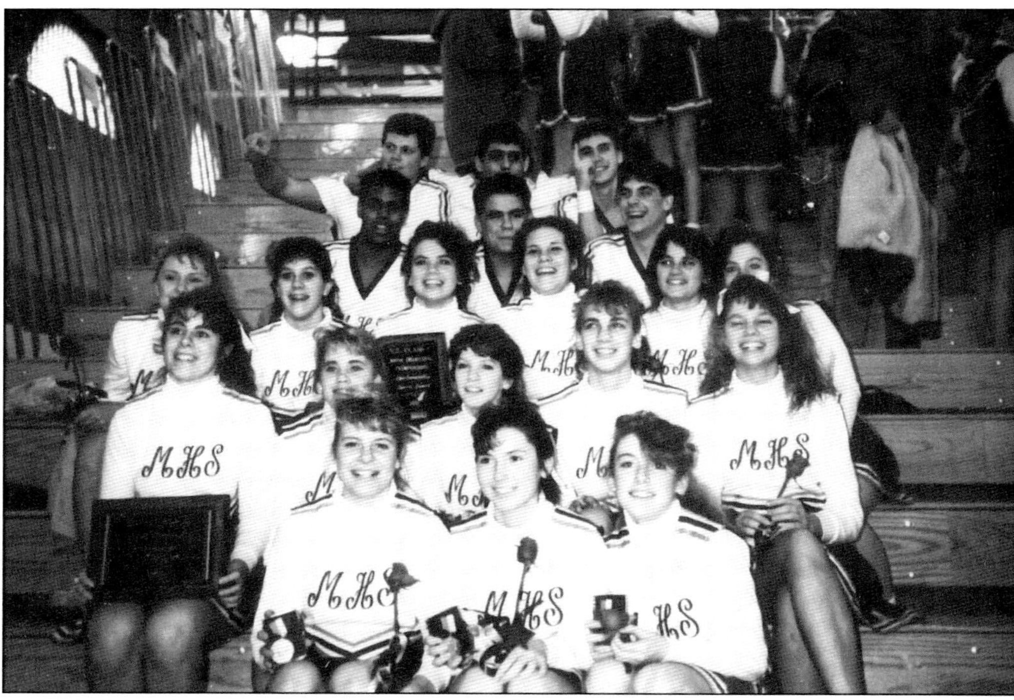

CHEERLEADERS. Merrimack can be very proud of its cheerleaders. Many of the students try out for the team and those that have been chosen have won several awards for their outstanding performances.

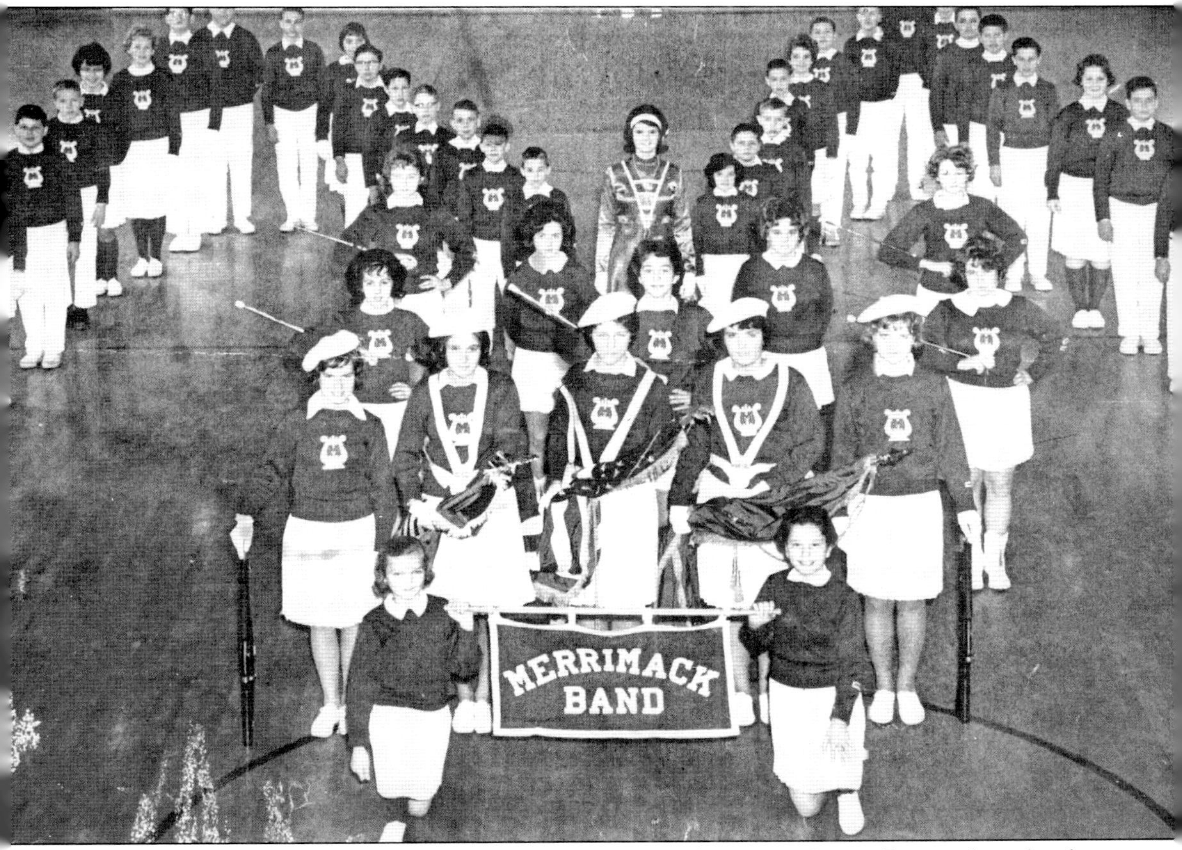

THE MERRIMACK SCHOOL BAND. Many years ago, when Mary Donnelly was the school music director, she saw the need for a school band. Through her efforts, Merrimack's first school band was formed. The band played and marched for local events and raised money to participate in the World's Fair in the 1960s. Now known as the Merrimack Tomahawks, the Merrimack High School Band has grown over the years. In addition, the uniforms and the banner have changed, and more flags have been added. They now perform at any event or parade held during the school year.

Class Motto:

Onward and Upward

Class Colors:
Blue and White

Class Flower:
White Rose

Class Roll:

GEORGE ALBERT-FRANCIS BELAND

HAZEL D. FISK
MARION E. FRENCH
FRANCES CHARLOTTE GREELEY
RUTH HASTINGS GREELEY
FLORENCE MABEL READ
ANGELENE ELIZABETH ROY
LILLIAN A. TREMBLAY
WESTON LYMAN WARRINER
ELIZABETH ROSE WATKINS
EDNA ANGEVINE WELCH
HERBERT W. WESTON
EARL BARLOW WISE

Fred W. Hall, Principal
Louis De Witt Record, Superintendent

The Class of Nineteen Twenty-four

McGaw Normal Institute

Commencement Exercises

Thursday Evening, June Fifth

eight o'clock

Merrimack Town Hall

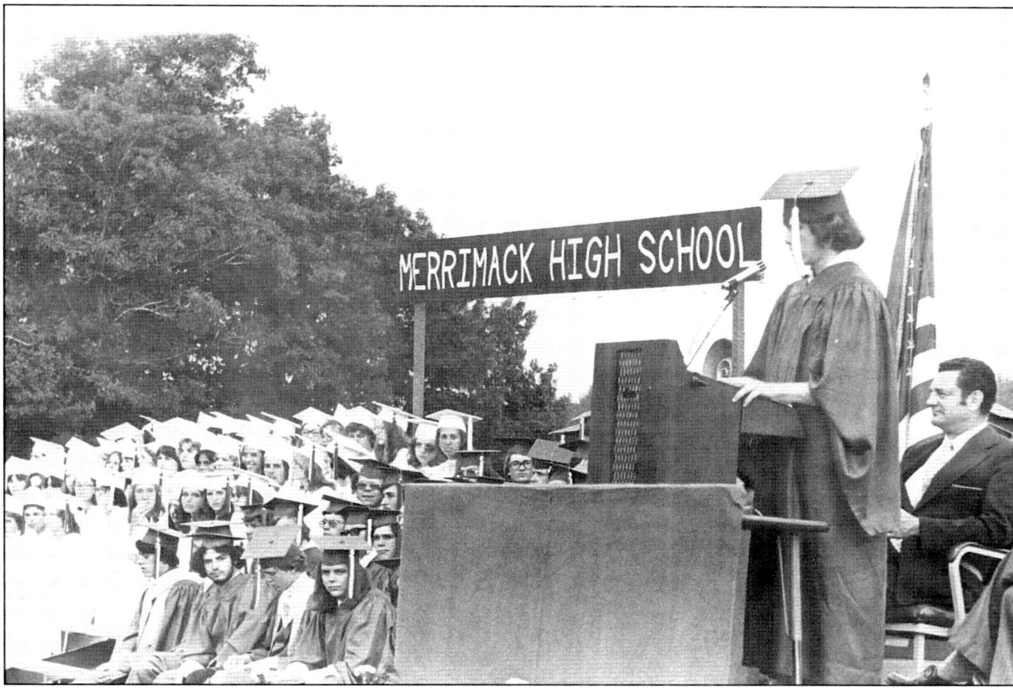

A MERRIMACK HIGH SCHOOL GRADUATION. Graduation ceremonies were held on the second floor of the Town Hall before the high school on McElwain Street was built. They were then held in the school gymnasium. When the classes became too large, the ceremonies were moved outside to the athletic field.

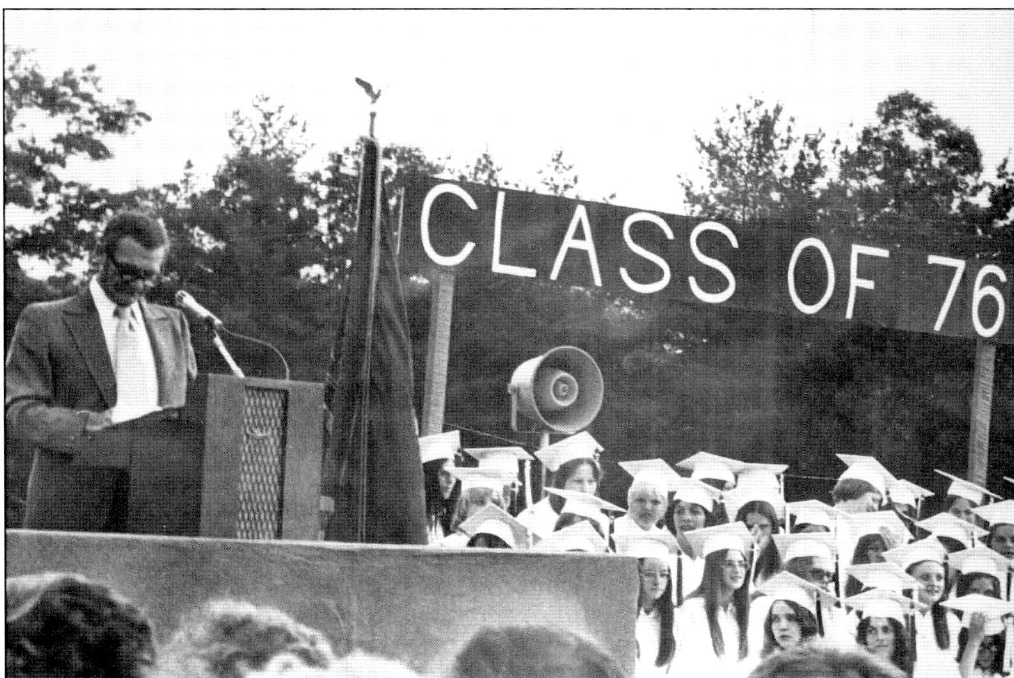

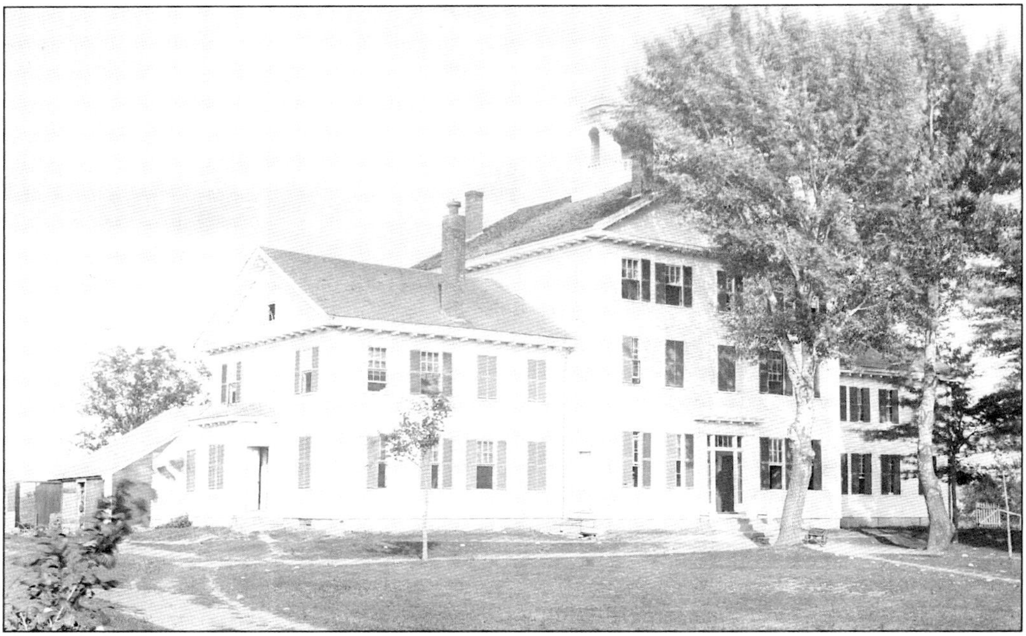

THE MCGAW NORMAL INSTITUTE. Built at the cost of $6,000, which was raised from selling shares, the McGaw Normal Institute on Depot Street became a reality in 1849. Robert McGaw was the largest shareholder. In 1872, when Robert McGaw died, he left the sum of $10,000 to turn the building into a high school.

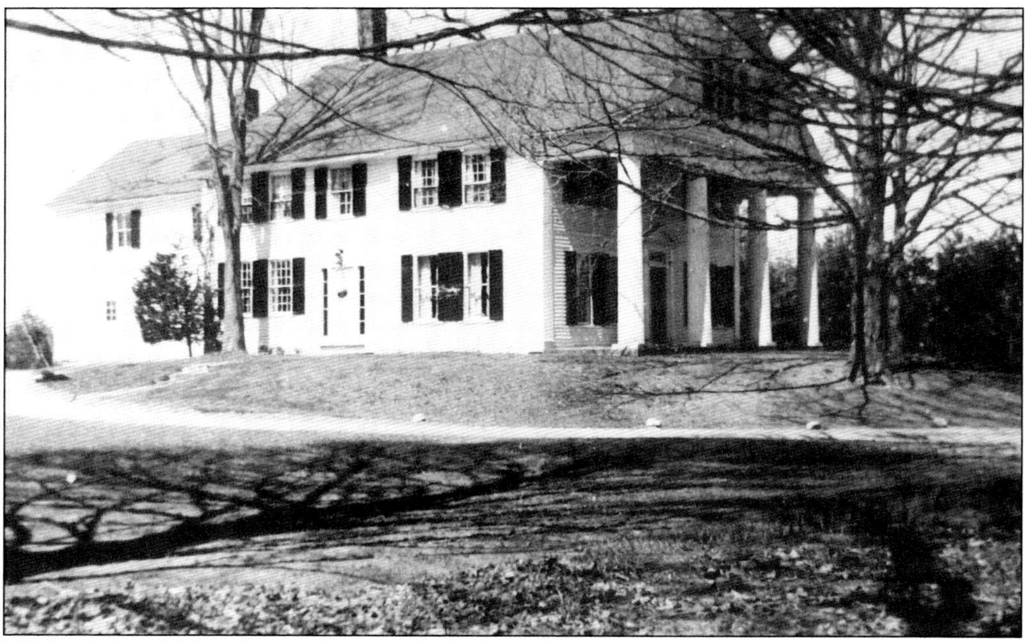

THOMAS MORE COLLEGE. A Catholic liberal arts college founded in 1978 now occupies the former Blanchard family home on Manchester Street. A library and dorm have been added to serve approximately ninety students. It is believed the original house was part of the underground railway that carried slaves to Canada.

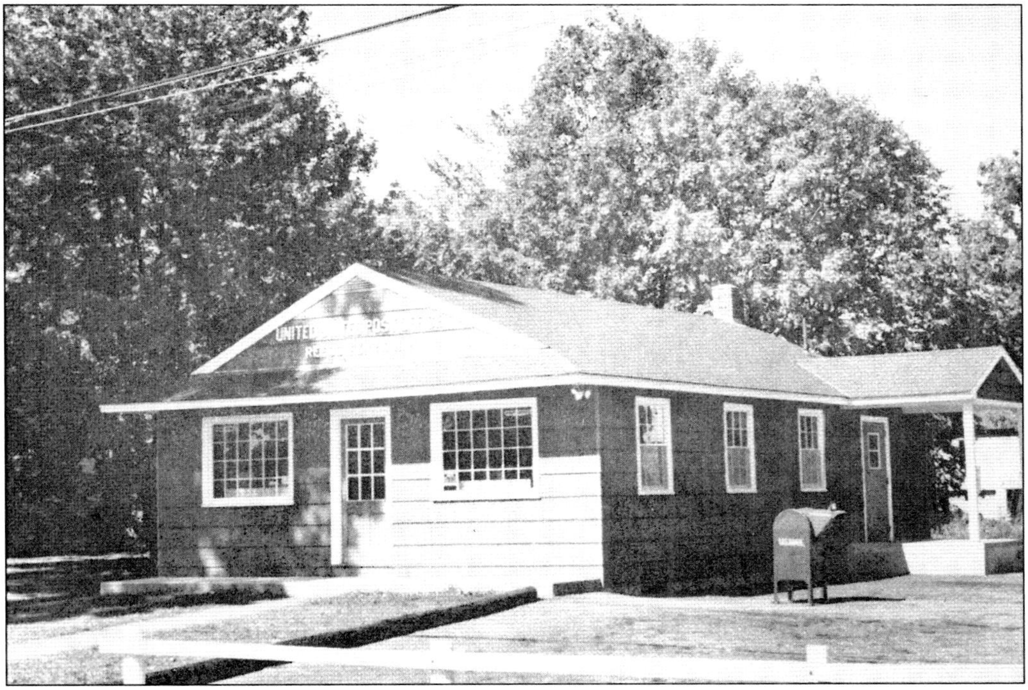

THE POST OFFICE. At one time there were four post offices serving Merrimack, located in neighborhood stores. As the town grew, the need for a central post office was seen and the present post office building was erected on Route 3 to serve all areas of Merrimack. This is the last post office in Reed's Ferry. Merrimack also has rural free delivery.

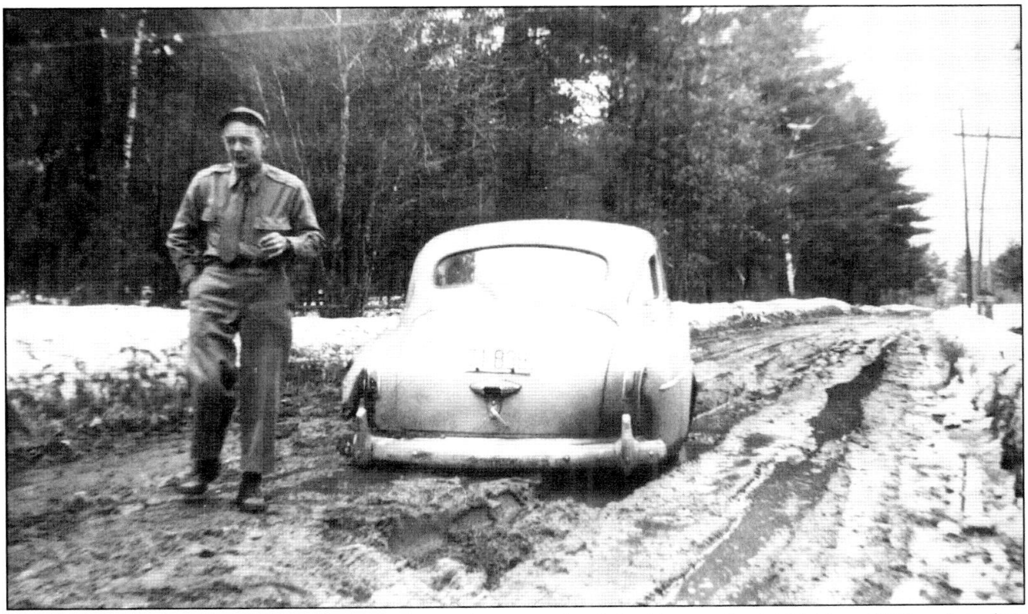

RURAL FREE DELIVERY. Not rain, nor sleet, nor hail shall stop the U.S. Post Office. Mud??? Maybe. In the spring of the year, Merrimack mailmen often got stuck in the mud on the many dirt roads in town.

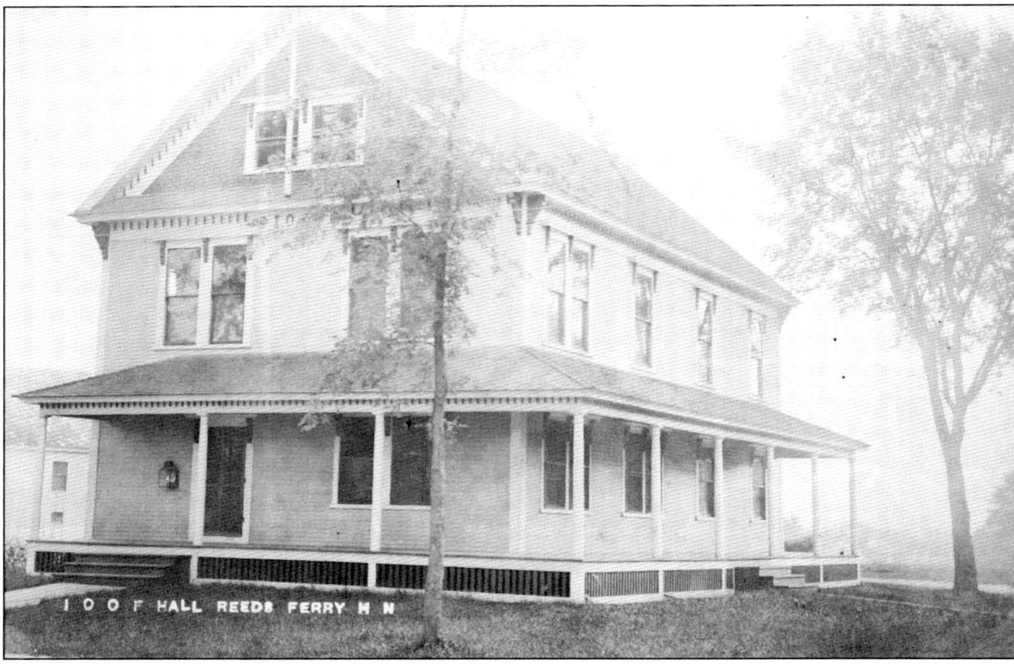

THE ODD FELLOWS HALL. Through the efforts of the charter members, a permanent home for the IOOF was built on Depot Street. Souhegan Lodge, as this chapter was known, disbanded in the 1970s. The hall has been used for many purposes and is currently the Merrimack Baptist Temple.

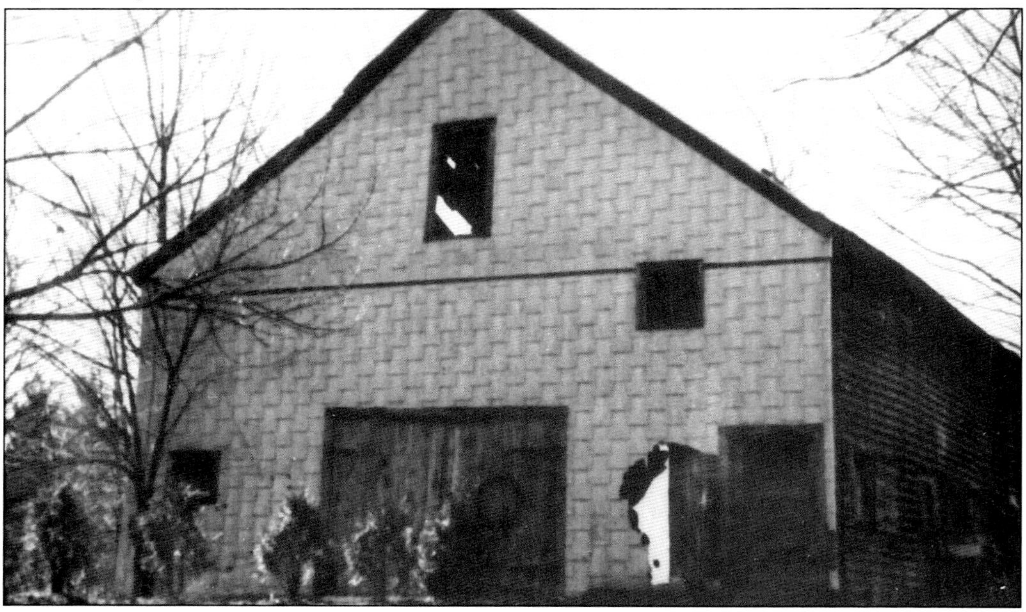

THE TOWN POOR FARM. Prior to the 1900s, people who had no one to care for them and who could not support themselves were sent to live on the poor farm. The second of Merrimack's poor farms was located on South Baboosic Lake Road. The farm system was discontinued in 1868. This farm became private property and was torn down in the 1980s.

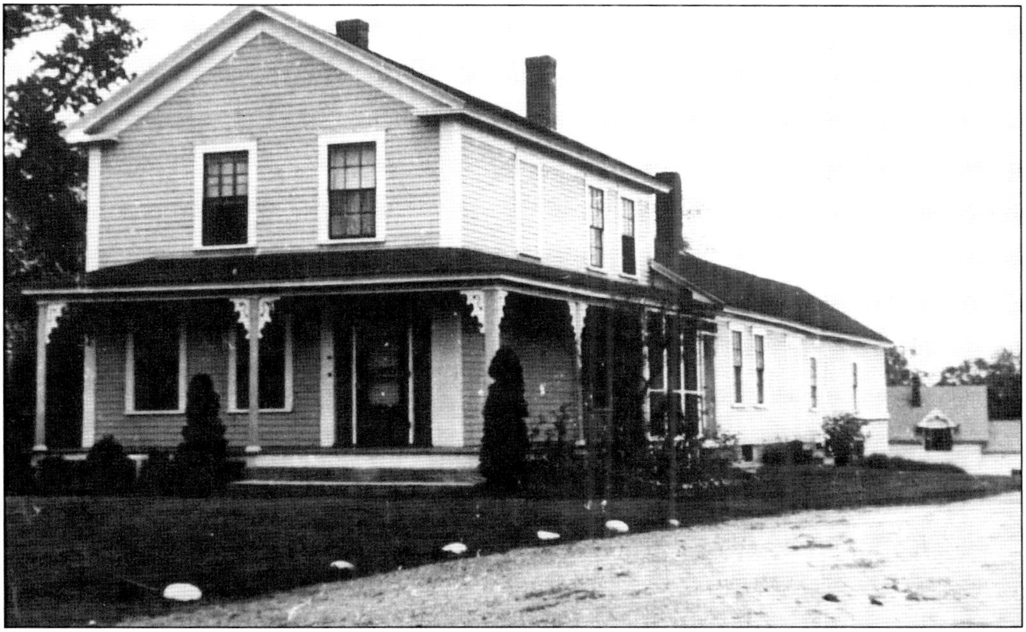

THE FISK FUNERAL HOME. This lovely old home on Route 3 was for many years a funeral home, with Charles Fisk as the undertaker. The first floor of the house was used for funeral services and the second floor was the living quarters for the Fisk family. A bank now occupies this site, adjacent to Fraser Square.

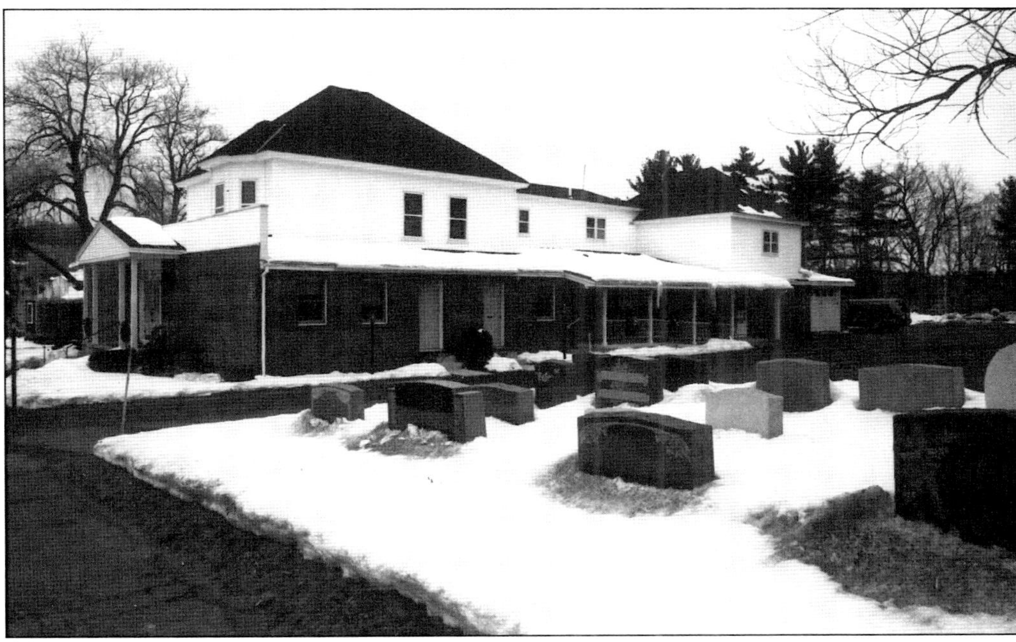

RIVET'S FUNERAL PARLOR. This funeral parlor was operated by an undertaker from Manchester from 1957 until 1963. In 1963 it was purchased by George and Jean Rivet. The Rivets remodeled the building in the early 1970s and again in 1992. Since George Rivet's death, his son Mark has run the family business.

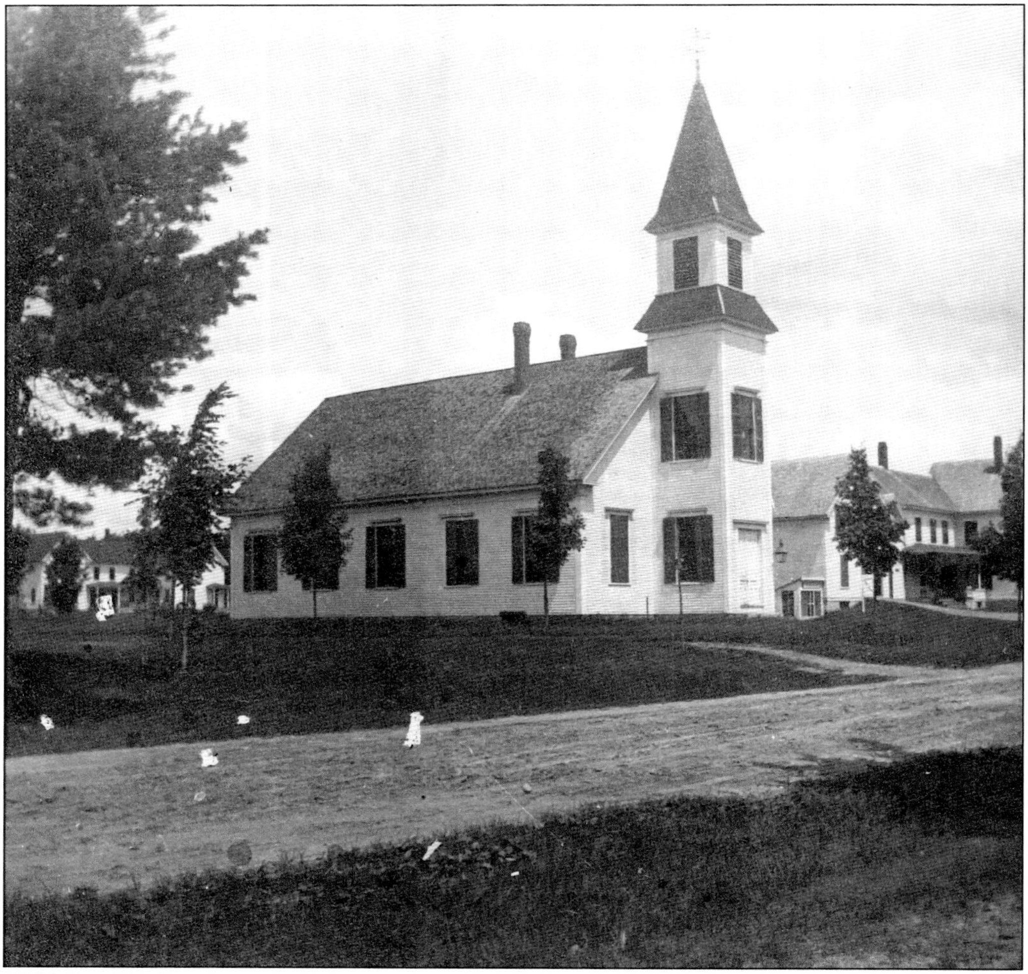

THE WHEELER CHAPEL. Jonathan Wheeler gave the Wheeler Chapel on Daniel Webster Highway to the people of Reed's Ferry for religious services and social events. As new churches and meeting halls were built, fewer and fewer people used the chapel and the upkeep became impossible. Trustees eventually decided to sell the property and the Faith Episcopal Church now owns the chapel.

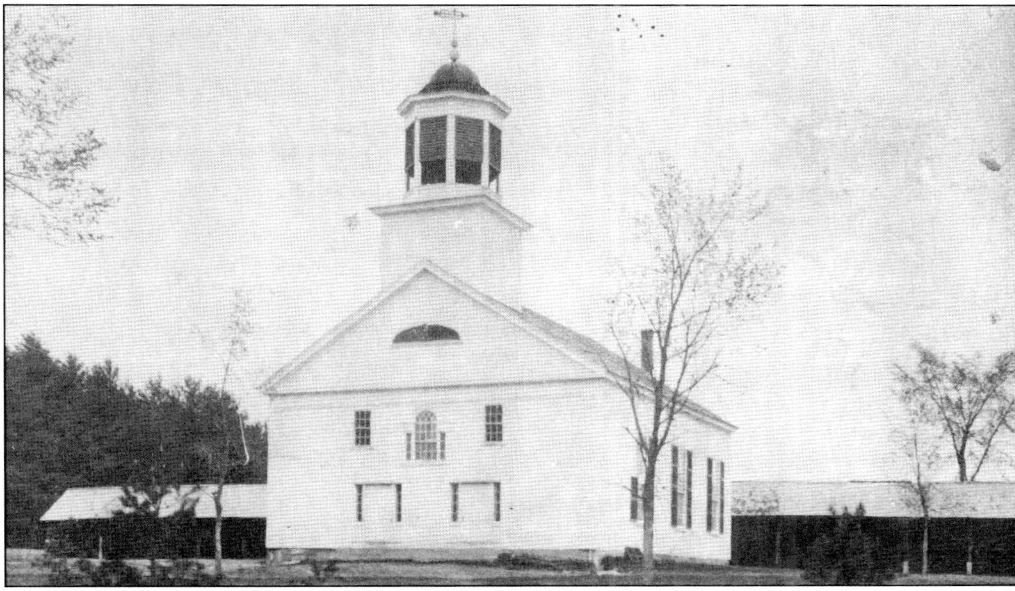

THE FIRST CONGREGATIONAL CHURCH. This church on Baboosic Lake Road is the home of the earliest congregation in Merrimack. The congregation first met in the meetinghouse on Meetinghouse Road. A more central location was desired and a new building was erected on the present site. The carriage sheds have been removed and a large addition added to the rear of the building.

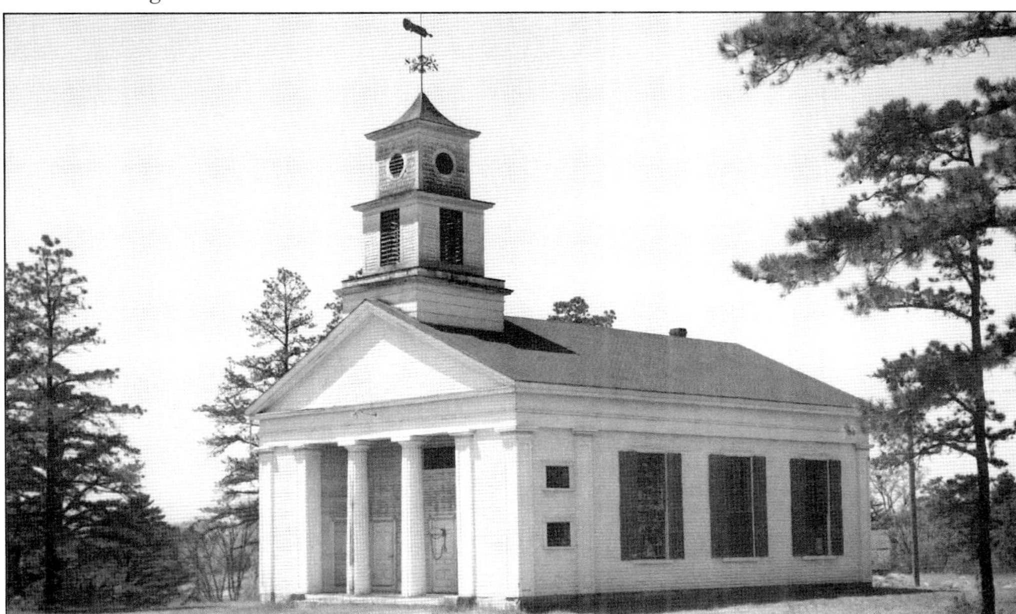

THE MERRIMACK VALLEY BAPTIST CHURCH. Travel and distance made it difficult for many residents in the South Merrimack area to attend church services, so in 1829 the first church building in Merrimack was erected on Boston Post Road. It was originally a Congregational church. The two church buildings are typical of New England churches and both have Joshua's Trumpet weather vanes.

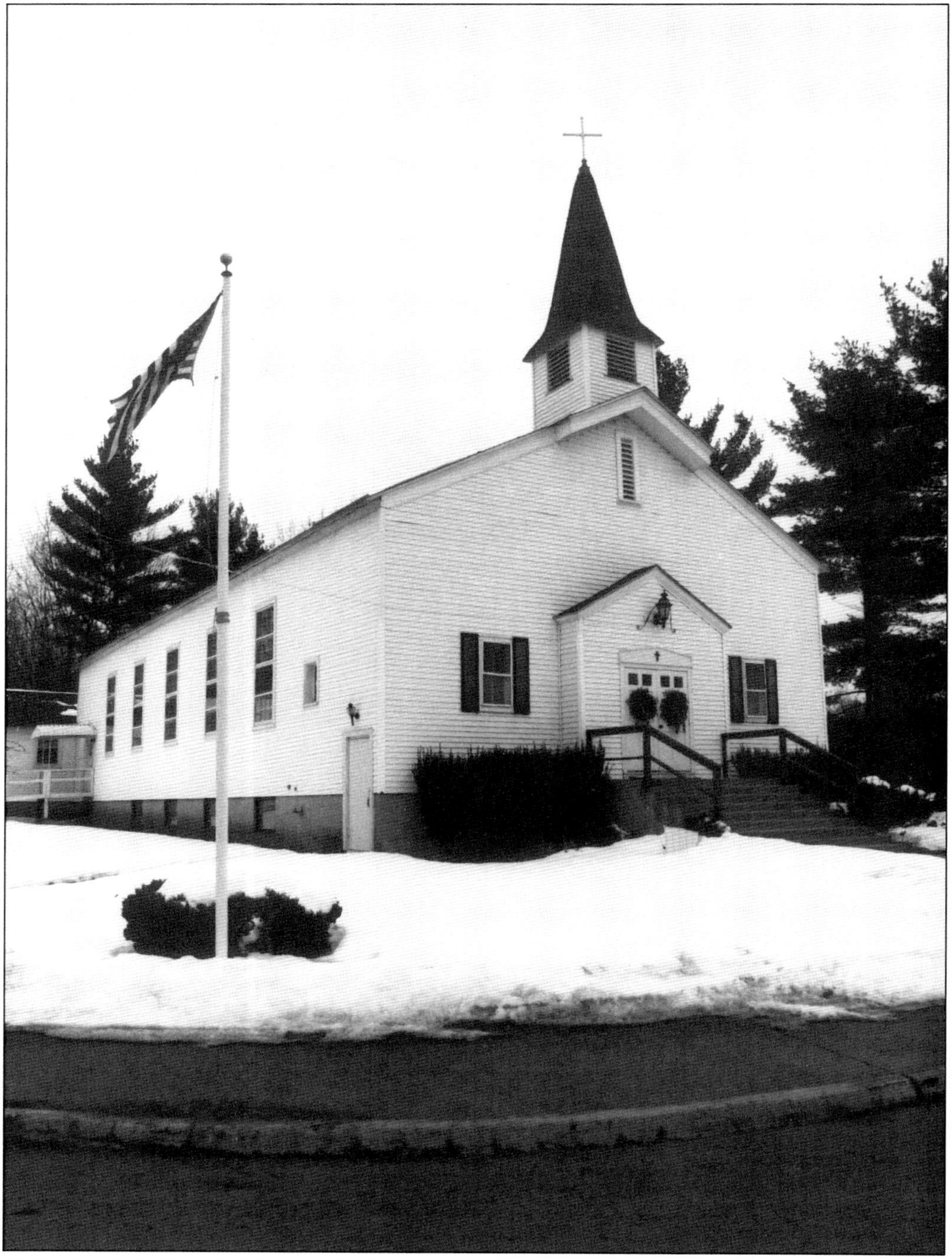

THE ST. JAMES UNITED METHODIST CHURCH. The Wesley Christian Fellowship officially became the St. James United Methodist Church in 1966. In 1968 the Grenier Field Chapel was purchased and moved to its present location on Route 3. During World War II, this chapel was the last worshipping place in the United States for many who went overseas from Grenier Field Air Base in Manchester.

Two

Notables

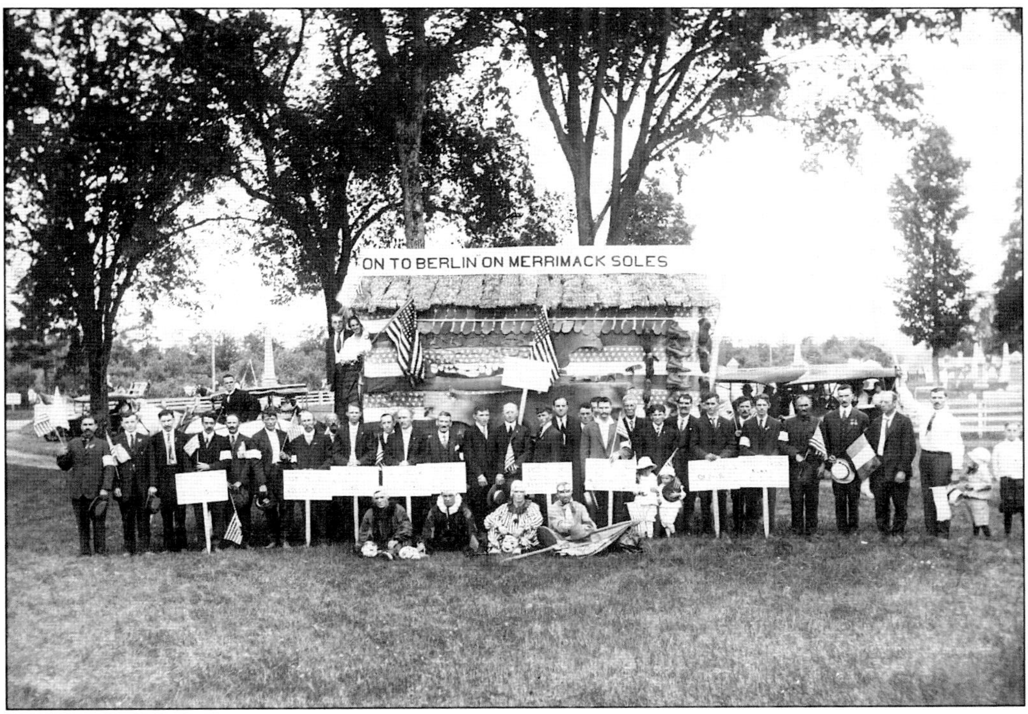

ON TO BERLIN. The soles of many military boots worn by the armed forces in World War I were made at a shoe shop in Merrimack.

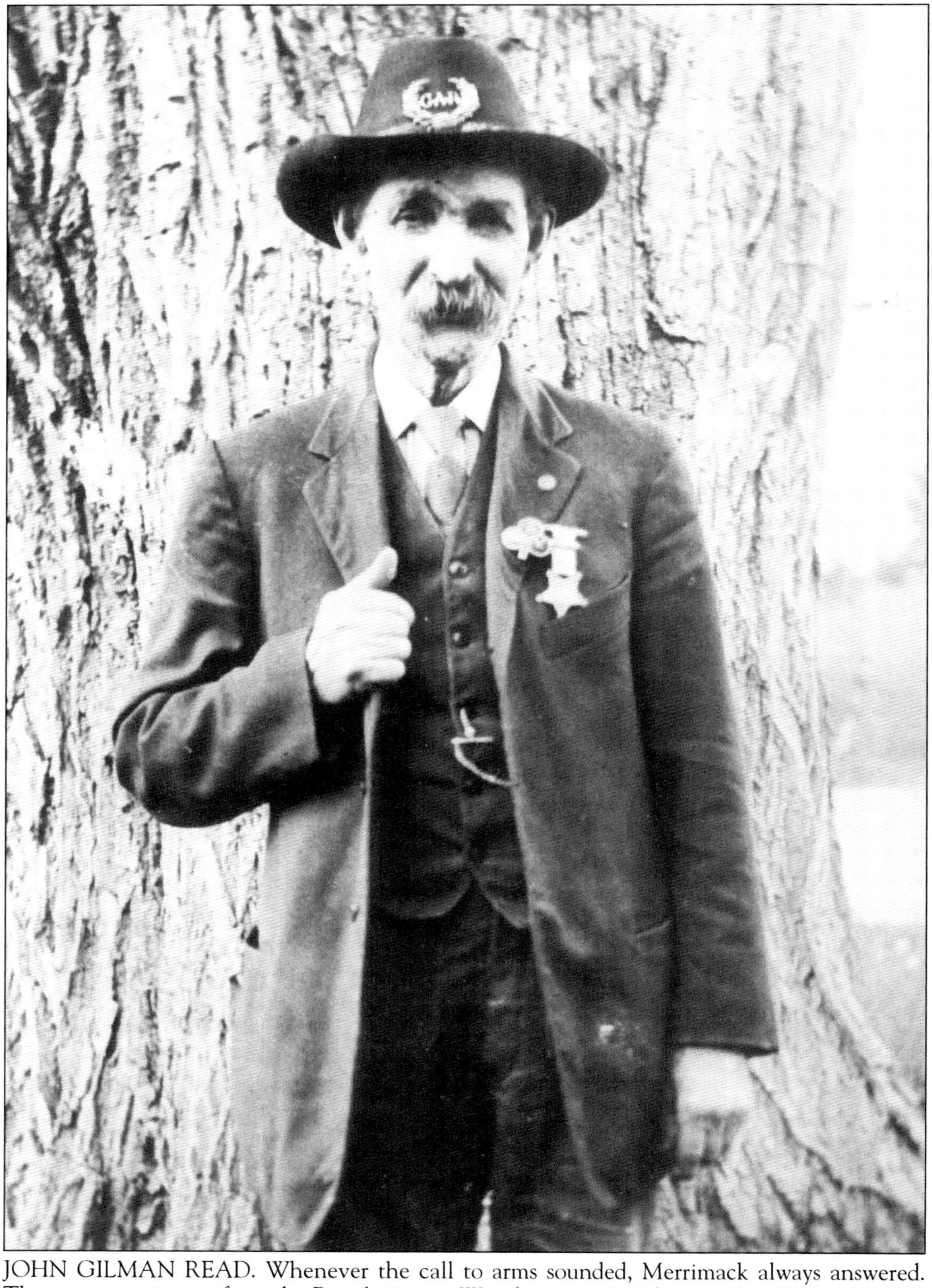

JOHN GILMAN READ. Whenever the call to arms sounded, Merrimack always answered. There are no pictures from the Revolutionary War; however, it is known that Merrimack had one casualty, a sixteen-year-old boy, Reuben Cummings. Among the many men from Merrimack who volunteered for the Civil War was John Gilman Read.

DUNCAN FRASER. World War I claimed the lives of two men from Merrimack. Duncan Fraser was one of them. He died in battle and lies buried somewhere in France.

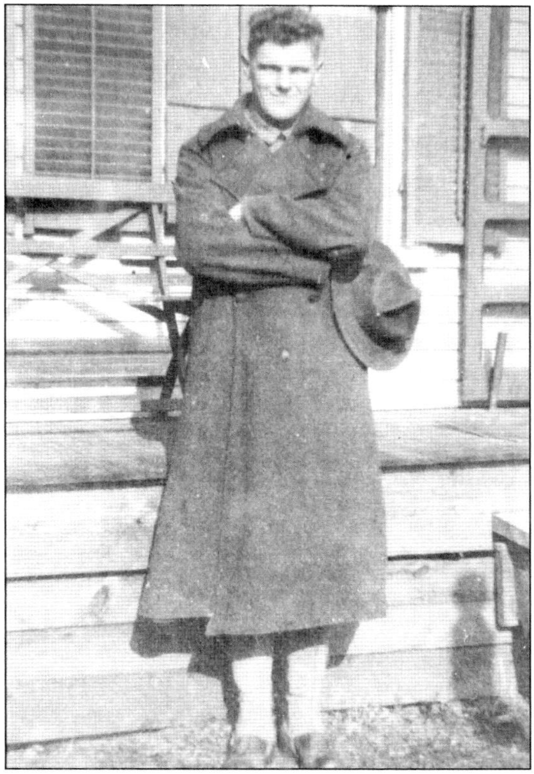

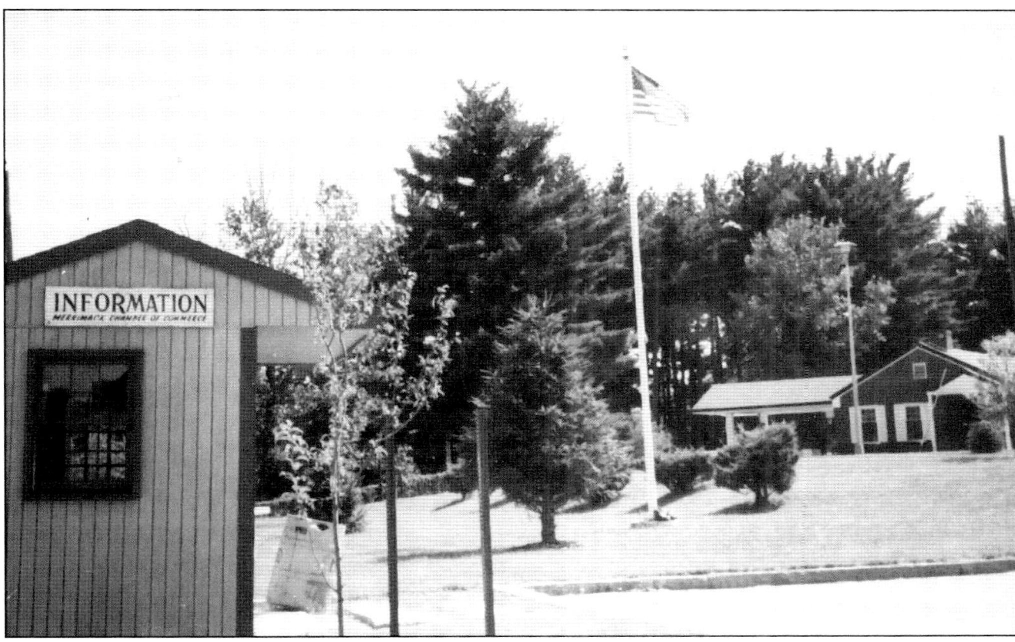

FRASER SQUARE. This piece of property was given to the town of Merrimack by the International Shoe Company. Located at the intersection of Route 3 and Railroad Avenue, it is now a town park dedicated to the memory of Duncan Fraser.

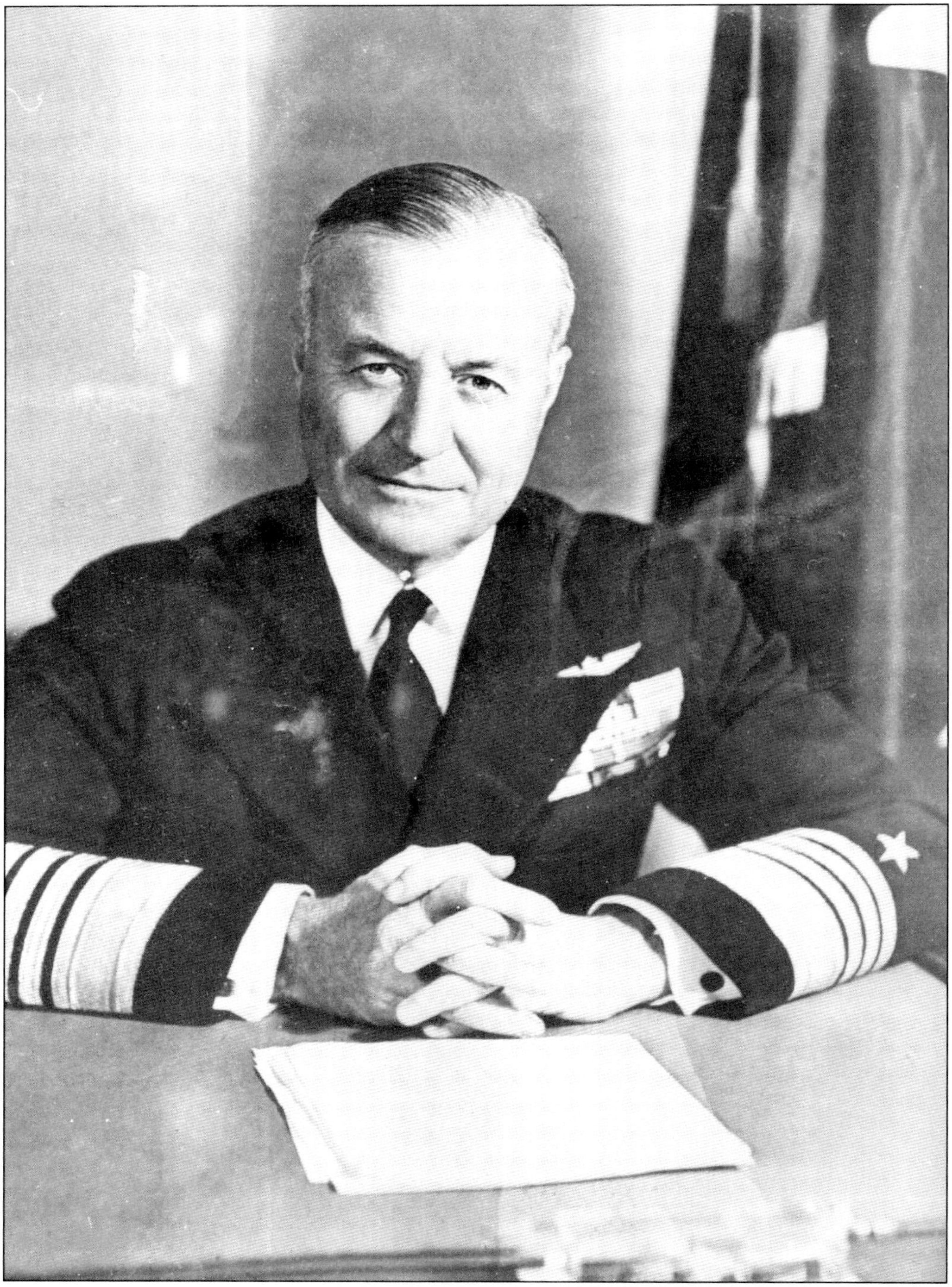

FORREST SHERMAN. Born on Depot Street in 1896, Forrest Sherman was the son of a headmaster of the McGaw Normal Institute. In 1942, he was captain of the aircraft carrier USS *Wasp* when it was sunk in the Solomon Islands by the Japanese. He later served as chief of naval operations. The destroyer USS *Forrest Sherman* was named in his honor in 1955.

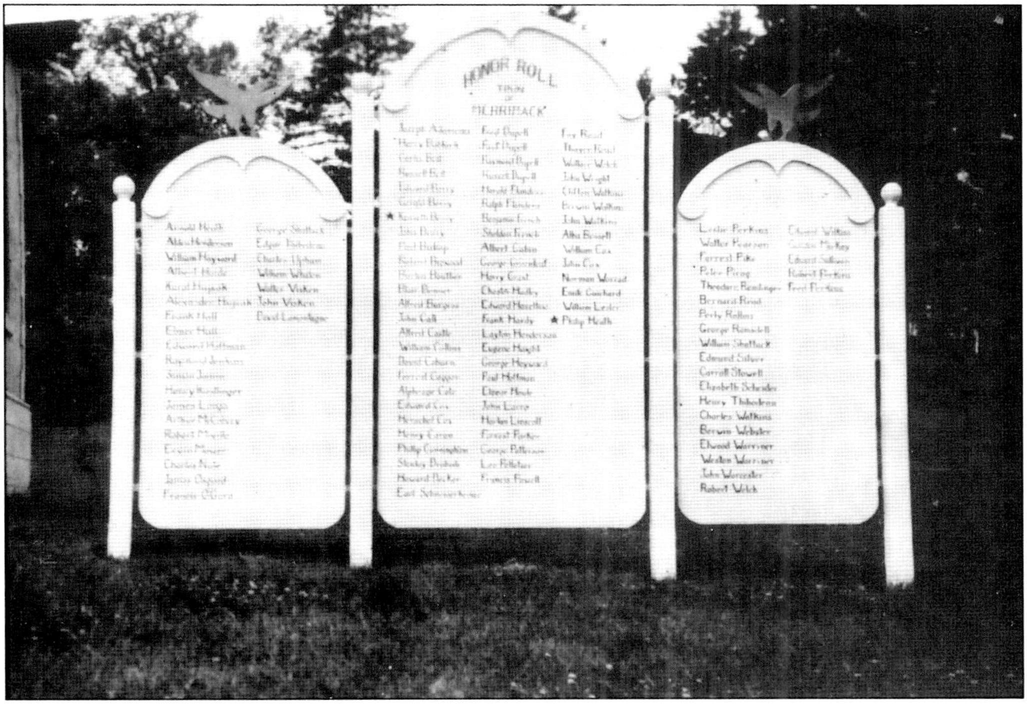

THE HONOR ROLL. This memorial to the World War II veterans of Merrimack stood for many years on the lawn of the Lowell Memorial Library. It was removed to be restored and never replaced.

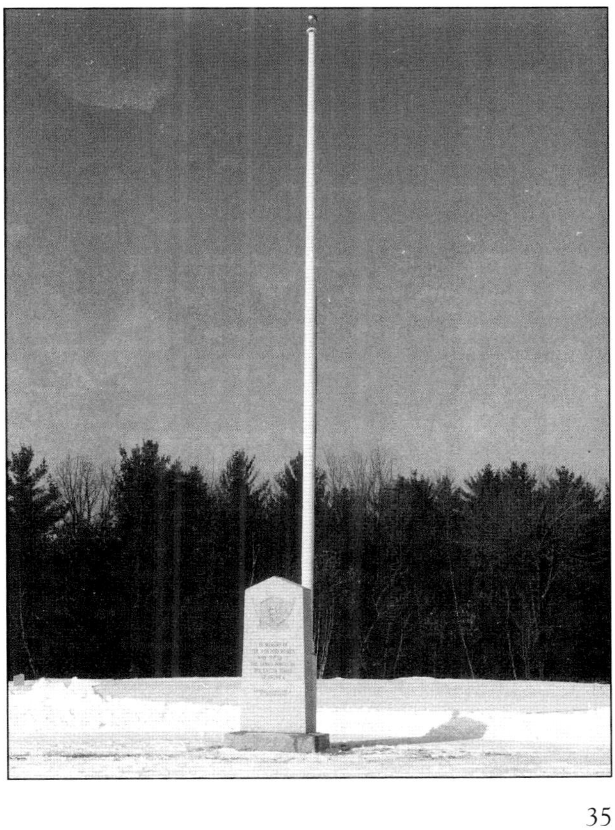

THE VETERANS' MONUMENT. Memorial Day services are held every year at the Veterans' Monument in Last Rest Cemetery. This memorial was erected by the American Legion Merrimack Post 98 and the Merrimack Veterans of Foreign Wars Post 8641.

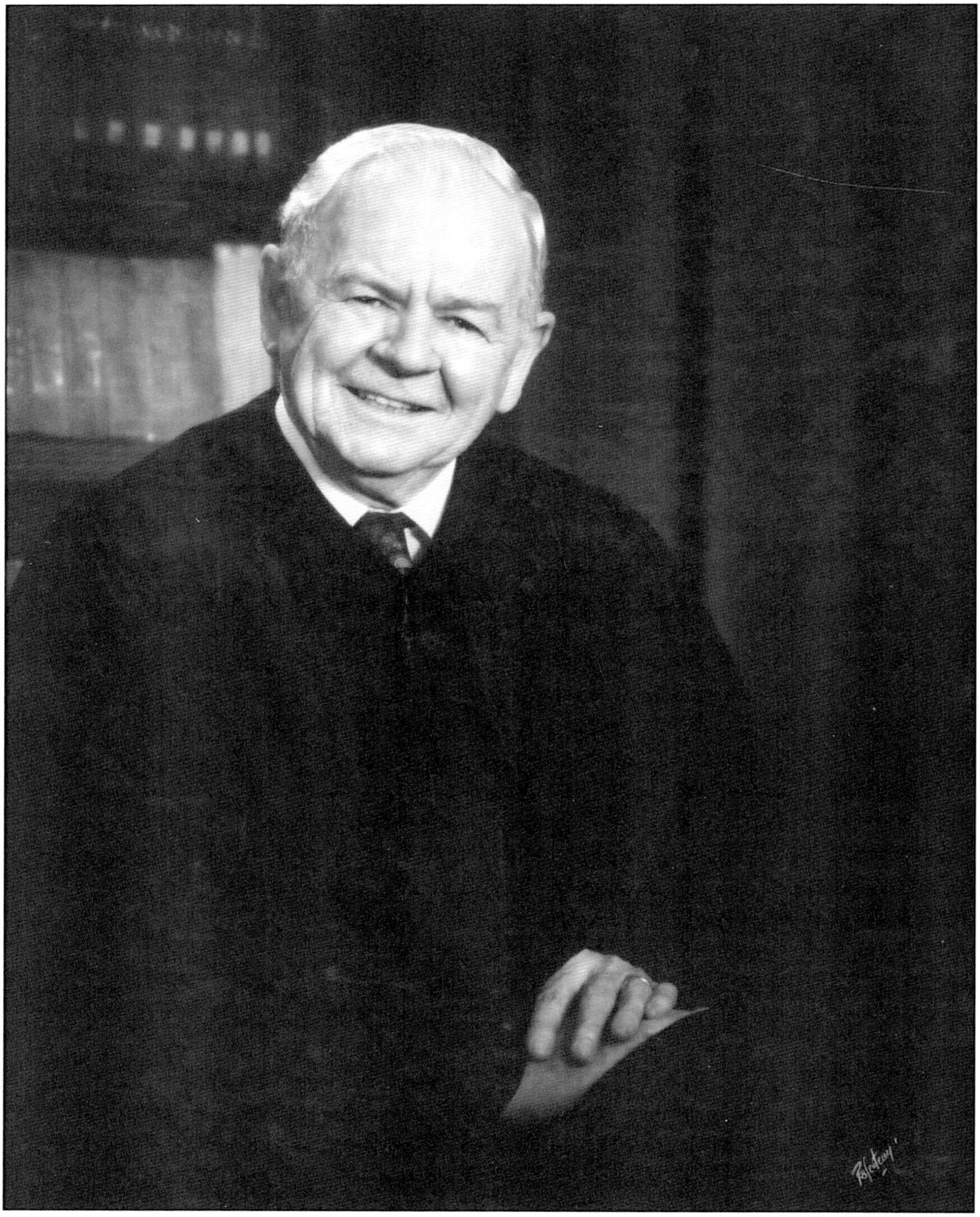

JUSTICE CHARLES MORRILL. Charles Morrill was appointed justice of the Merrimack District Court system in 1962. The only requirements to be a justice are that the person be "learned, wise and discreet." Justice Morrill, however, had a law degree and practiced in Merrimack for many years. The towns of Merrimack and Bedford share the Merrimack District Court system. Court is held on the second floor of the west wing of the Merrimack Town Hall.

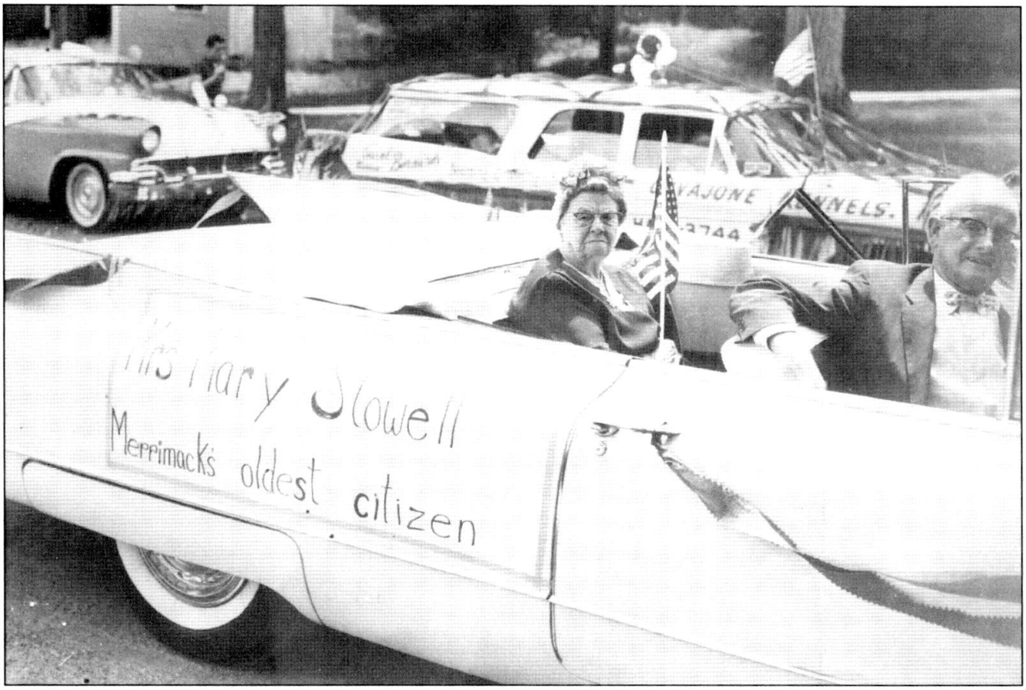

MERRIMACK'S OLDEST CITIZEN. For many years Merrimack honored its oldest citizen with the presentation of the Boston Post Cane. The cane was lost several years ago, but the oldest citizen is still honored and rides in the July Fourth parade. Shown here are two of the former oldest citizens, Mary Stowell and Olive Bell.

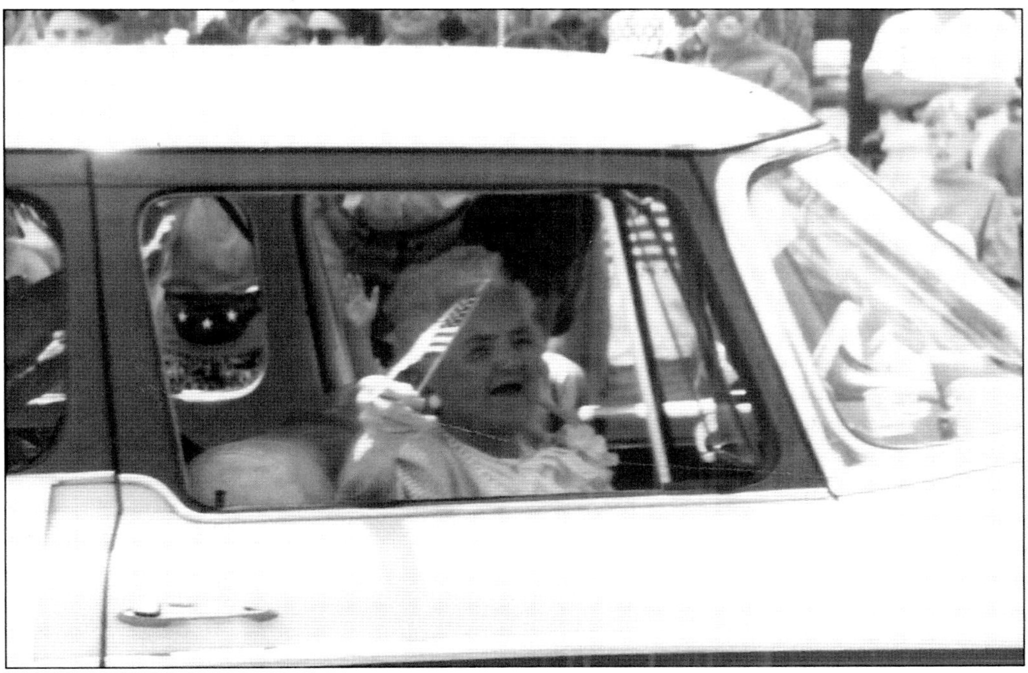

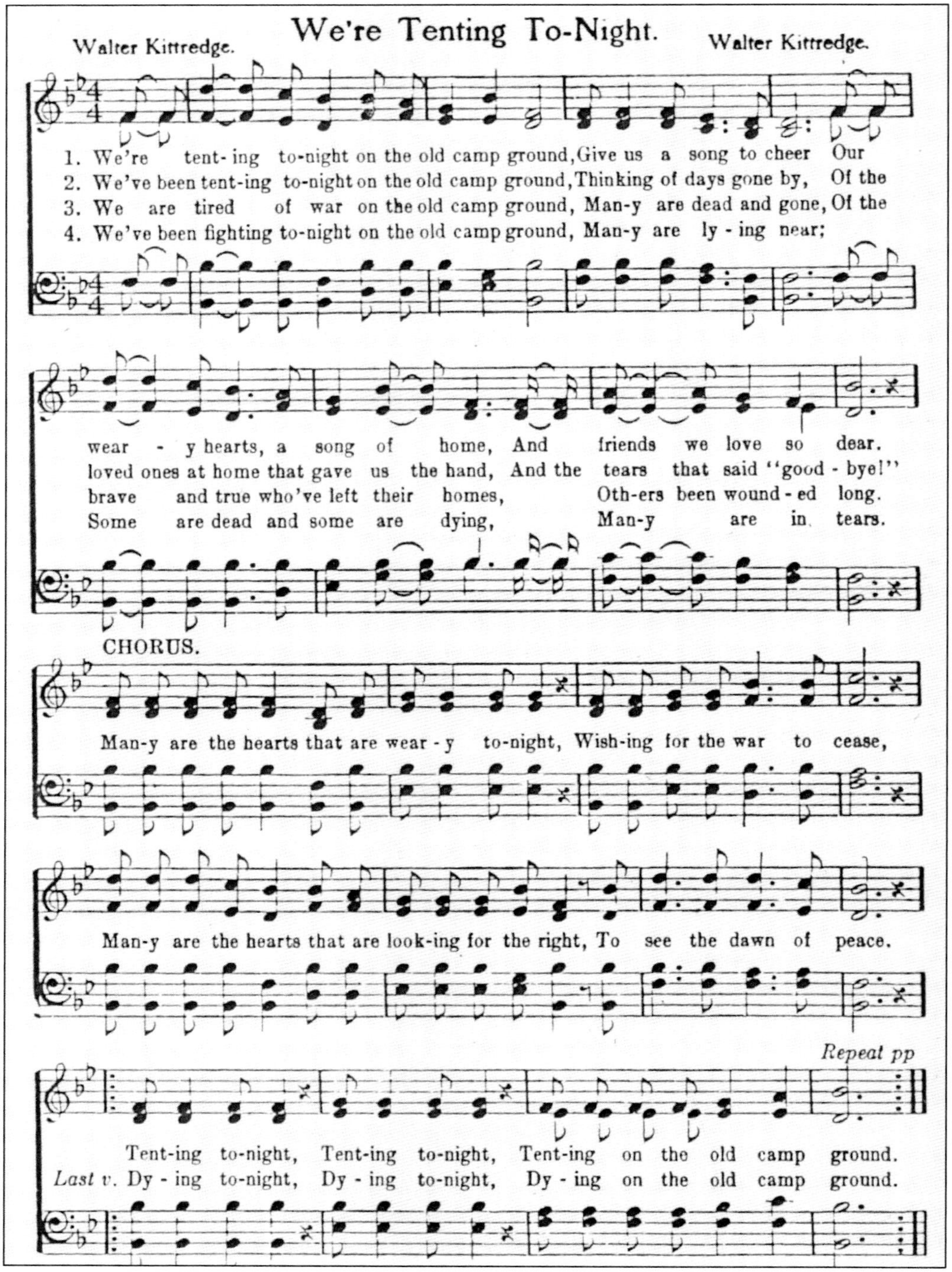
We're Tenting To-Night.
Walter Kittredge.
Walter Kittredge.
1. We're tent-ing to-night on the old camp ground, Give us a song to cheer Our
2. We've been tent-ing to-night on the old camp ground, Thinking of days gone by, Of the
3. We are tired of war on the old camp ground, Man-y are dead and gone, Of the
4. We've been fighting to-night on the old camp ground, Man-y are ly-ing near;
wear-y hearts, a song of home, And friends we love so dear.
loved ones at home that gave us the hand, And the tears that said "good-bye!"
brave and true who've left their homes, Oth-ers been wound-ed long.
Some are dead and some are dying, Man-y are in tears.
CHORUS.
Man-y are the hearts that are wear-y to-night, Wish-ing for the war to cease,
Man-y are the hearts that are look-ing for the right, To see the dawn of peace.
Repeat pp
Tent-ing to-night, Tent-ing to-night, Tent-ing on the old camp ground.
Last v. Dy-ing to-night, Dy-ing to-night, Dy-ing on the old camp ground.

WALTER KITTREDGE. A minstrel, author, and composer, Walter Kittredge is famous for writing the Civil War song "We're Tenting Tonight." He often performed at the Merrimack House (McConihe's Tavern), and was known as the "Minstrel of Merrimack."

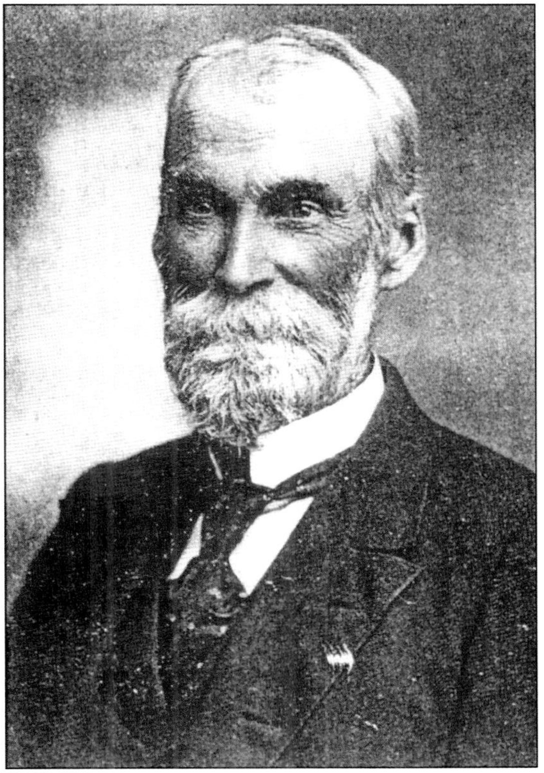

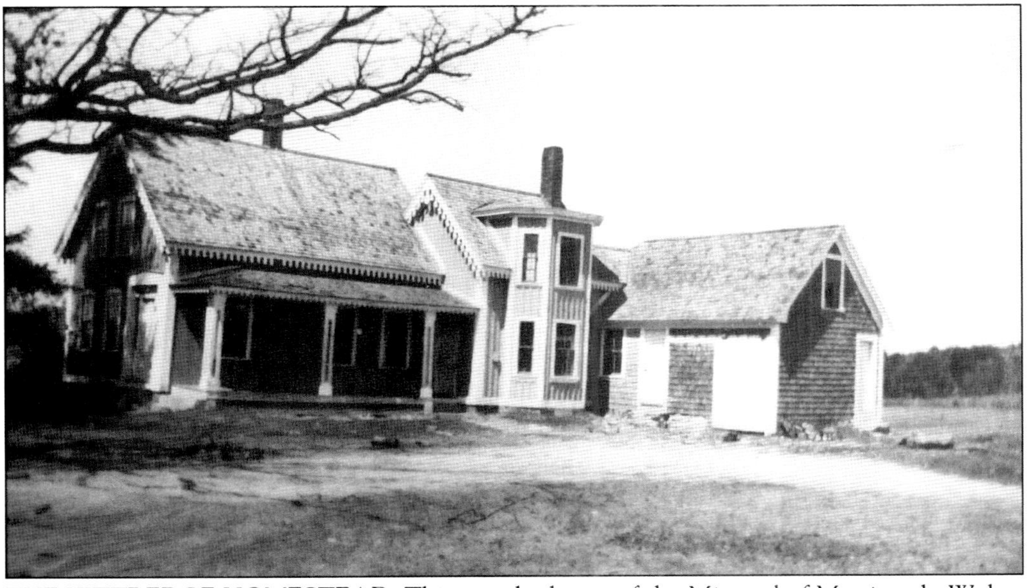

THE KITTREDGE HOMESTEAD. This was the home of the Minstrel of Merrimack, Walter Kittredge. Many of his songs were written in this house. The house no longer exists, having been destroyed by a fire.

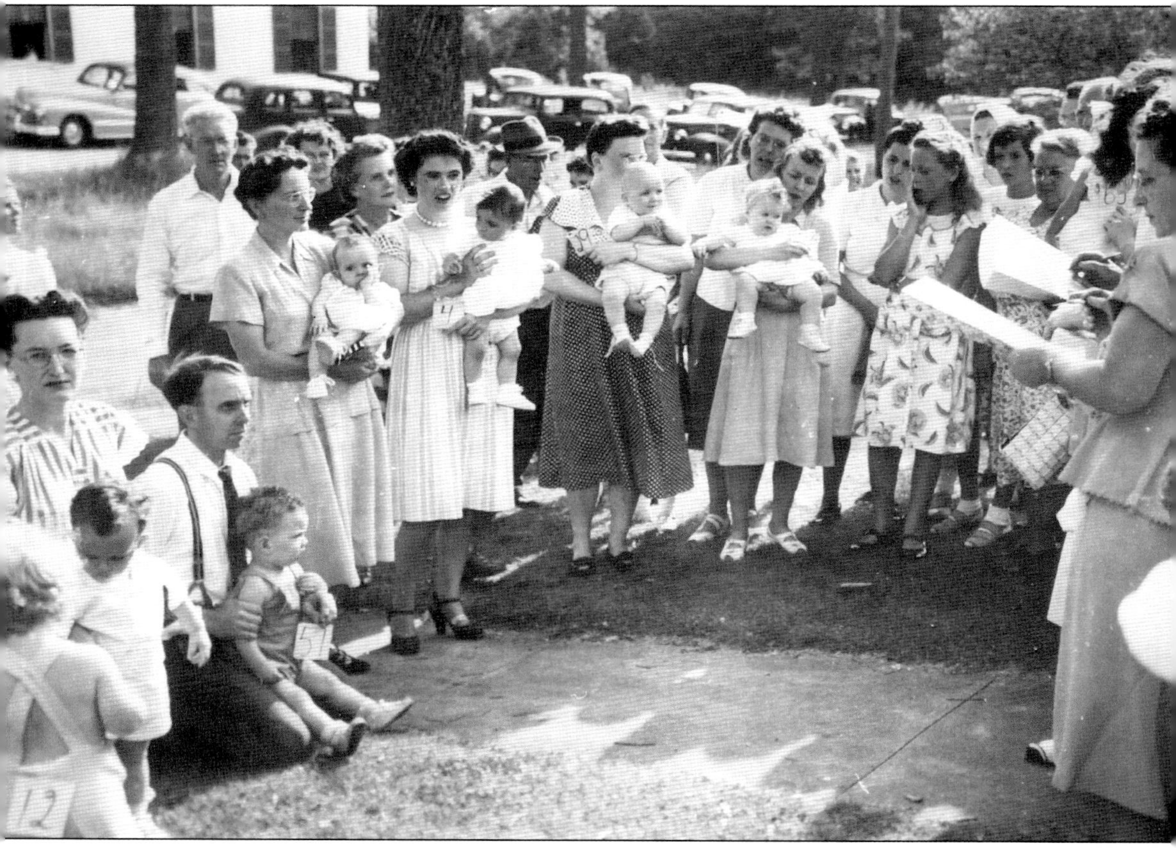

BEAUTY PAGEANTS. Merrimack may never have had a Miss America, but it has had its share of beauties. There is no record as to who won this beauty contest. Maybe the judges couldn't decide.

Three

Food and Lodging

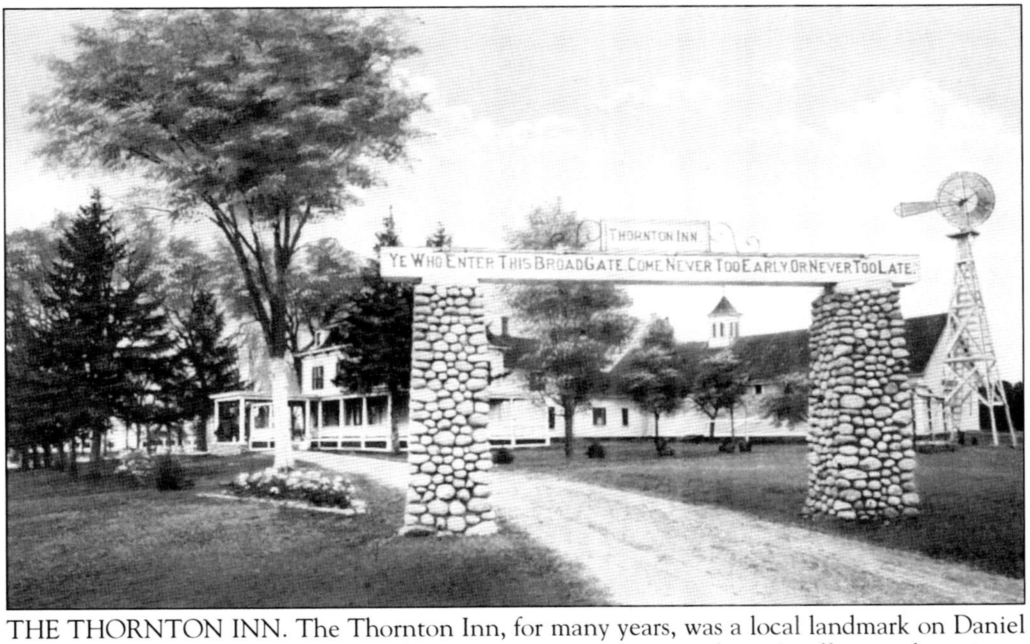

THE THORNTON INN. The Thornton Inn, for many years, was a local landmark on Daniel Webster Highway, and it has served as an inn, a restaurant, a doctor's office, and a private home. It is now an office complex.

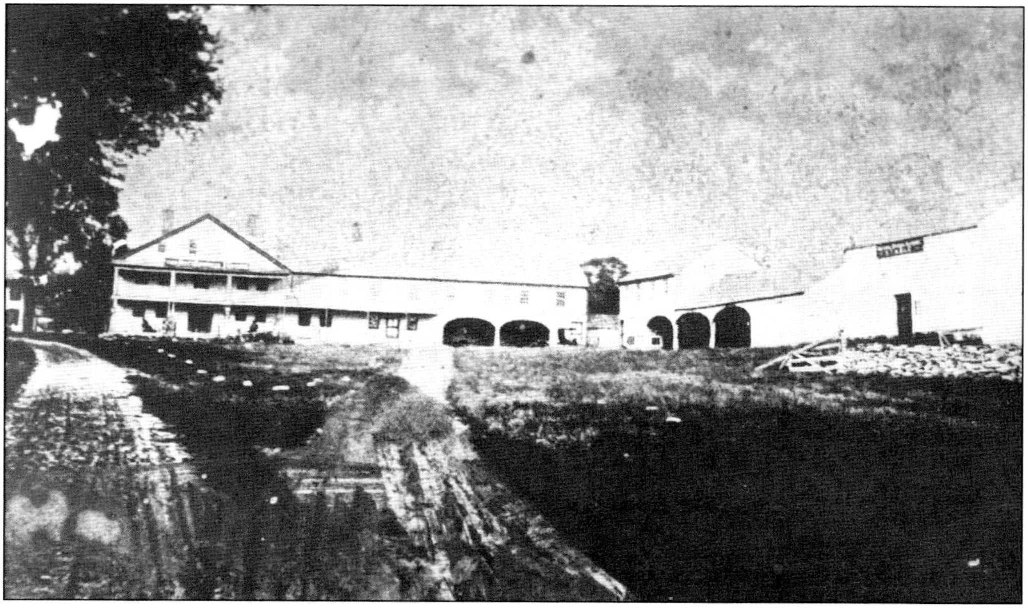

THE ROCKINGHAM HOUSE. Built prior to 1780 by Oliver Farwell, this tavern stood on Naticook Road near the intersection of Route 101A. Known as the Rockingham House, it had a floating dance floor and was quite a famous place. Merrimack's only remaining tavern was destroyed by a fire in 1931.

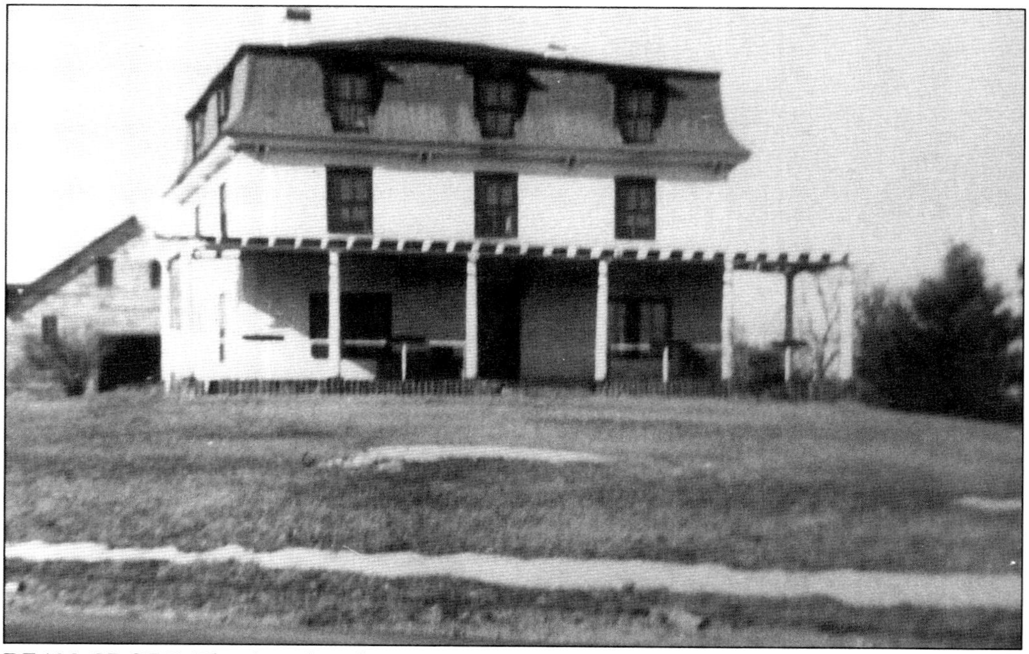

DEAN CROFT. This boarding house was rumored to be the most notorious place between Boston and Concord. It stood between the Merrimack River and Route 3, and was often frequented by travelers. It was torn down and replaced by a bank.

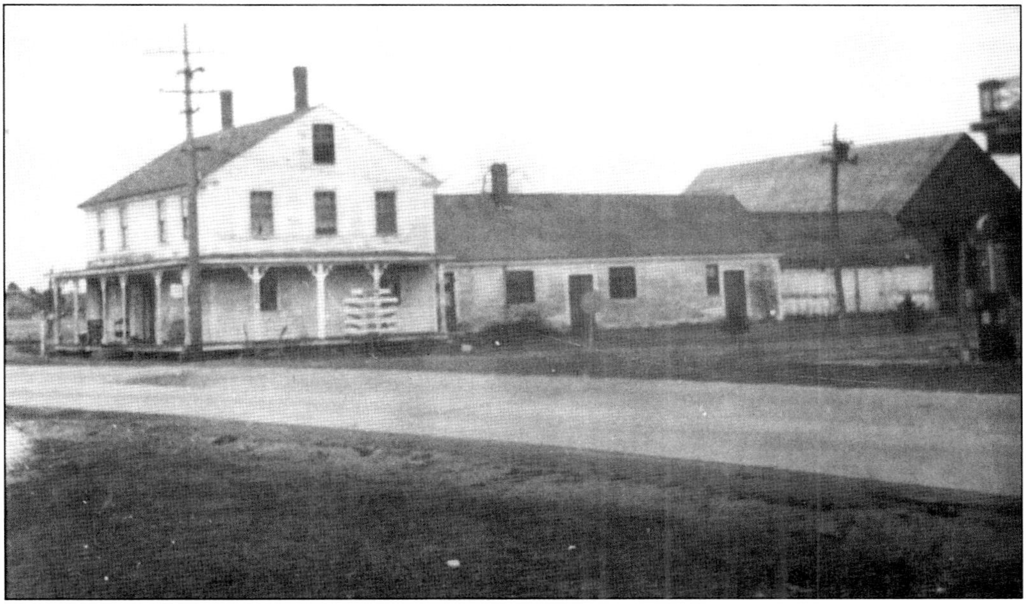

MCGAW'S TAVERN. The small Cape-style section of this house was known as McGaw's Tavern. It was located on Route 3, west of the Merrimack River near Reed's Ferry landing, and was often frequented by river travelers. The front of the house was added later and at one time it housed the post office. The site is now a gas station.

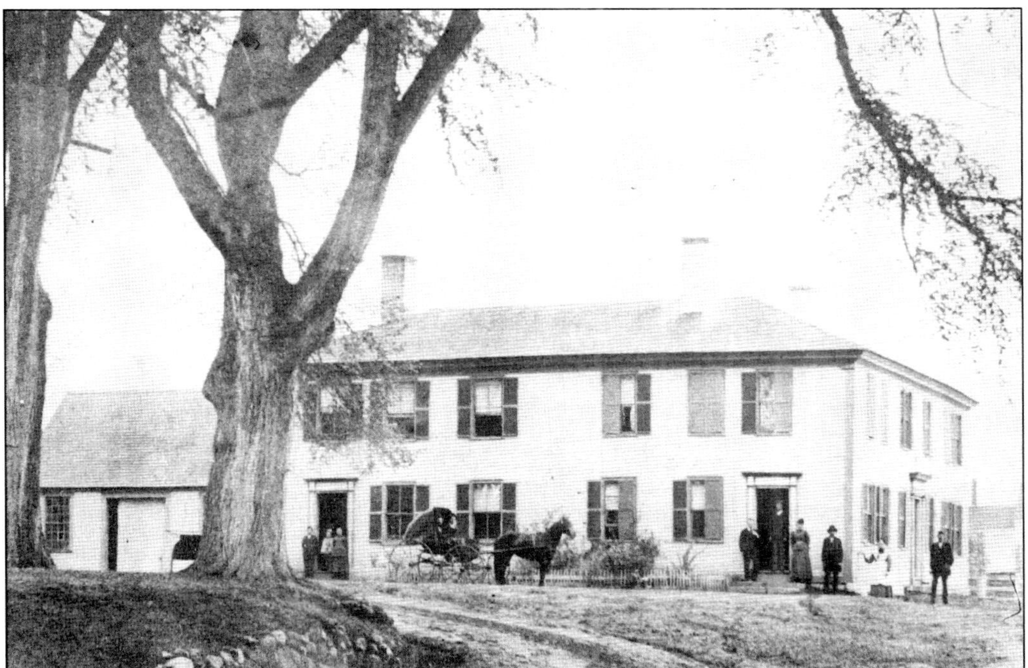

MCCONIHE'S TAVERN. This tavern, also known as Nevin's Tavern and the Merrimack House, was located where the library is now. It was moved to the other side of Daniel Webster Highway when the library was built and is now a private home.

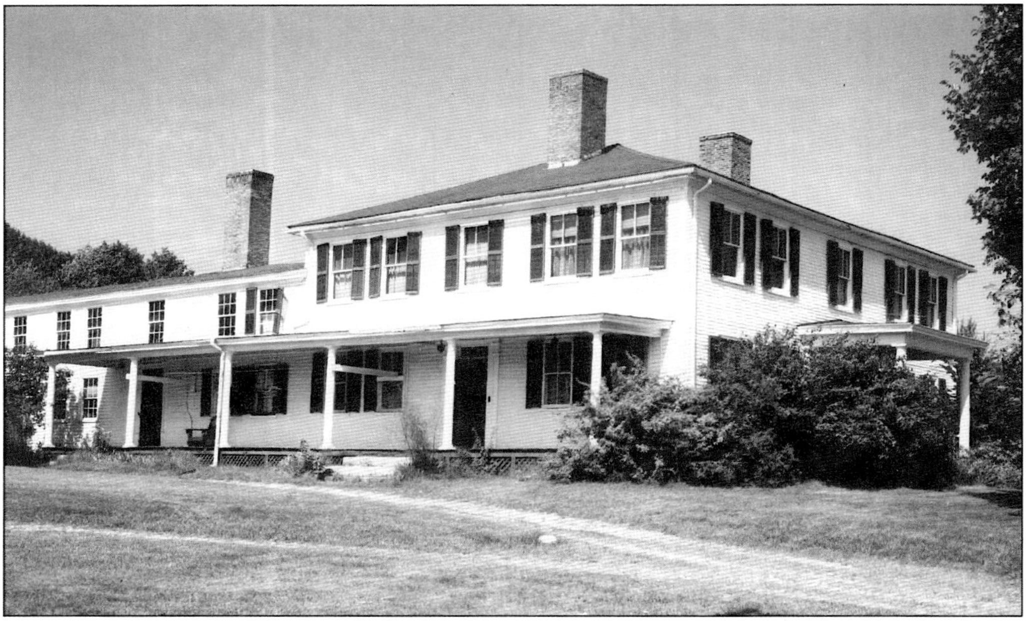

RIDDLE'S TAVERN. Isaac Riddle built this tavern in 1807 for the use of the stockholders and officers of Riddle's Mills. The second floor of the building could be converted from a large ballroom to individual rooms by the use of sliding panels. Located on Daniel Webster Highway, it later became a private home and then the Country Gourmet Restaurant and Cafe.

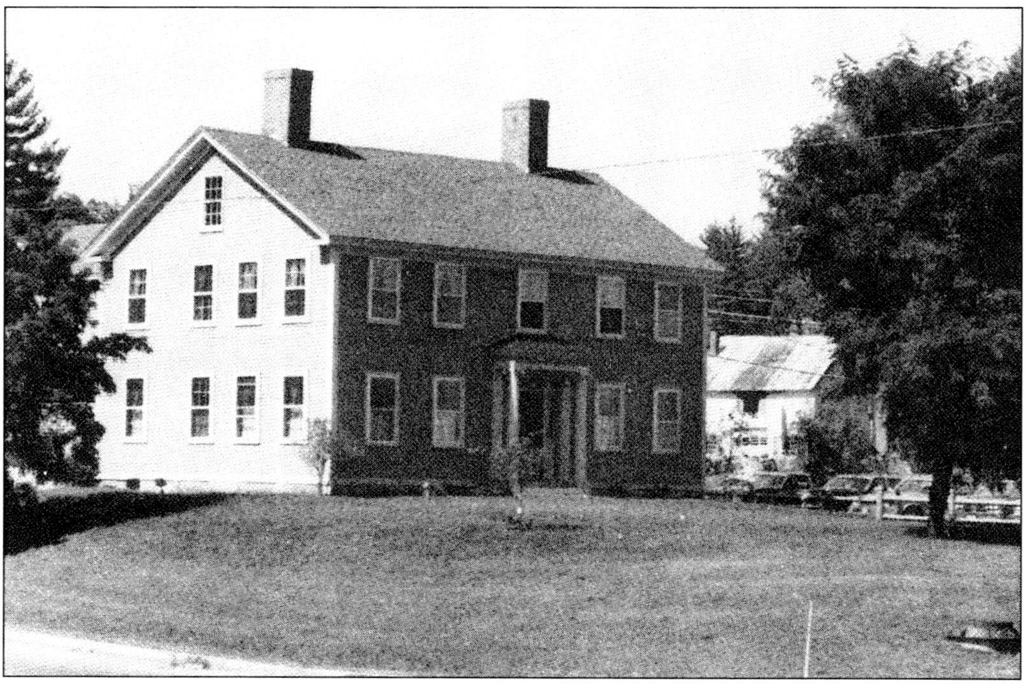

HANNAH JACK TAVERN. James Thornton operated this tavern in the early 1800s. It was built by his father, Matthew Thornton, who signed the Declaration of Independence. It has been a private home, a doctor's office, and an apartment house. It is currently a restaurant.

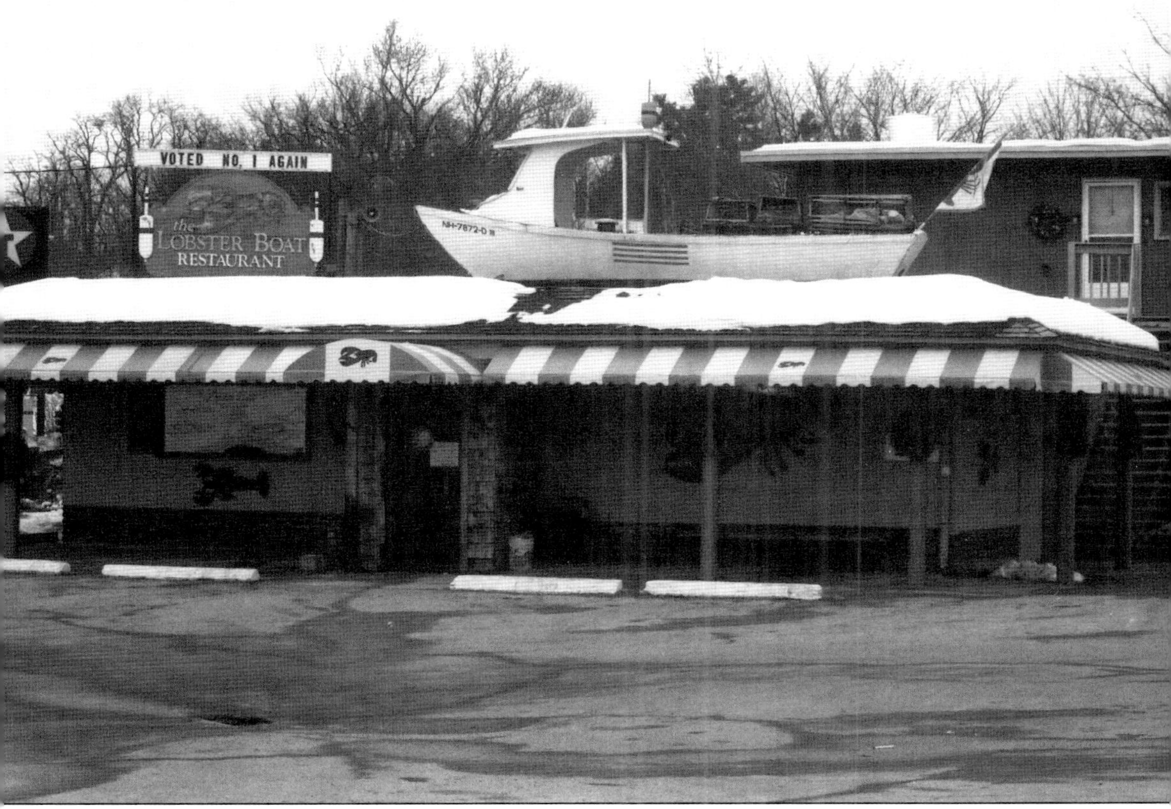

THE LOBSTER BOAT. Washington may not have slept in Merrimack; however, it is rumored that President Jackson did. We do know for sure that Vice President Quayle ate here; his picture hangs on the wall of this restaurant on Route 3 to prove it.

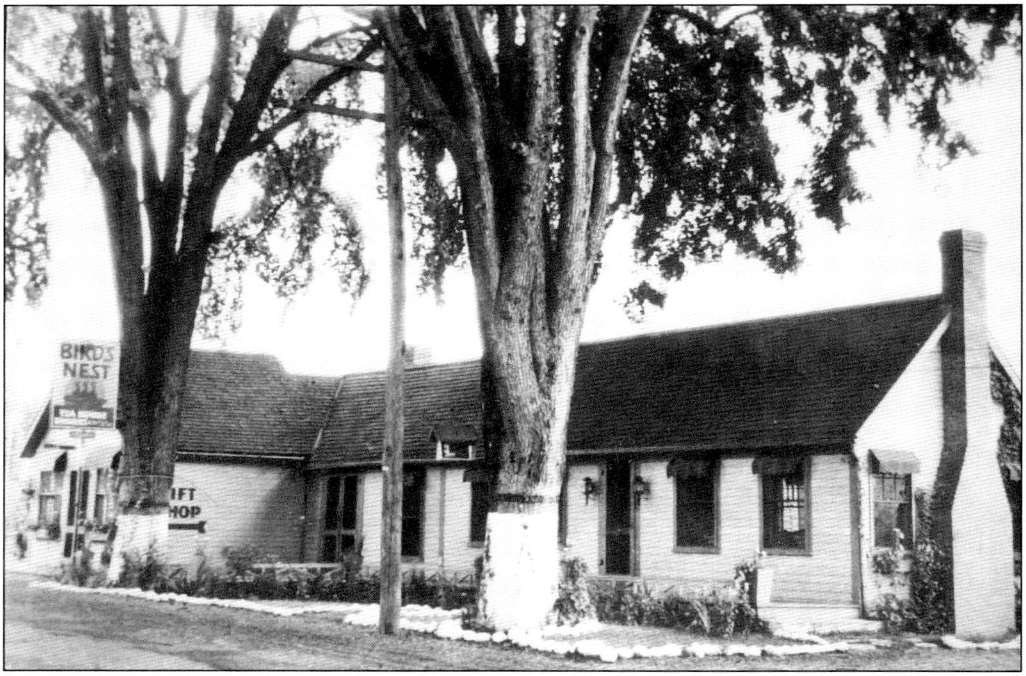

THE BIRD'S NEST TEA HOUSE. The charming little eating establishments along Route 3, where one could stop for afternoon tea, have become a thing of the past.

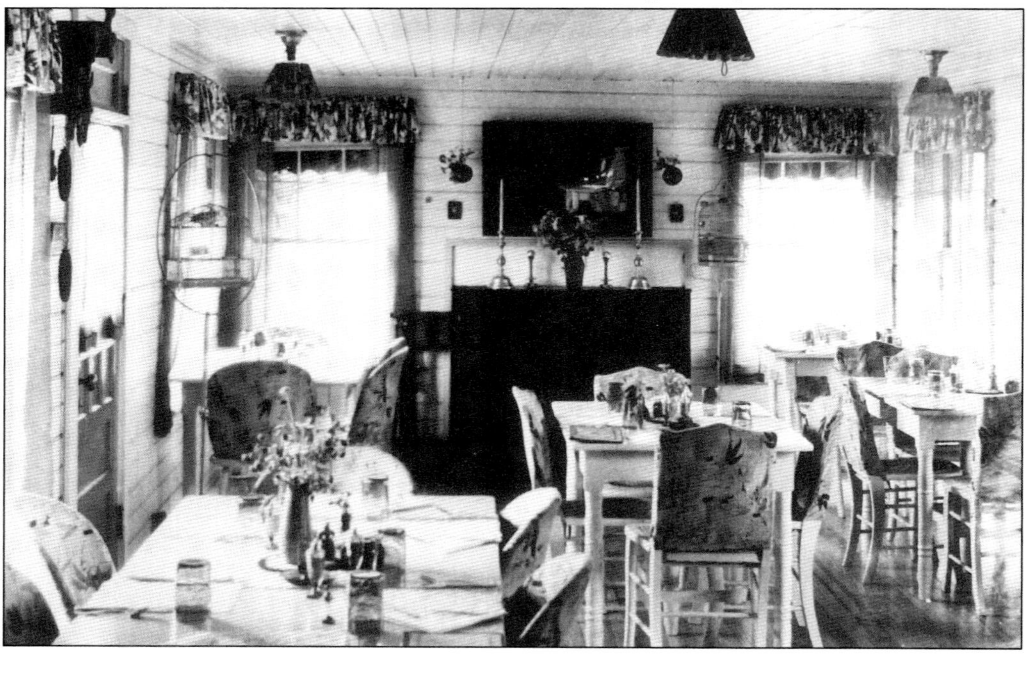

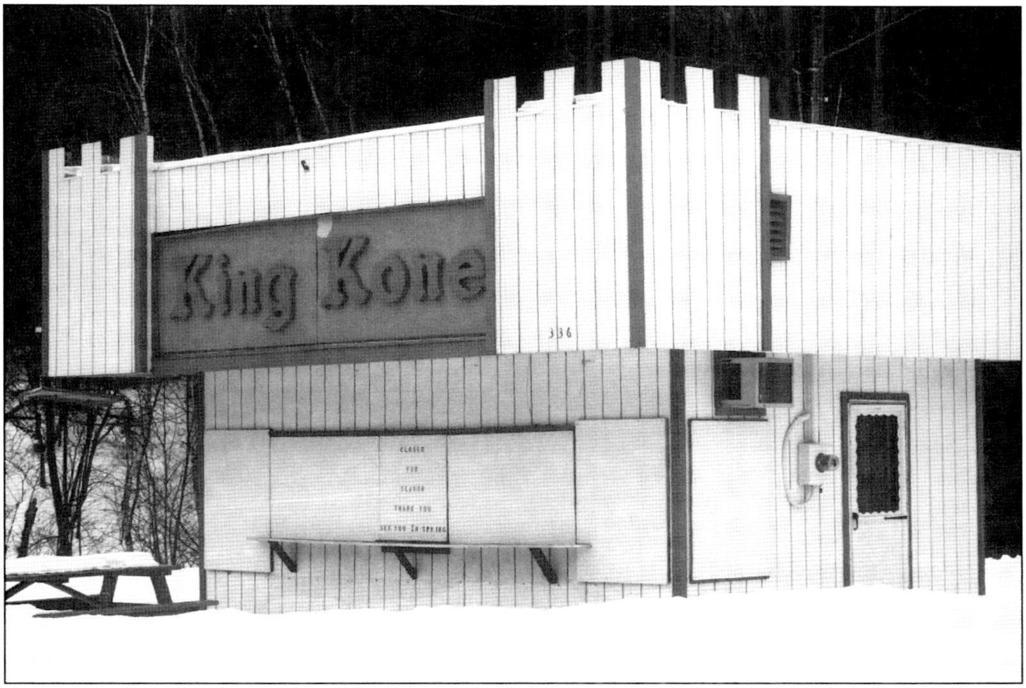

KING KONE. Merrimack's most popular ice cream stand is located on Daniel Webster Highway. Summer begins and ends with the opening and closing of King Kone.

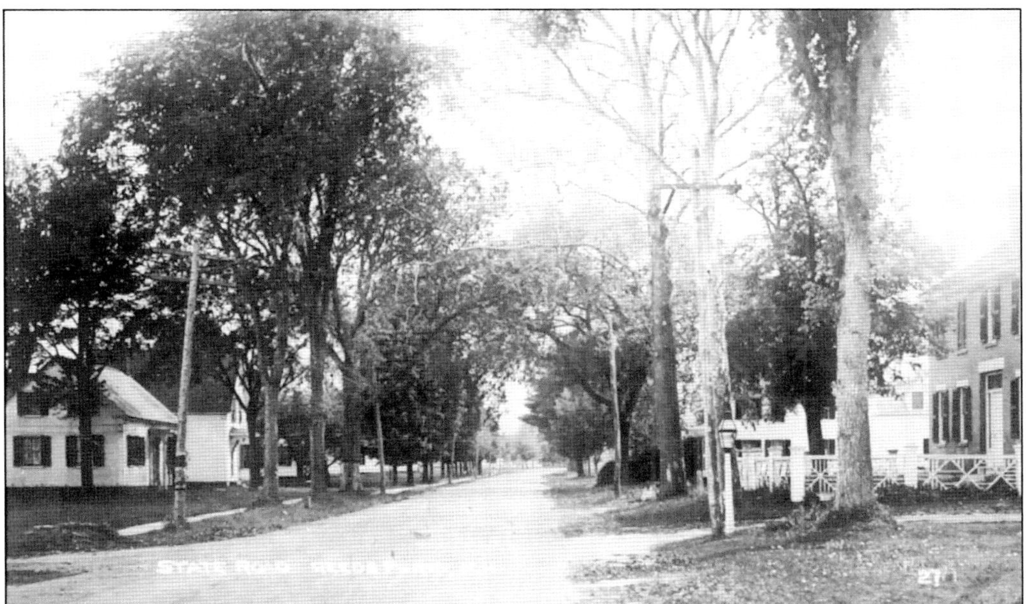

TORTILLA FLAT. A Mexican restaurant, located in the northern section of town, was established by combining the two houses on the left side of this picture. They were the former homes of Doctor Butterfield and Town Clerk Claude Maker.

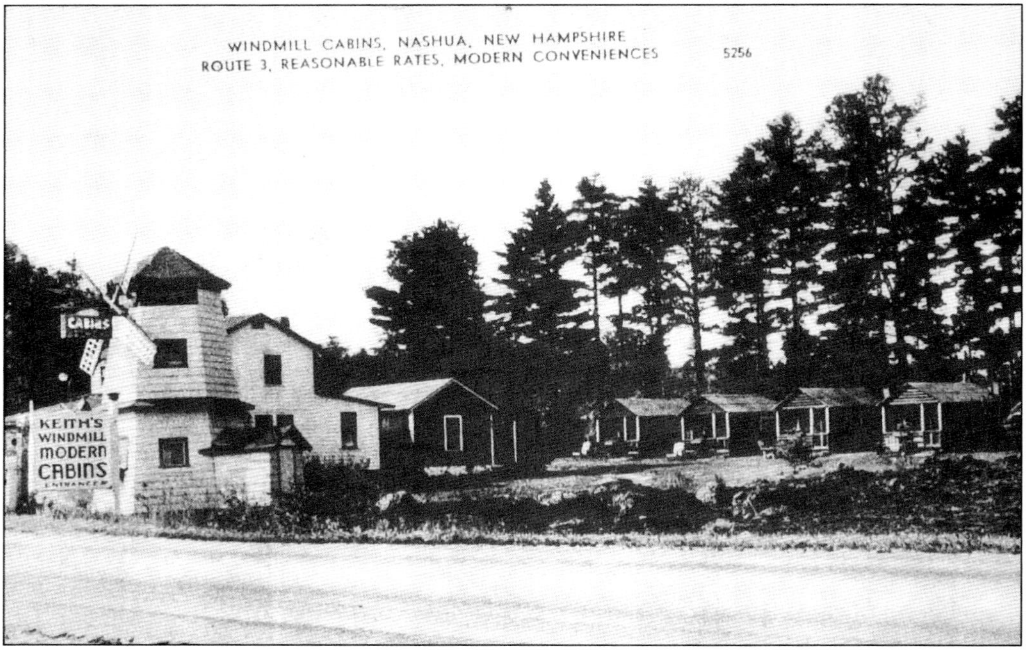

THE WINDMILL CABINS. Because of the postal address, the Windmill Cabins were often thought to be located in Nashua. However, being located across Daniel Webster Highway from where the Nashua Corporation is now, they were definitely in Merrimack.

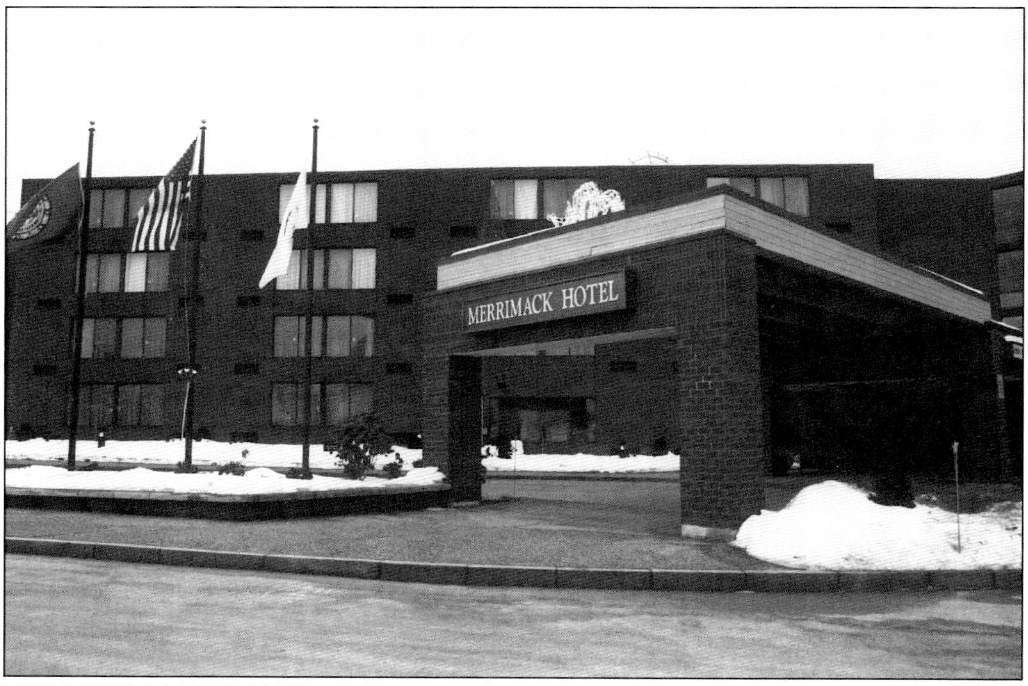

THE MERRIMACK HOTEL. Following in the tradition of providing a respite to travelers, the Merrimack Hilton was built as a two hundred-room luxury hotel with a gourmet restaurant, convention center, and coffee shop. It is now the Merrimack Hotel.

Four

Disasters

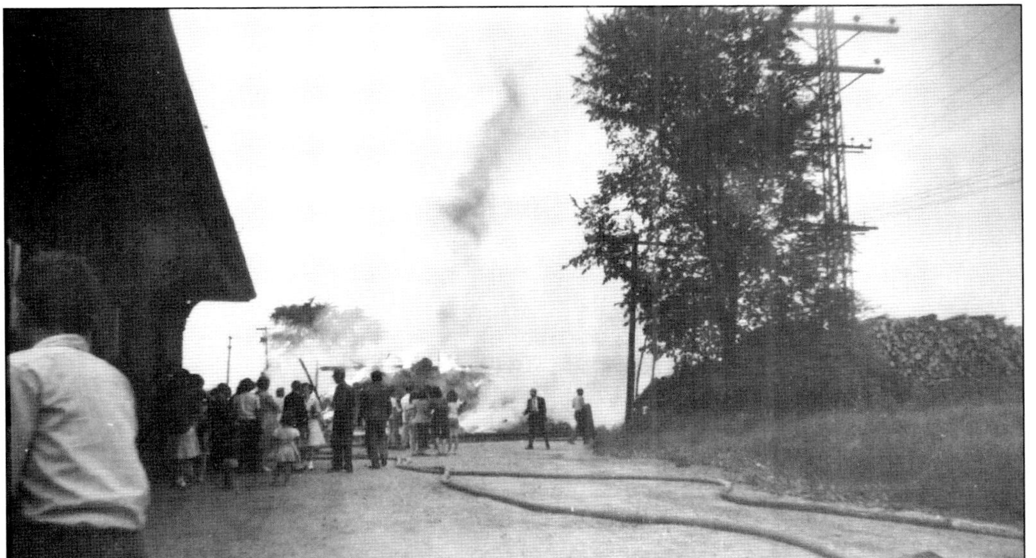

HASELTINE'S EXCELSIOR SHOP. Excelsior, a stripped-wood packing material, is prone to fire. This shop was the scene of three fires, the last of which, in 1946, burned it to the ground. The lumber, however, was saved. It was located next to the train tracks at the end of Railroad Avenue.

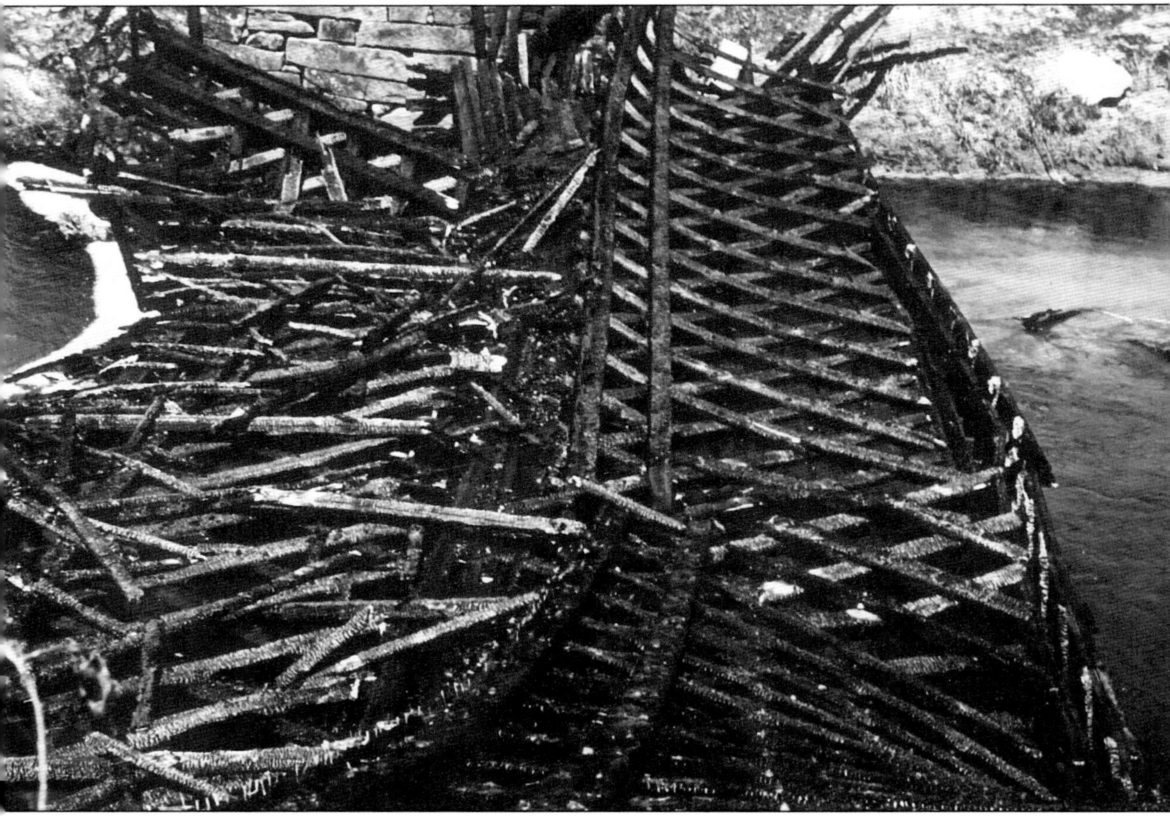

COVERED BRIDGES. Merrimack was fortunate to have two covered bridges. Both the Turkey Hill Bridge and Field's Bridge spanned the Souhegan River. Within one year, in the 1960s, both were destroyed by arsonists.

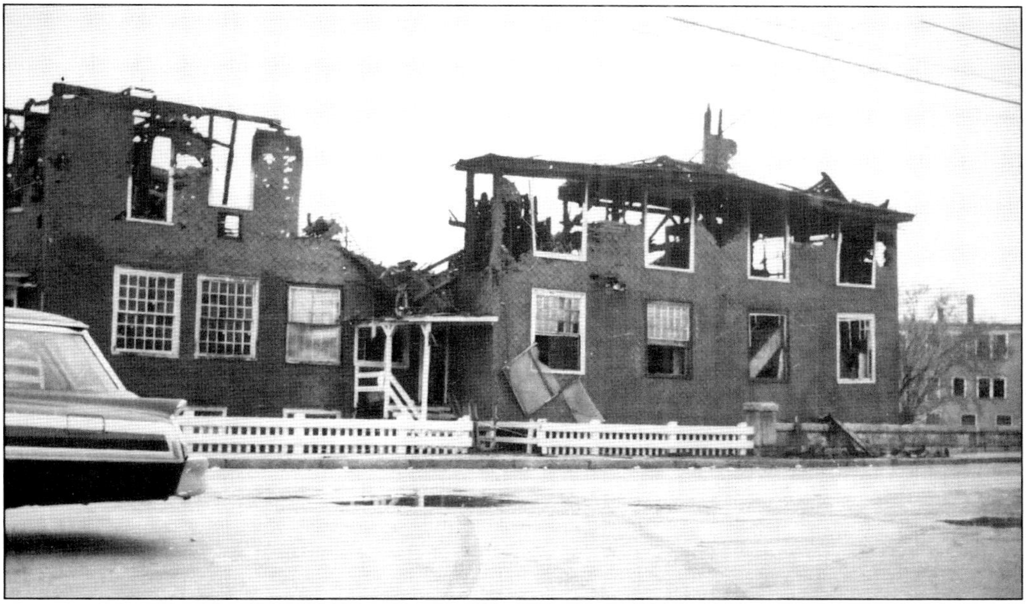

THE GATE CITY POULTRY PLANT. A spectacular fire destroyed this poultry plant in the 1950s. Because of the building's proximity to the chemical plant on Route 3, the fire caused some frantic moments for residents and firefighters.

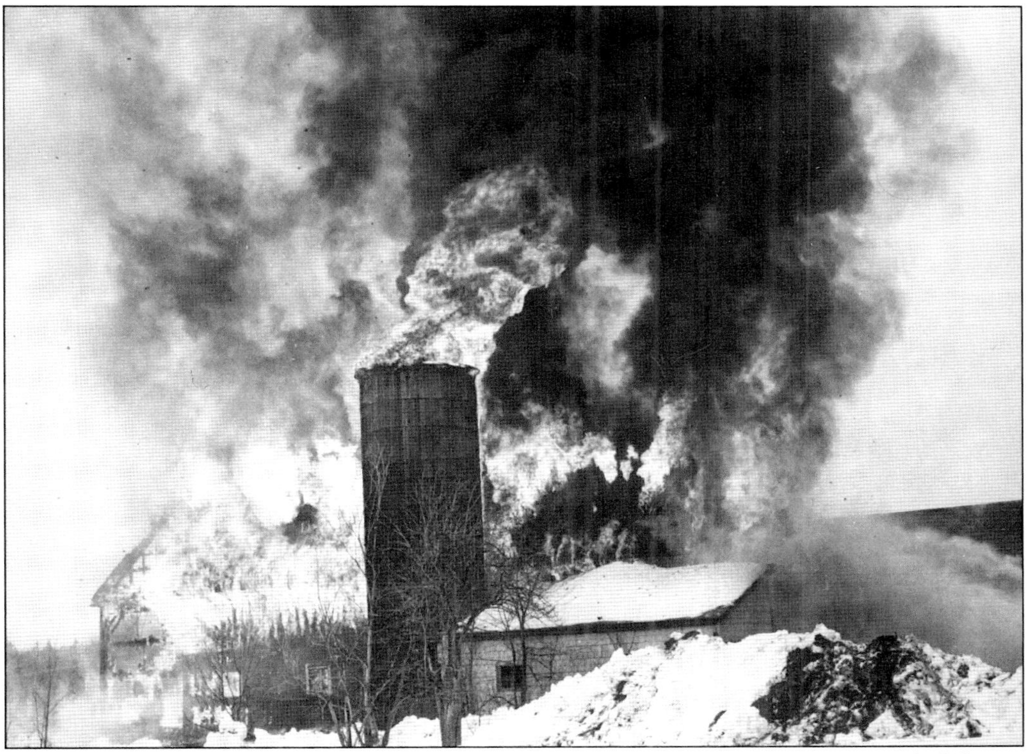

THE NIKILAS ANAGNOSTOU FARM. This property, located on Bedford Road, fell into disrepair and was burned as a training exercise for the fire department in 1973.

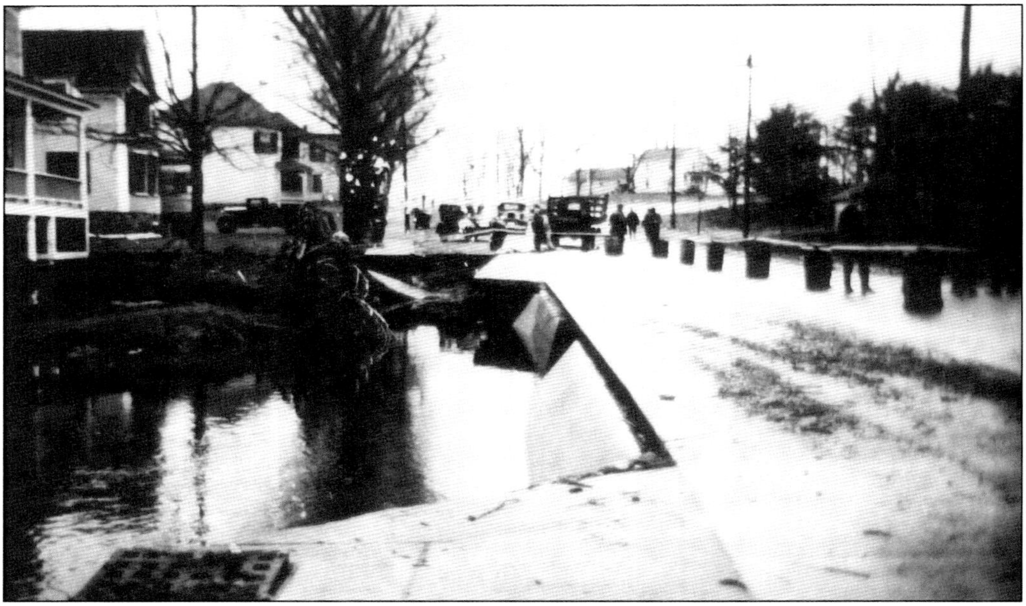

THE 1936 FLOOD. The winter of 1936 was a harsh one with much snow. When the snow melted and the spring rains came, the Merrimack and Souhegan Rivers overflowed their banks. Severe damage was done to the highway near the Central Fire Station. The bridge was destroyed and had to be replaced.

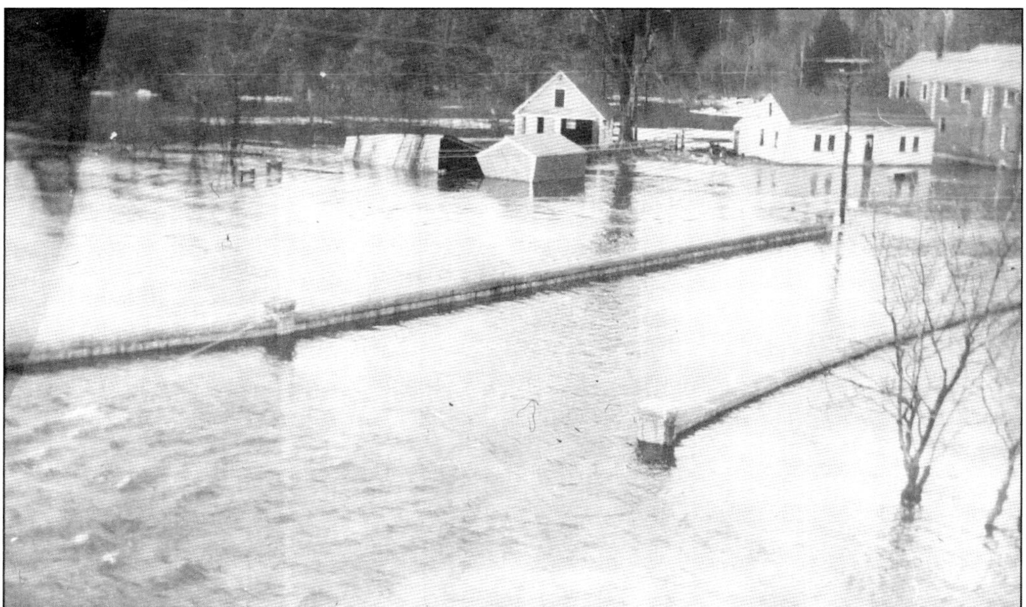

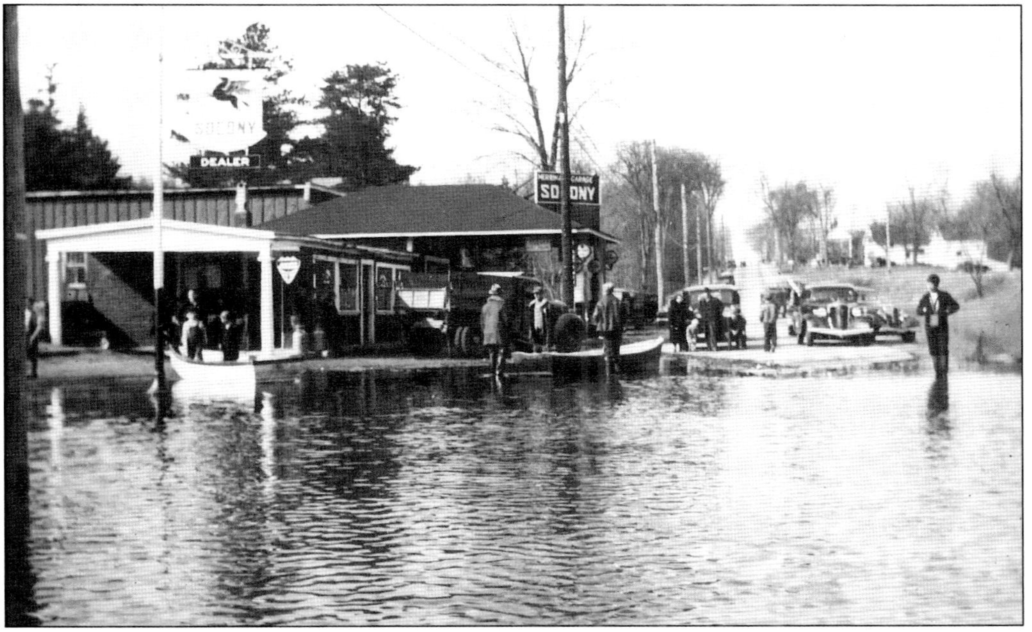

GRAMMIE AMES'. Greenleaf's Store and Station was located where Connell's Shopping Mall is now. Many fondly remember it as Grammie Ames'.

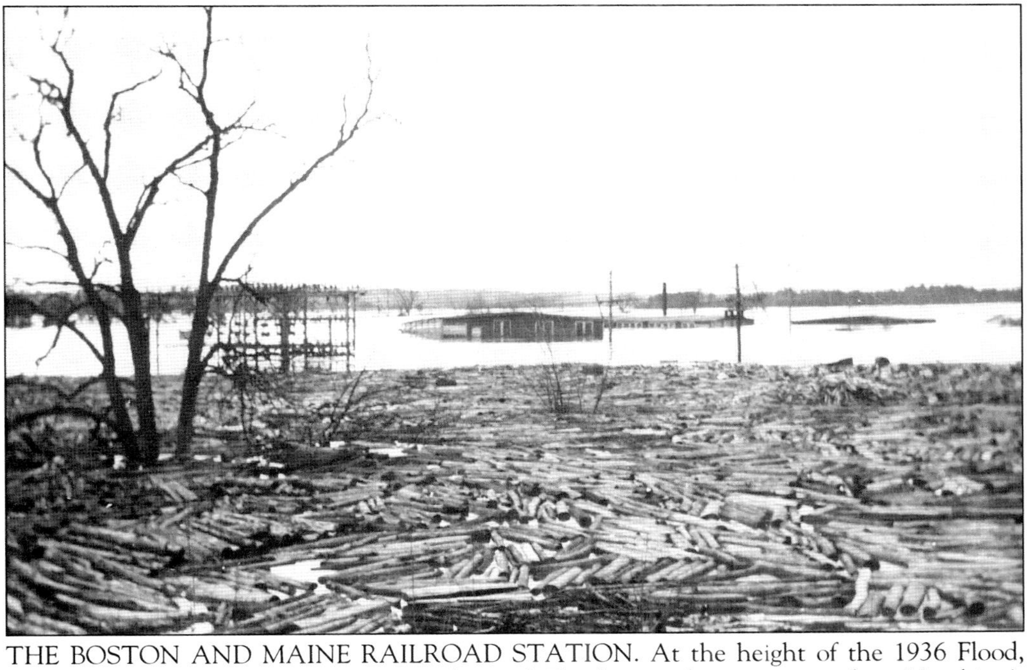

THE BOSTON AND MAINE RAILROAD STATION. At the height of the 1936 Flood, all that could be seen of the depot was the roof. The logs in the picture are from Haseltine's Excelsior Shop next to the depot.

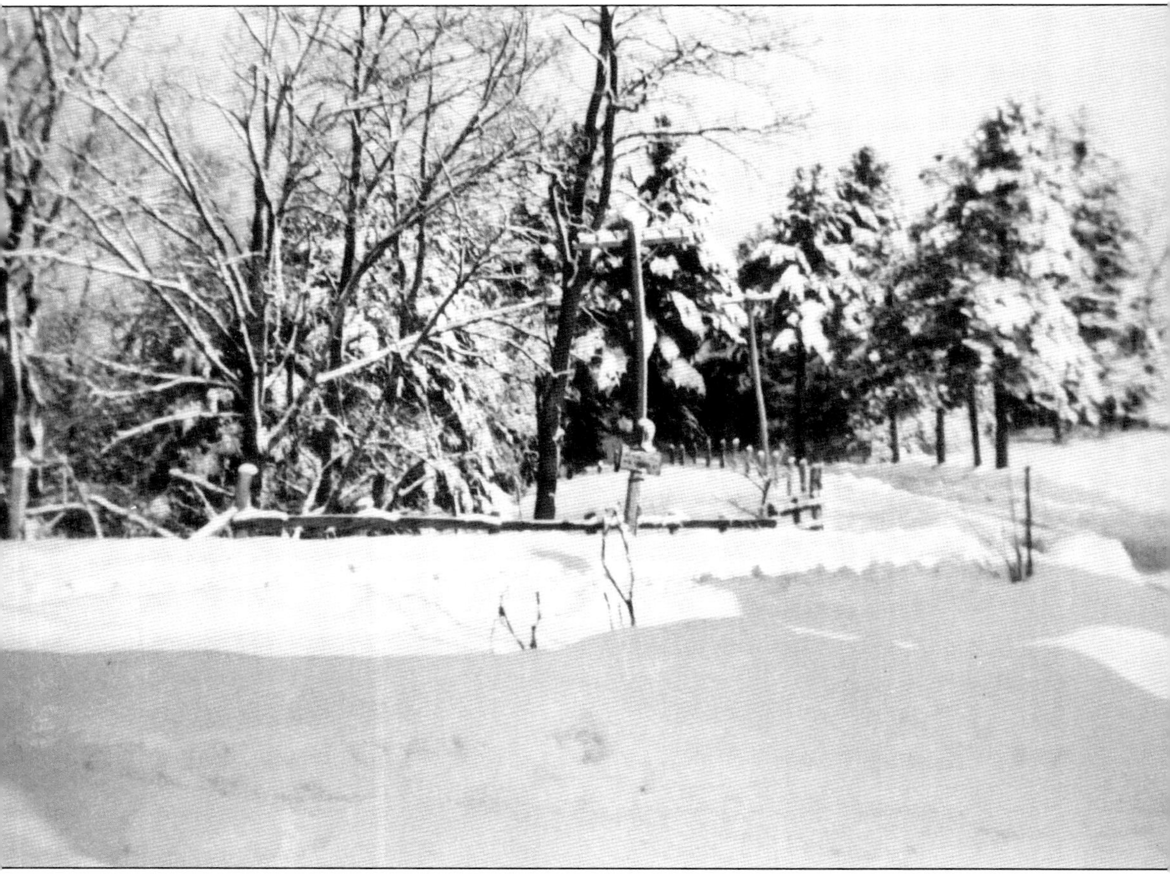

THE BLIZZARD OF 1940. This photograph of Meetinghouse Road, just after a big snow storm, shows where the road used to run. It now runs on the other side of the cemetery.

Five

Transportation

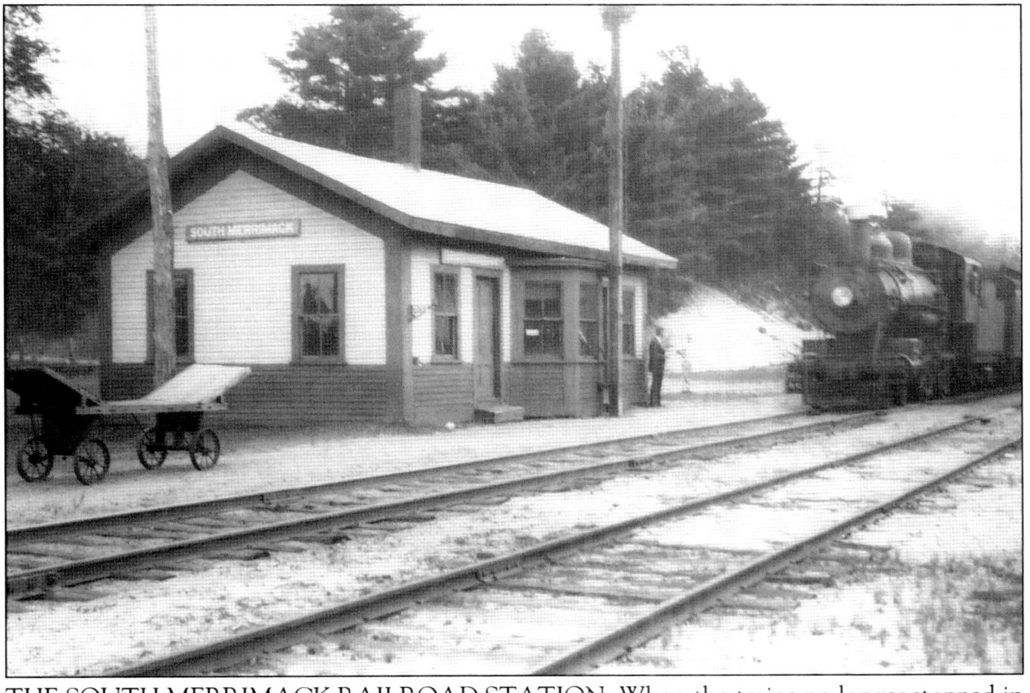

THE SOUTH MERRIMACK RAILROAD STATION. When the trains no longer stopped in South Merrimack, this station was no longer needed. Rather than tear down a perfectly good building, it was moved to Boston Post Road and remodeled into a private home.

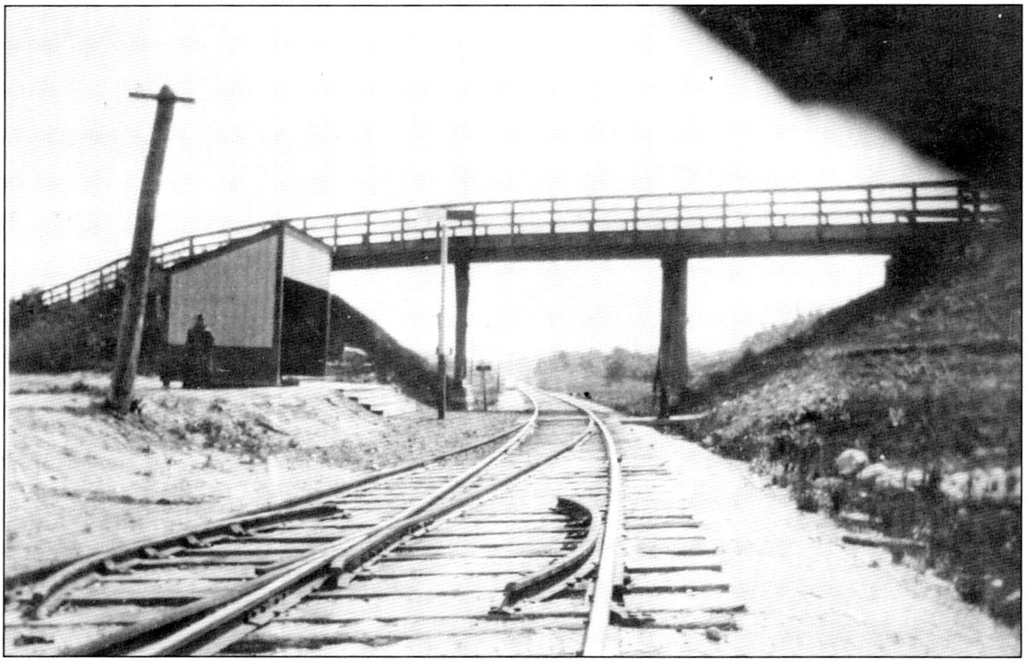

THE STOWELL ROAD STATION. This simple railroad station was the pick up and drop off point for local farmers' produce and for passengers on the line from New Boston through Manchester. Bill Fisk, the engineer on the last run, stated in his diary: "Last passenger train June 13, 1931. Tracks all tore up in 1935."

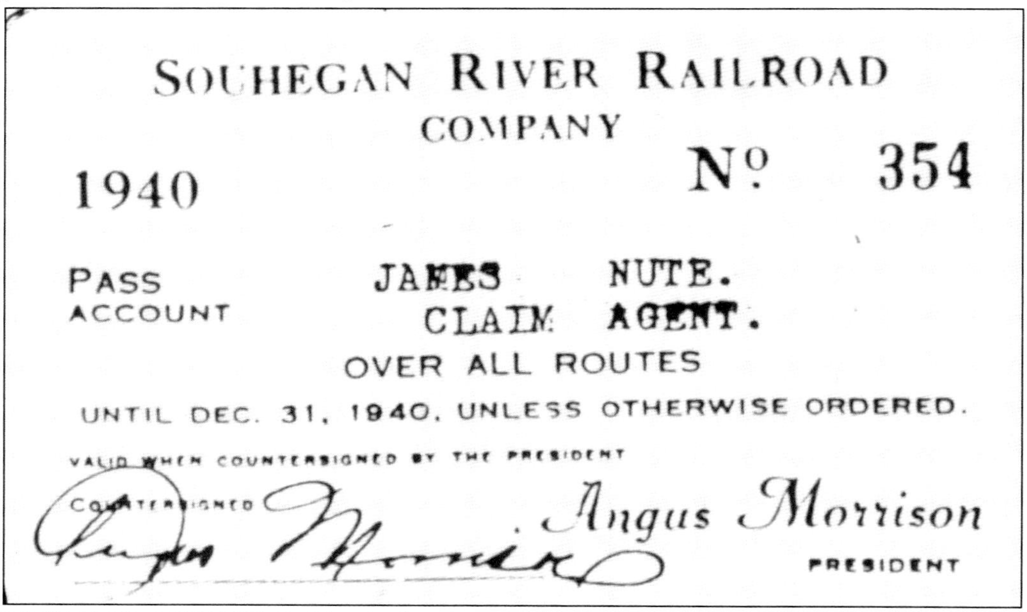

SOUHEGAN RIVER RAILROAD
COMPANY

1940 No 354

PASS ACCOUNT JAMES NUTE.
CLAIM AGENT.

OVER ALL ROUTES

UNTIL DEC. 31, 1940. UNLESS OTHERWISE ORDERED.

VALID WHEN COUNTERSIGNED BY THE PRESIDENT

COUNTERSIGNED

Angus Morrison
PRESIDENT

TICKET TO NOWHERE. The Souhegan River Railroad was all make-believe. Some of the town's men started a "Card Club" as entertainment for themselves in 1940. They filled all the positions needed for the railroad and issued authentic-looking annual passes. Angus Morrison was the president and James Nute was the claim agent.

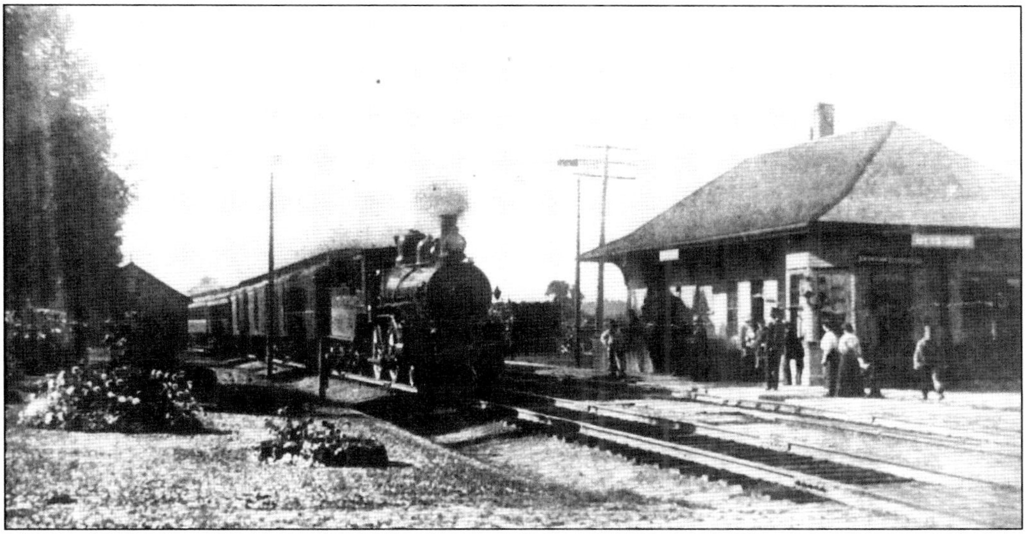

THE MERRIMACK RAILROAD STATION. The railroad came to Merrimack in the late 1850s. Prior to that, the rivers were the main means of travel. Two of the Boston and Maine Railway stations are shown here; the Merrimack station is still standing on Railroad Avenue.

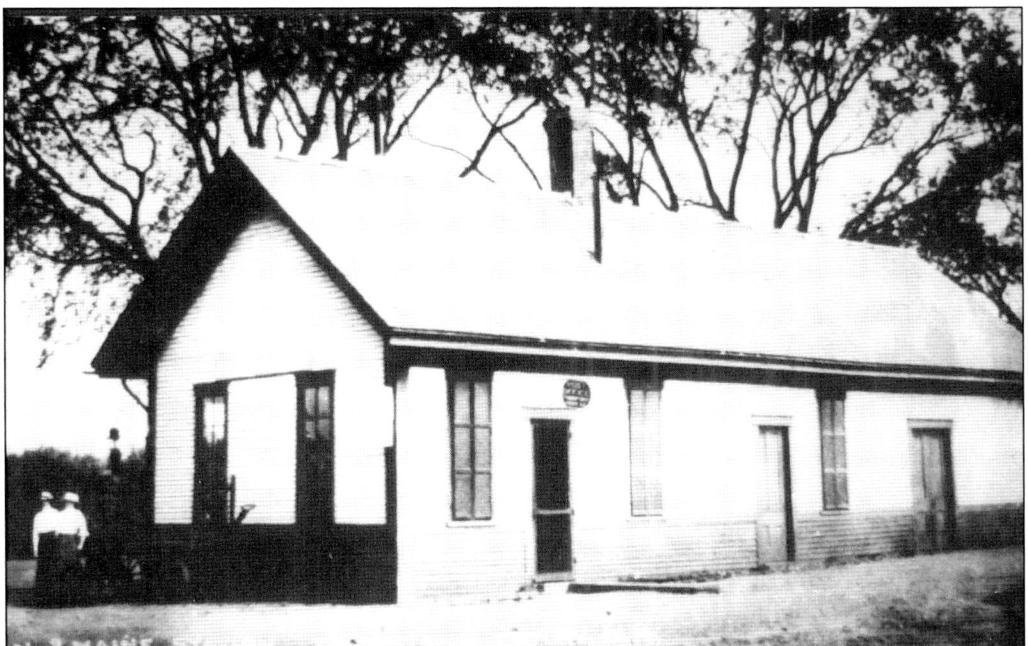

THE THORNTON'S FERRY RAILROAD STATION. Once located on Griffin Street, this station no longer exists. The trains still run through Merrimack but do not stop for passengers.

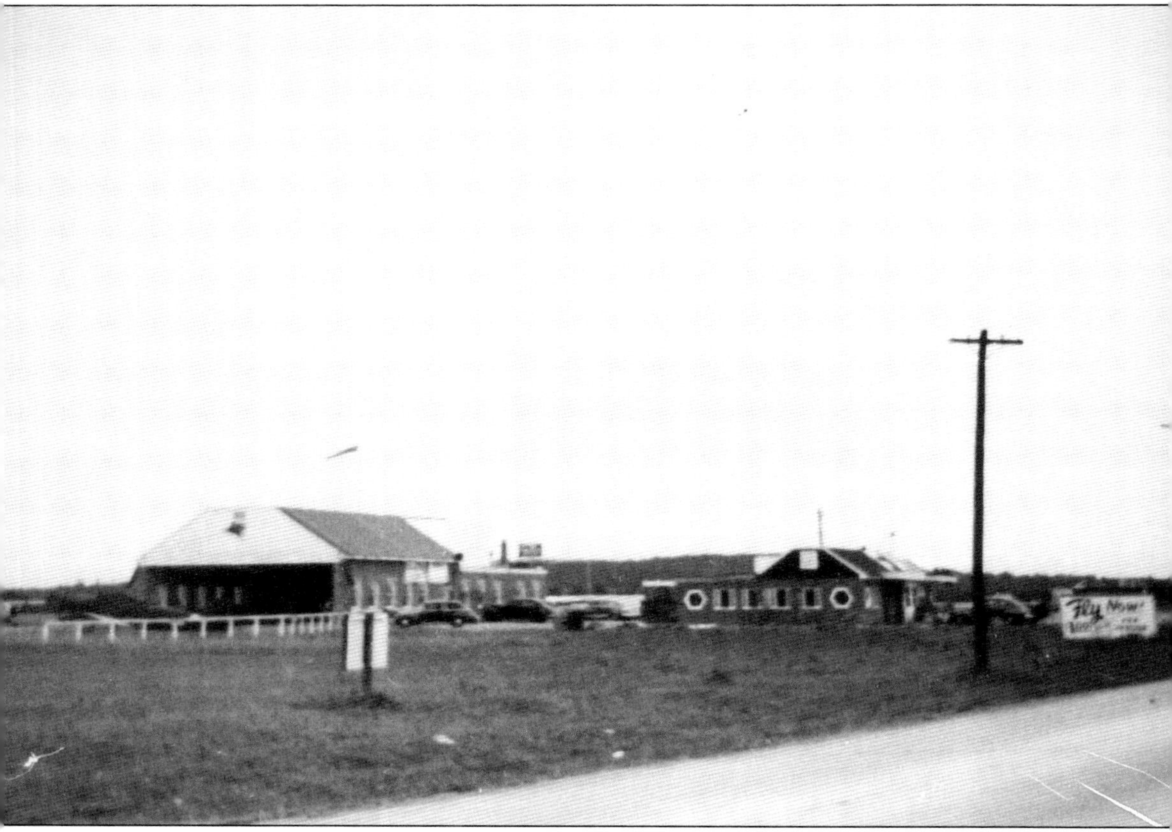

DANIEL WEBSTER AIRWAYS. Many small planes could be seen landing or taking off from here. There was also a lunchroom at the facility. When Sanders Associates bought the property, the airport was closed. They also purchased property north of this where the drive-in theater used to be.

Six

Recreation

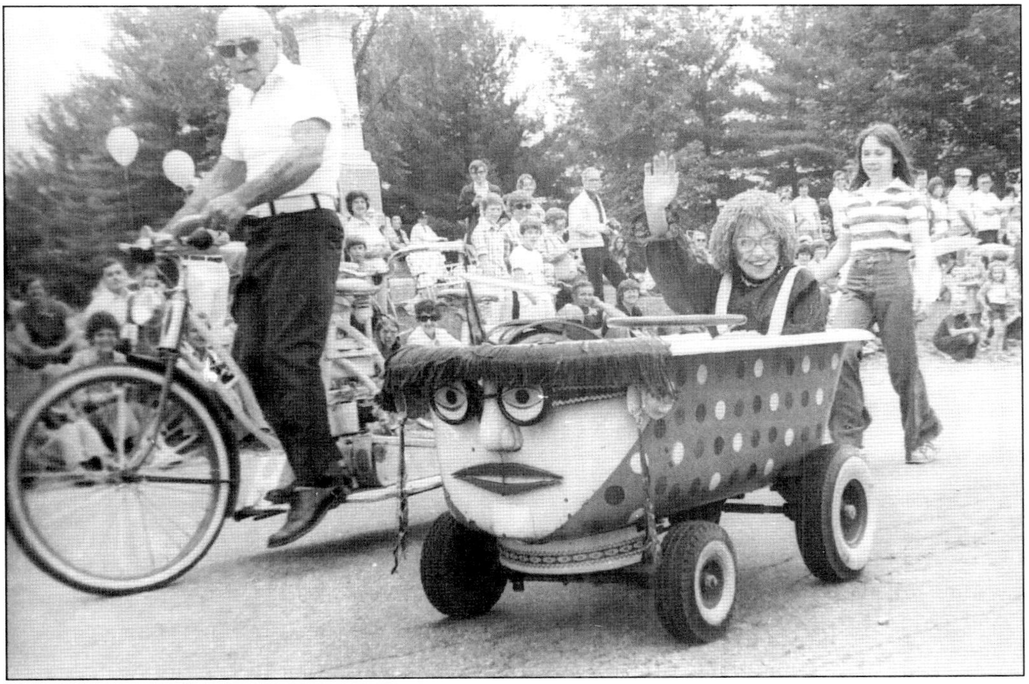

A JULY FOURTH PARADE ENTRY. Some people can afford to ride in limousines, others only on bicycles: and then there are people like this, who ride in bathtubs.

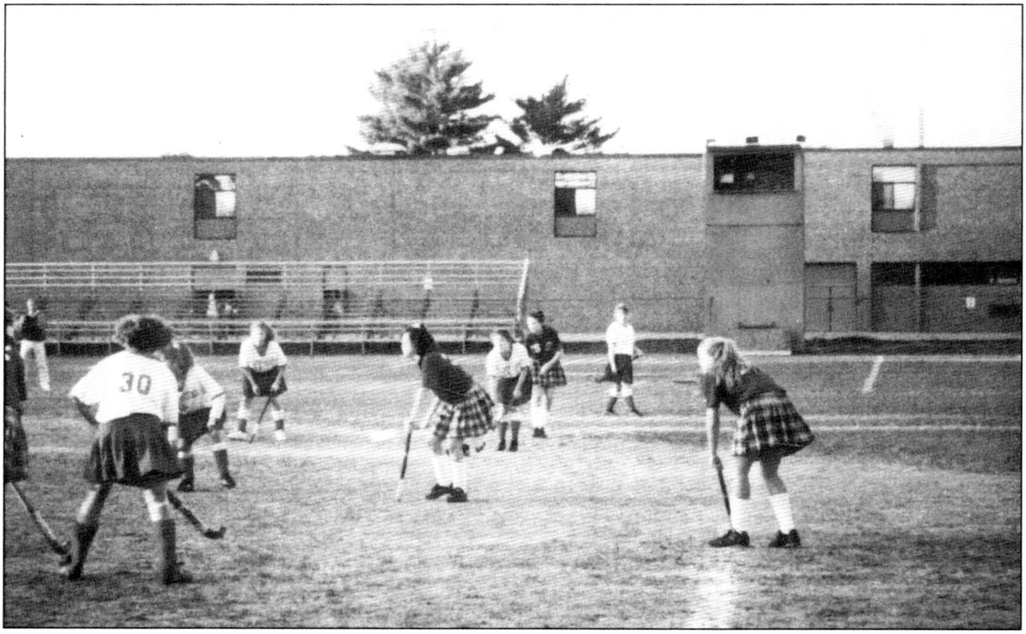

FIELD HOCKEY. Sports programs make up a big part of the high school's extra curricular activities. Girls' field hockey, established in 1978, consists of eleven players per team and is played on a smooth grass field at the high school.

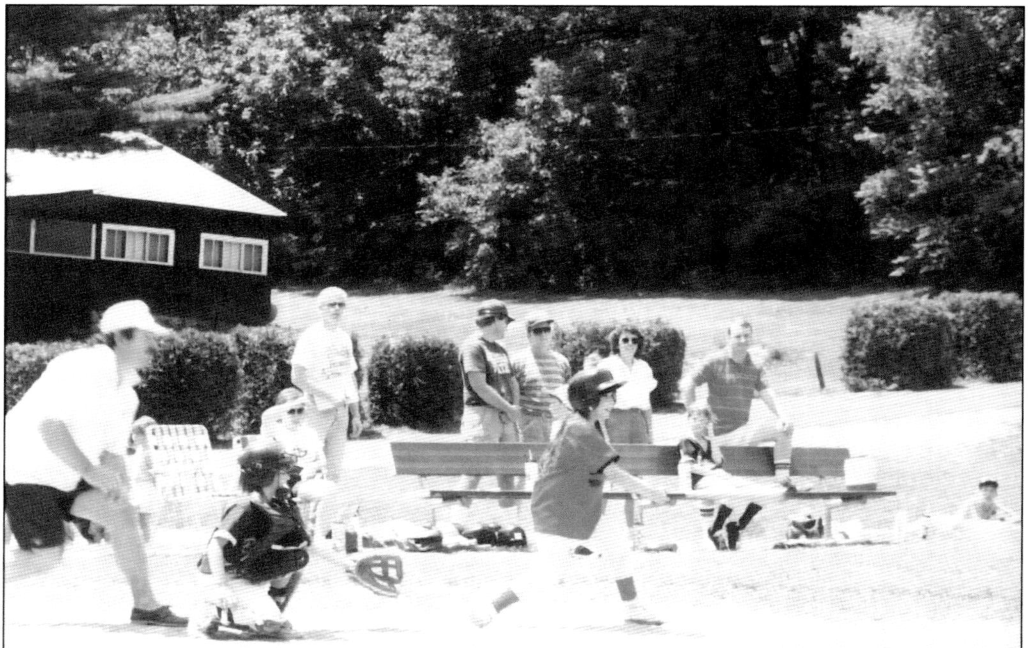

SOFTBALL. Girls, age six to eighteen, make up four leagues that play every spring at Reed's Ferry, Turkey Hill, Wasserman Park, and on school fields. There are no boys' softball teams; however, mens' softball is extremely popular in Merrimack. Most of the mens' teams are sponsored by local businesses.

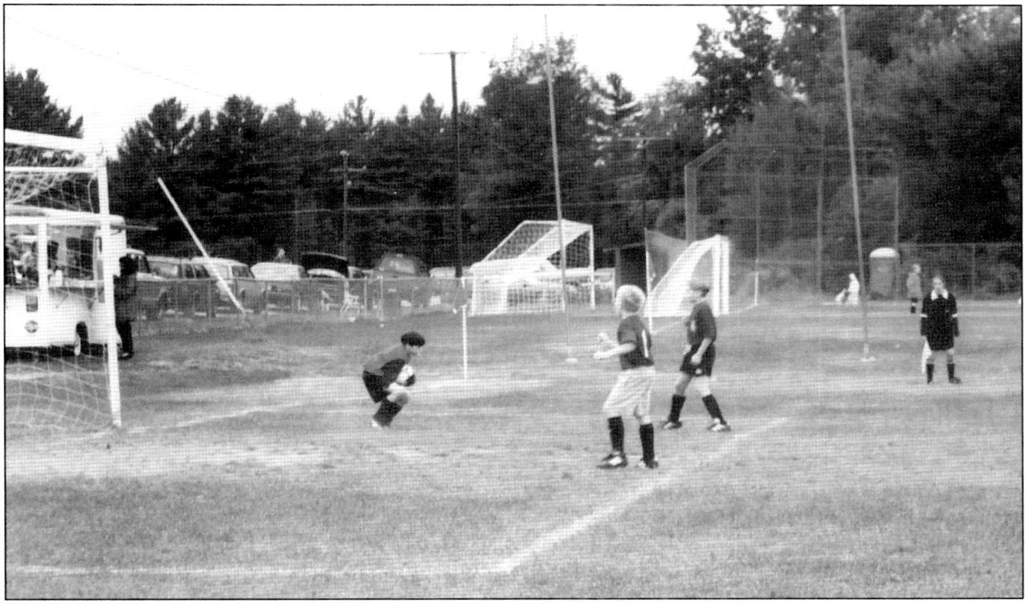

SOCCER. Soccer is played year-round in Merrimack. In-town Recreation League games are played in the fall at various fields in town, such as this one at the Reed's Ferry School. Soccer teams from Merrimack also compete with neighboring towns. Organized indoor teams as well as a introductory soccer camp, held at Reed's Ferry, have been added to the annual program.

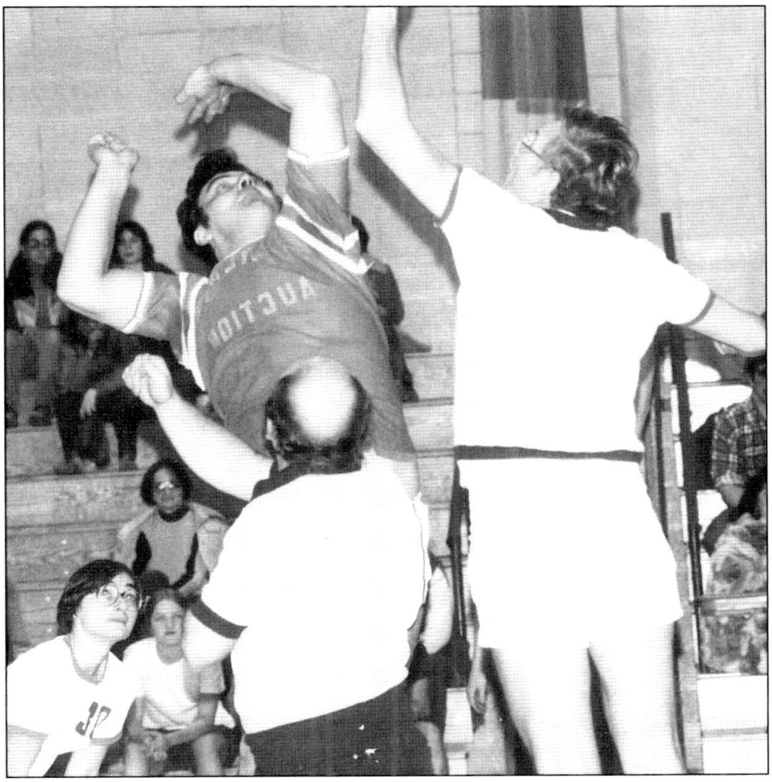

BASKETBALL. Merrimack teachers play the Merrimack Police Department in an exhibition game at the high school.

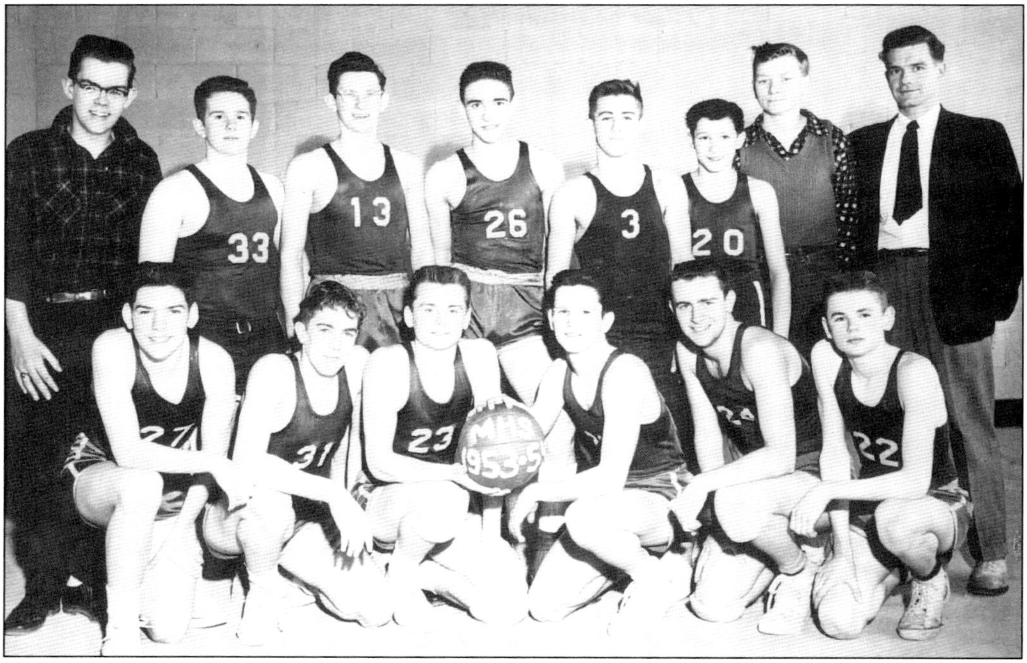

HIGH SCHOOL BASKETBALL. Before the high school gymnasium was built in the late 1950s, the only place to play basketball was on the second floor of the Town Hall. Students from all levels of high school participated.

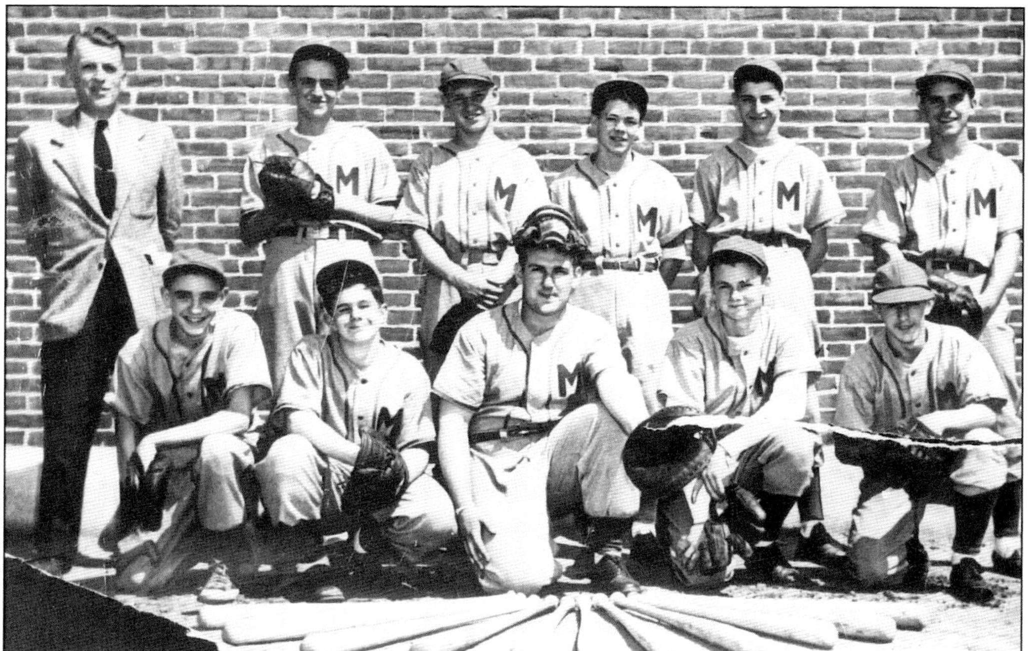

HIGH SCHOOL BASEBALL. Having no athletic field of their own, high school baseball players, in the 1950s, played on a privately-owned field at the back of what is now Connell's Shopping Mall.

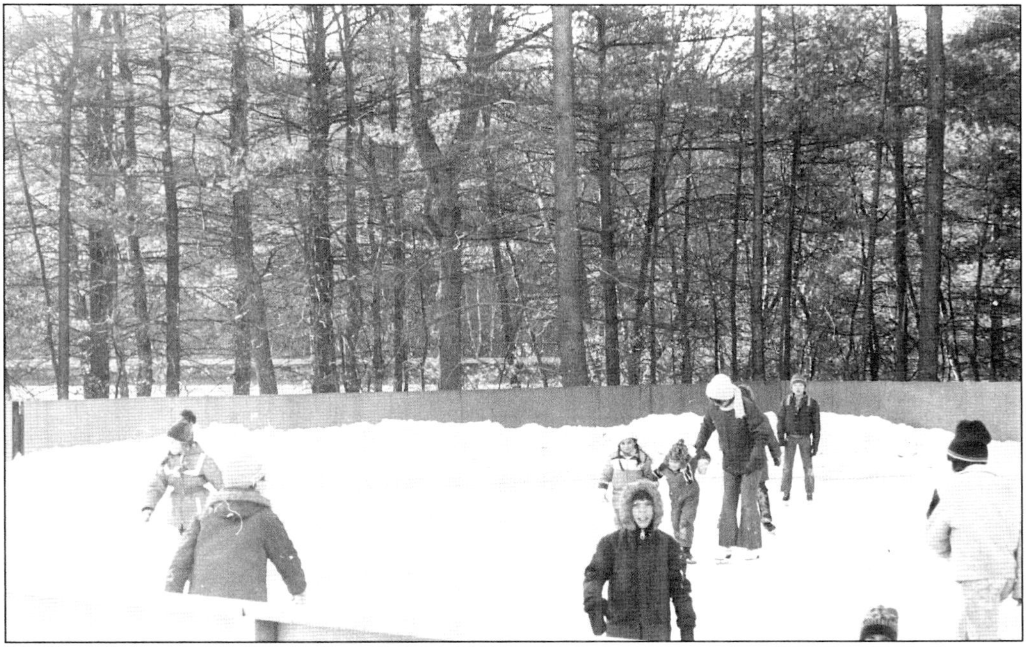

THE ICE SKATING RINK. Merrimack's public ice skating rink is located on O'Gara Drive, across from the middle school. The rink is flooded as soon as the weather is cold enough and is open until spring thaw.

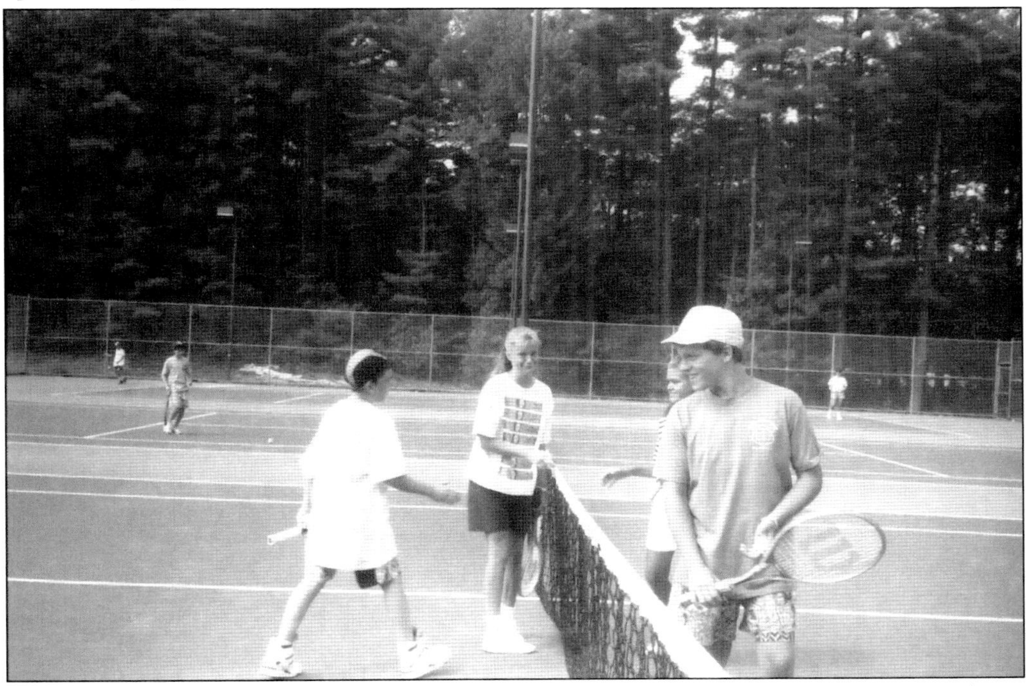

THE WASSERMAN PARK TENNIS COURTS. The tennis courts at Wasserman Park are available for anyone to use whenever the park is open. Tennis lessons are given at the courts under the direction of the Merrimack Parks and Recreation Department.

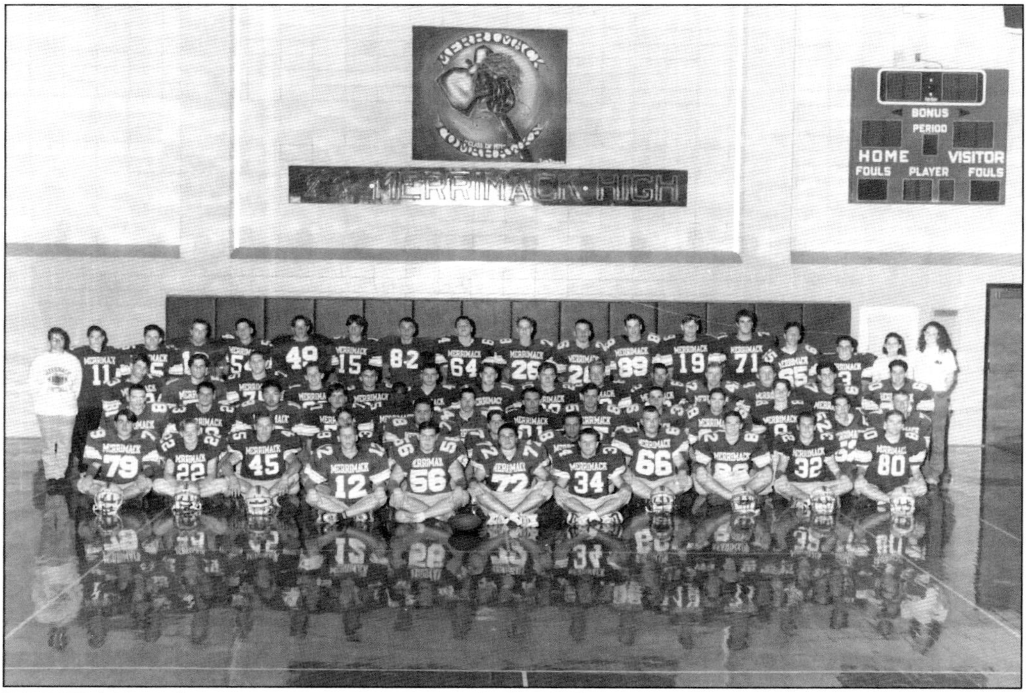

FOOTBALL. Like most sports in Merrimack, football starts at an early age with Pop Warner, and continues through high school. Merrimack High School now participates in the annual Turkey Bowl held on Thanksgiving Day. The Merrimack High School cheerleaders are always visible at the games.

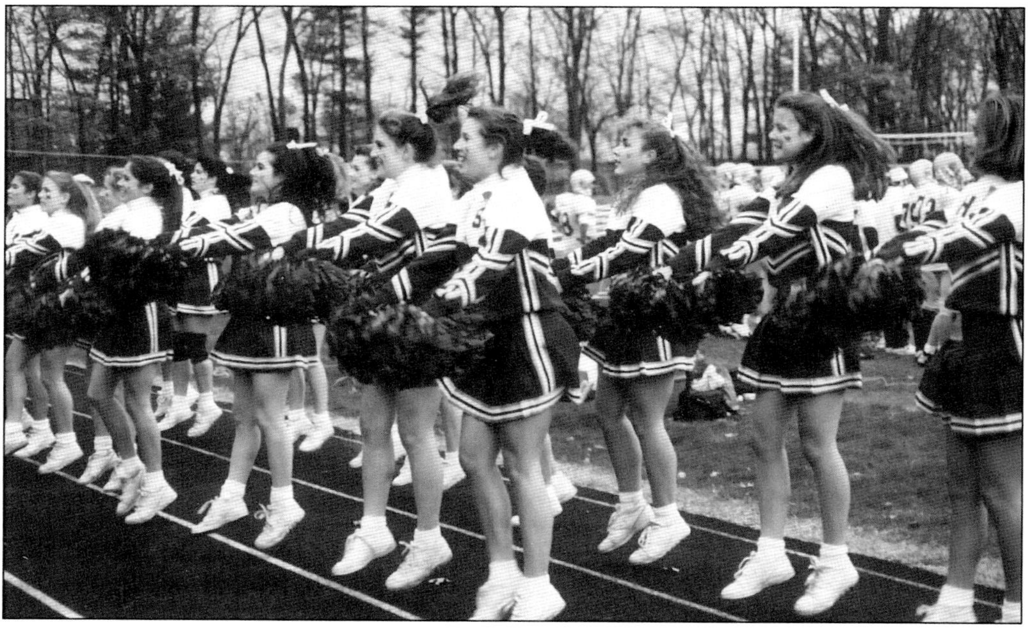

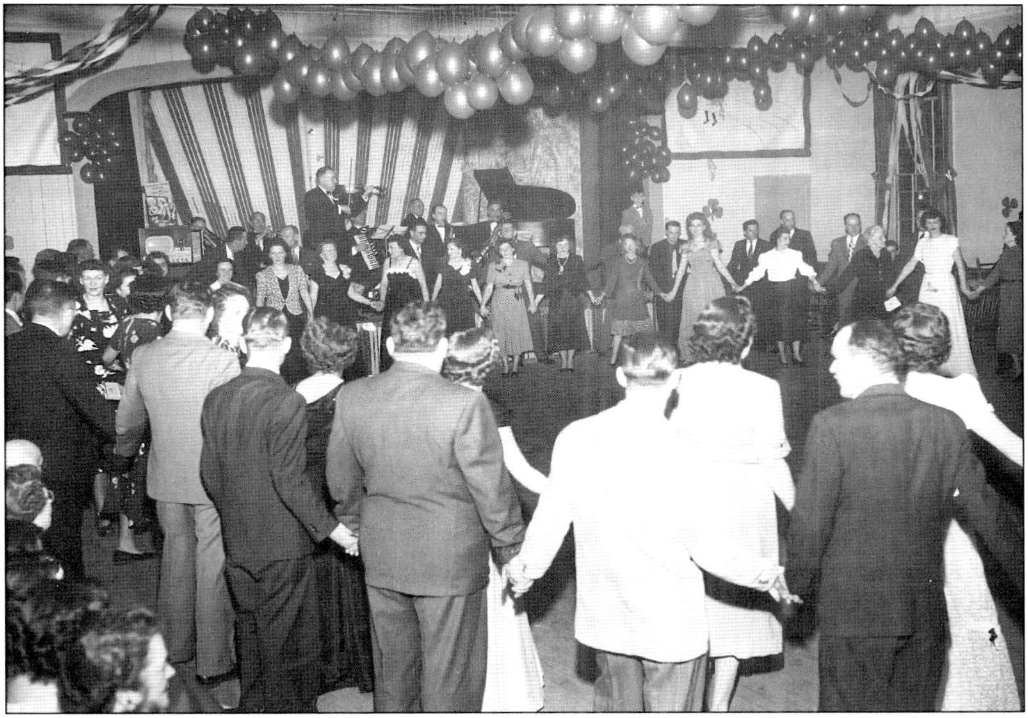

BALLROOM DANCING. Dances were very popular in the 1940s and '50s, with several held during the year at the Town Hall. One New Year's Eve there was a fire in town just as the dance began. The men, being volunteer firemen, left the dance to fight the fire, which left the women only each other to dance with.

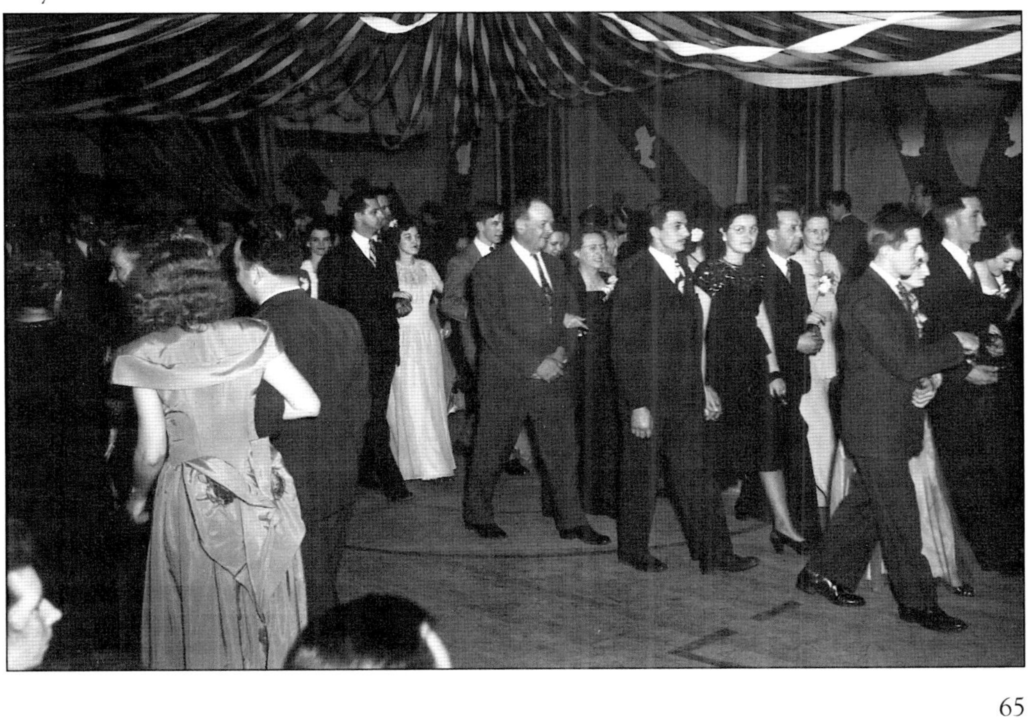

Reeds Ferry

Women's Club

1995 - 1996

Yearbook

Founded 1925

MOTTO

"To Do This Village Good"

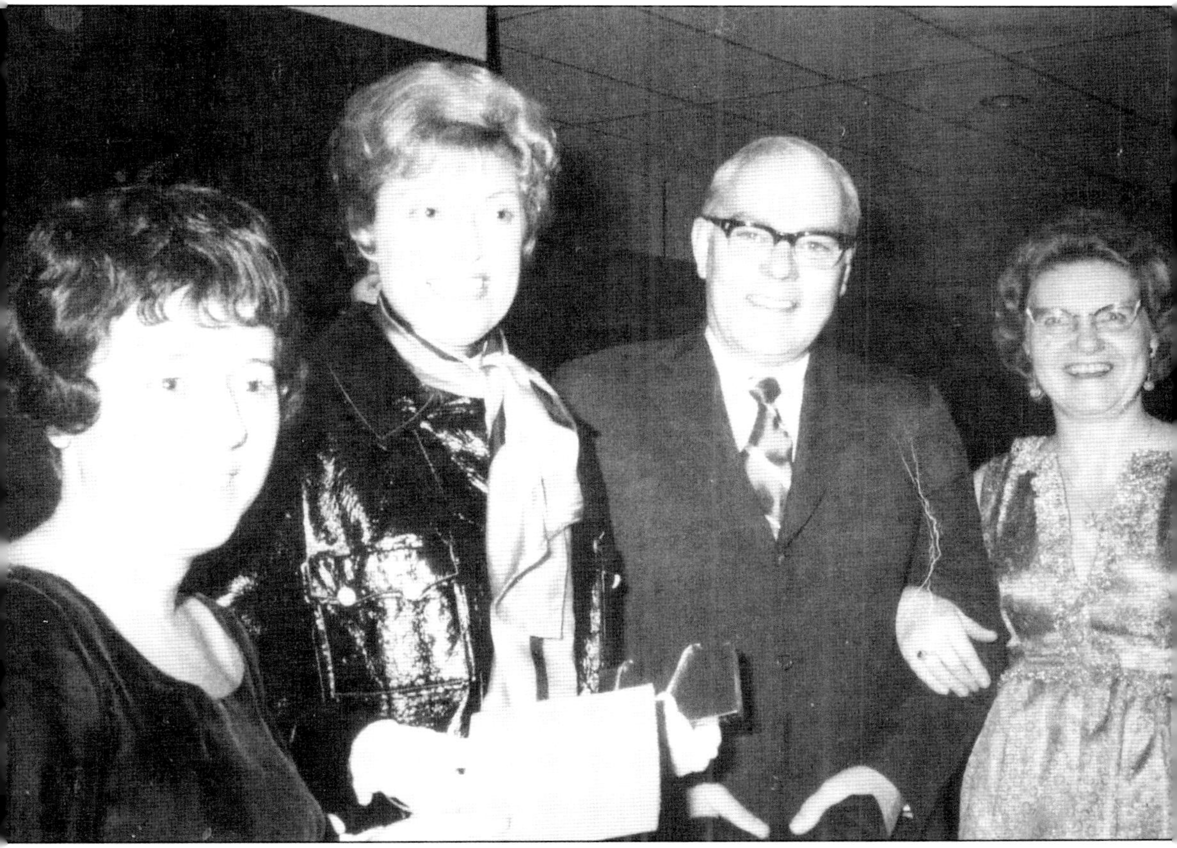

THE REED'S FERRY WOMENS' CLUB. The Reed's Ferry Womens' Club was founded in 1925. Their Silver Tea was one of the social events of the year and it was quite an honor to attend. They also held a Charity Ball as a fund-raiser every year.

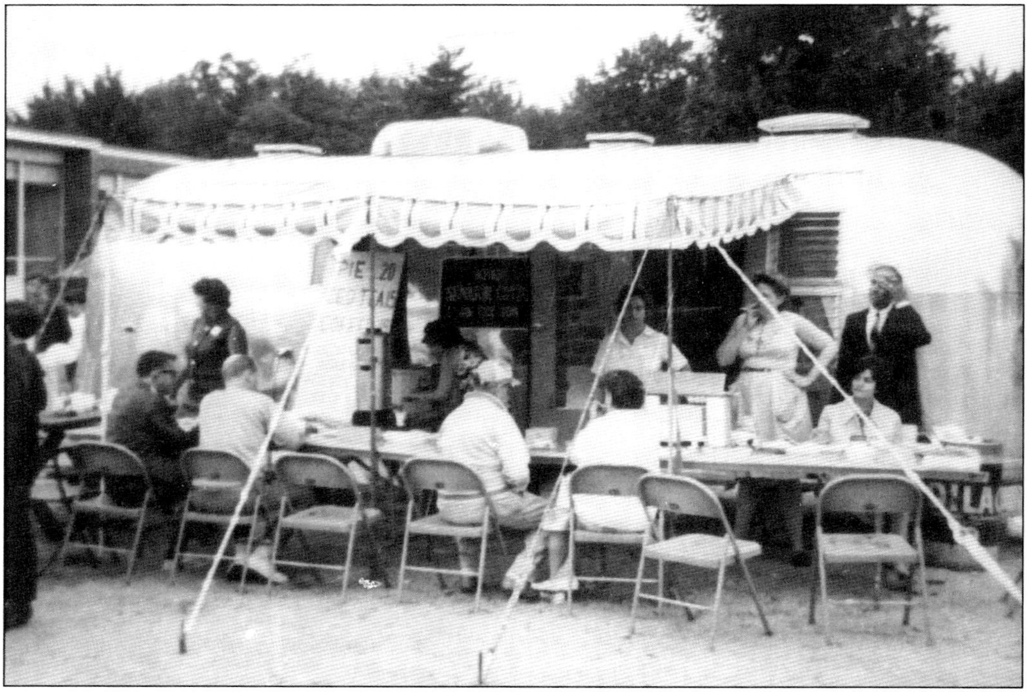

THE MERRIMACK REPUBLICAN WOMENS' CLUB. The Womens' Club was organized in September 1966. There are currently thirty-eight members, including six charter members. Funds for activities of the club are raised through events at the July Fourth celebration.

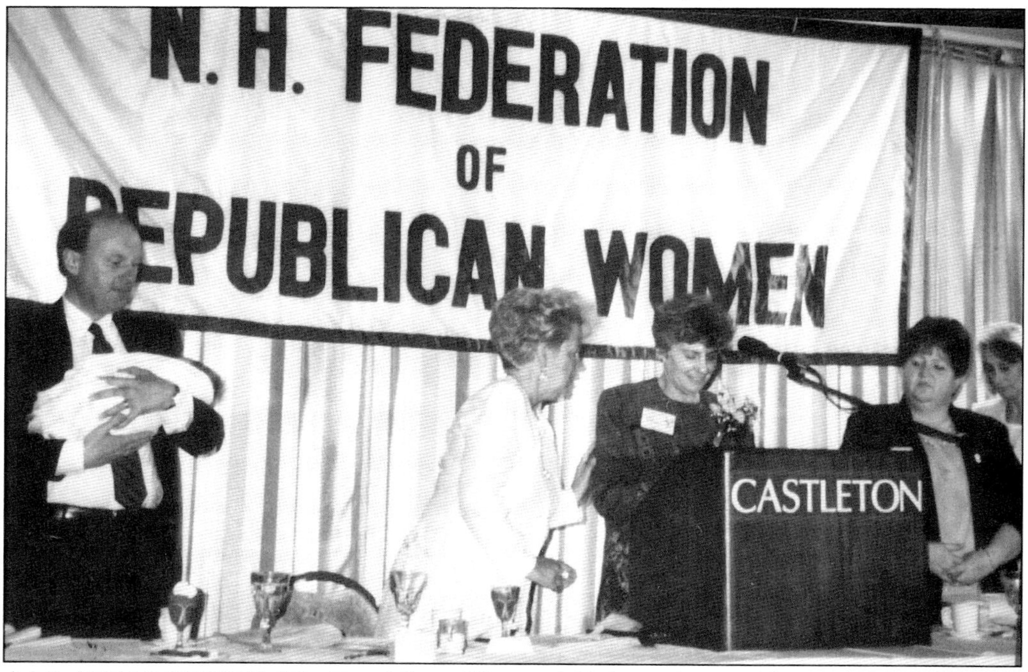

A LILAC LUNCHEON. The Republican Womens' Club was honored by a very special person at one of their lilac luncheons: the son of Governor Steve Merrill.

A Pair of Country Kids

3 Act Comedy

Presented By Senior Class of McGaw

MERRIMACK TOWN HALL

Friday Dec. 15, 1939 8 P.M.

Dancing 10 - 12 Refreshments on Sale

Music By Joe Gladysz

Admission 35c

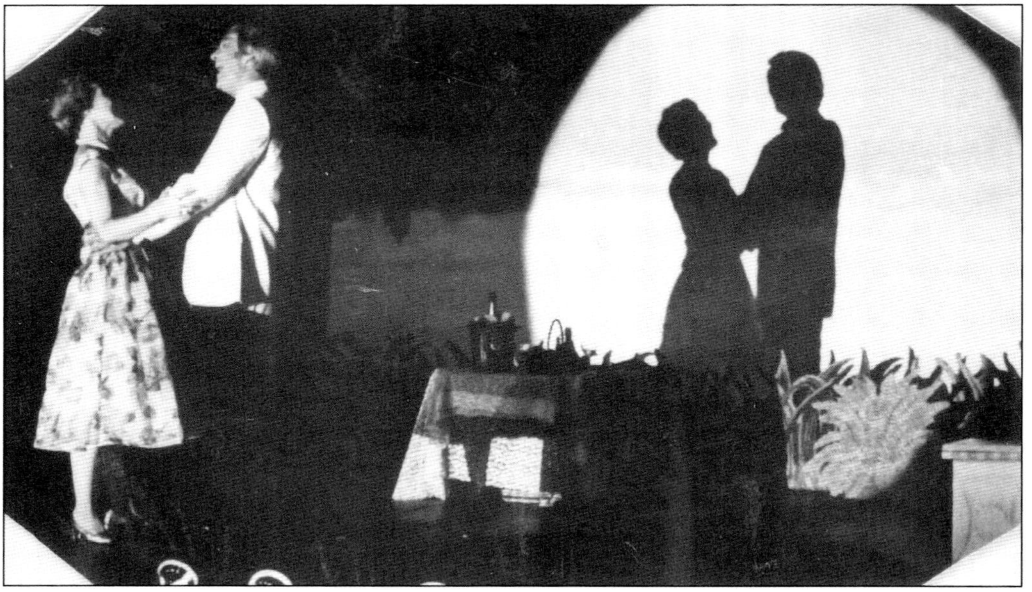

MERRIMACTORS. Merrimack has had several theater groups over the years. One of the more prominent ones was the Merrimactors. Beginning in the early 1970s, they performed for almost ten years in the all-purpose room of the middle school. Two performances a year were staged, including such plays as *South Pacific*, *Arsenic and Old Lace*, and *A Connecticut Yankee in King Arthur's Court*.

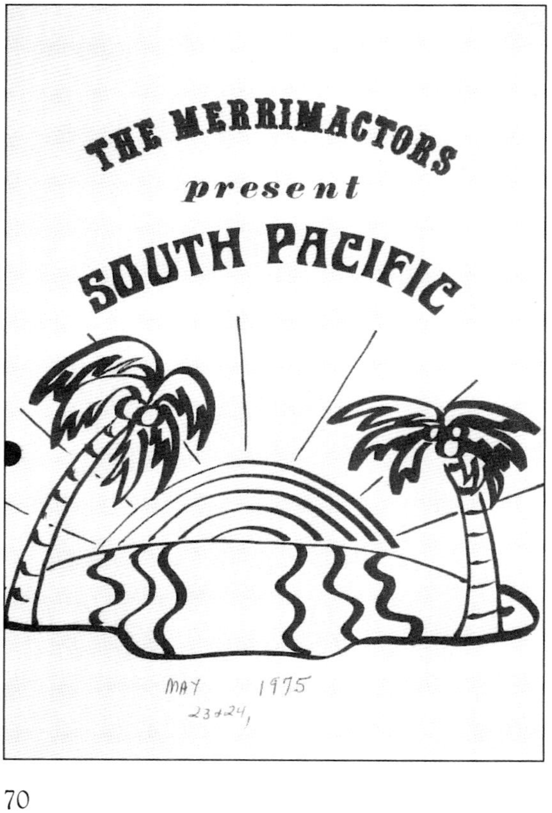

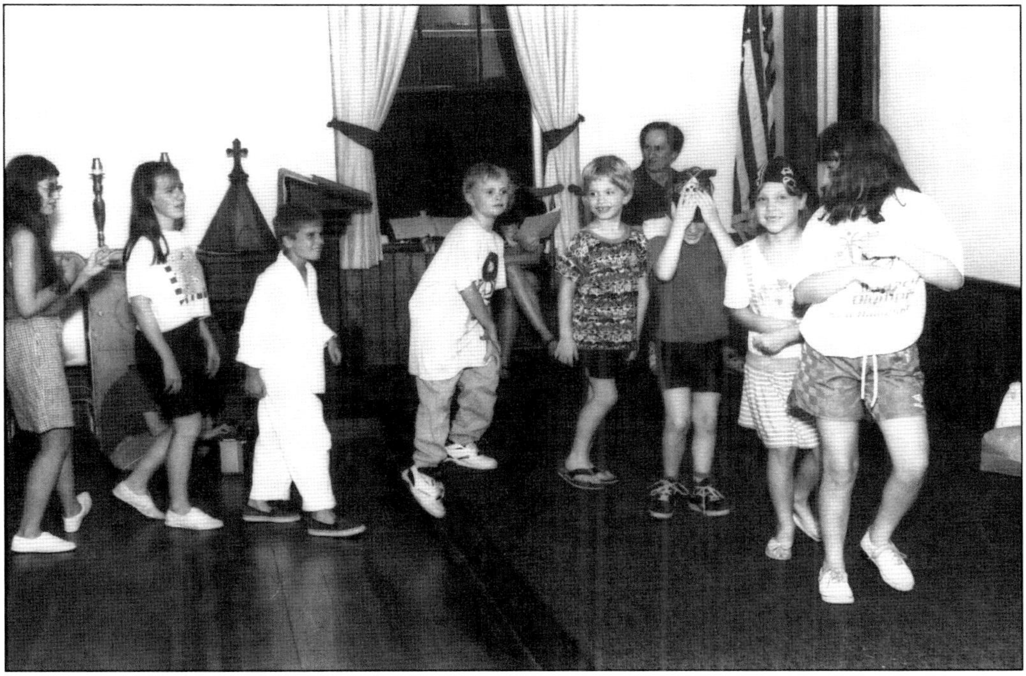

YOUNG STARS. In the summer of 1992, the first Young Actors Community Theatre was founded. The "Dancing Pirates" are shown here, rehearsing for their first play.

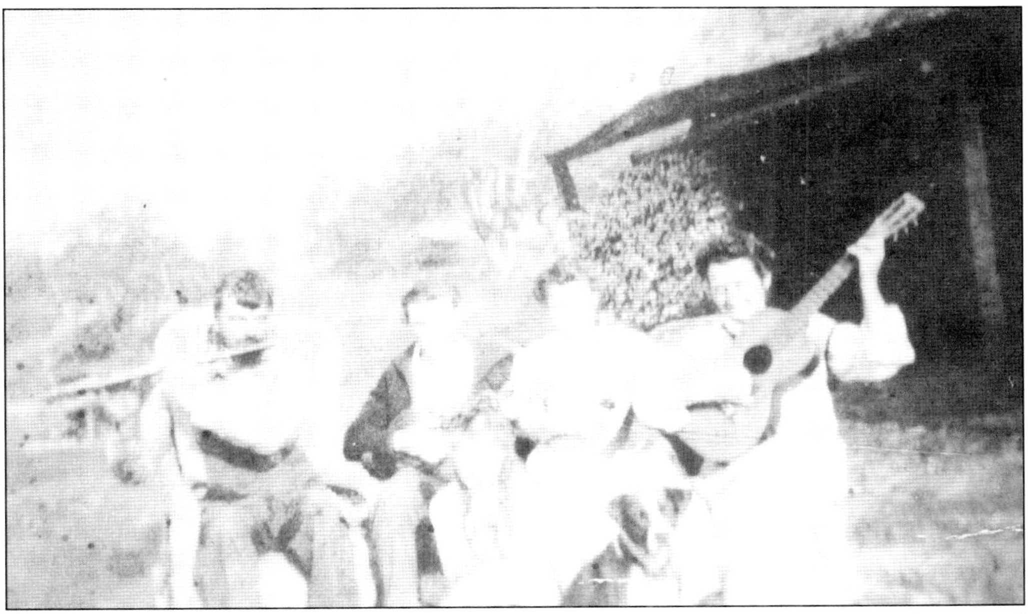

A FAMILY BAND. Shown here is the Schneiderheinze family band. Everyone played a musical instrument except the family dog, who may or may not have been the vocalist.

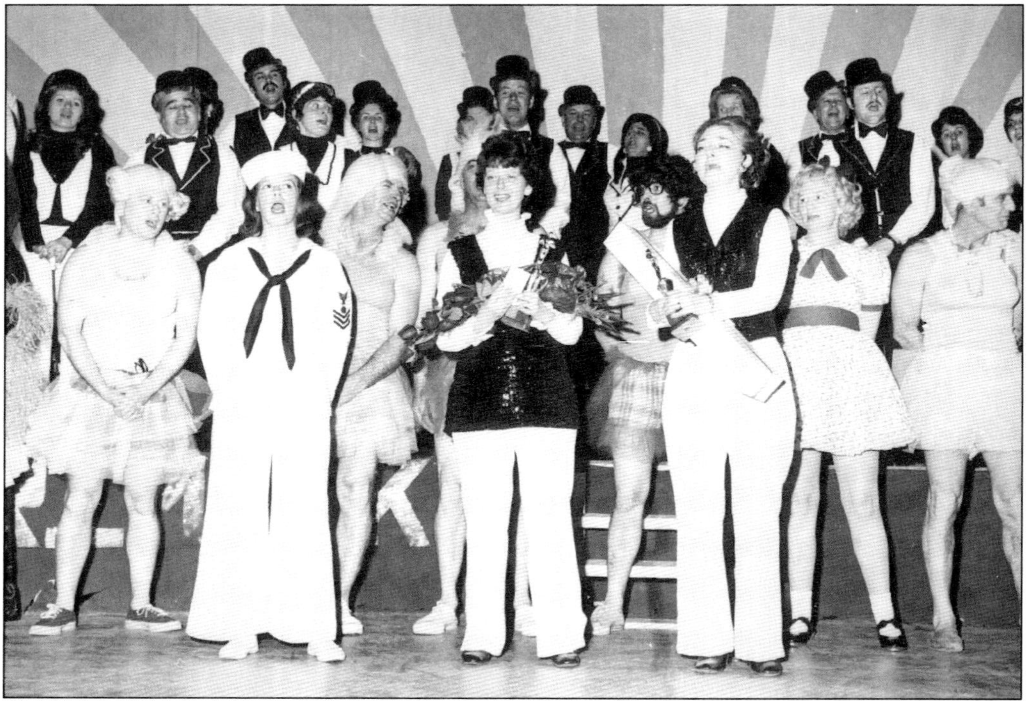

VARIETY SHOWS. From ballerinas to sailors to chorus girls, Merrimack loved a good show and staged many talent nights, minstrel shows, and plays. They were strictly amateur nights and anyone was welcome to perform.

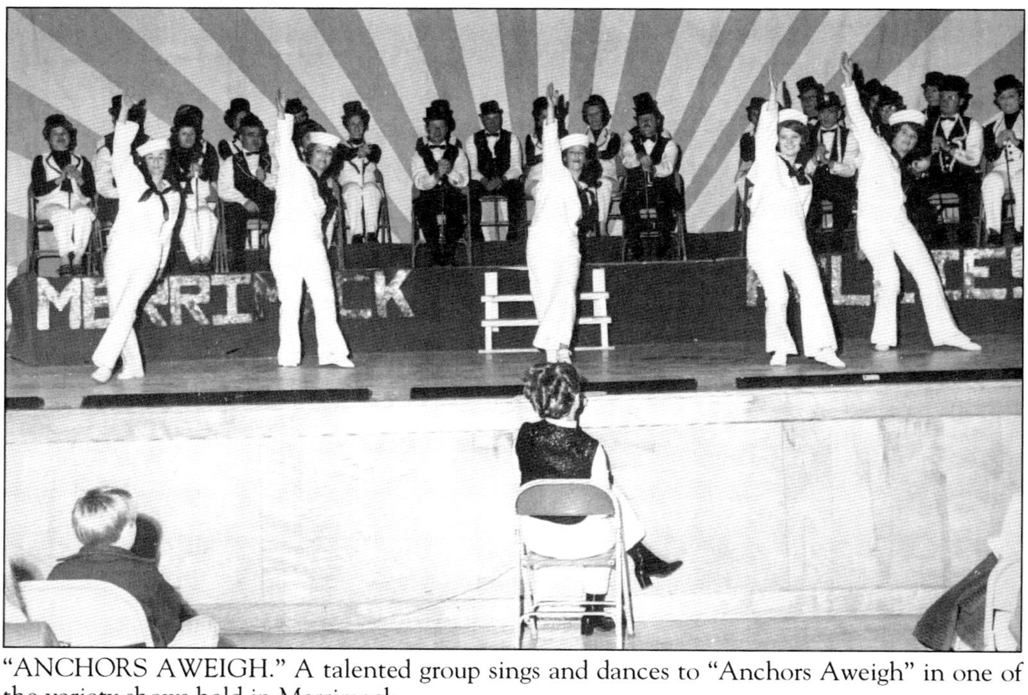

"ANCHORS AWEIGH." A talented group sings and dances to "Anchors Aweigh" in one of the variety shows held in Merrimack.

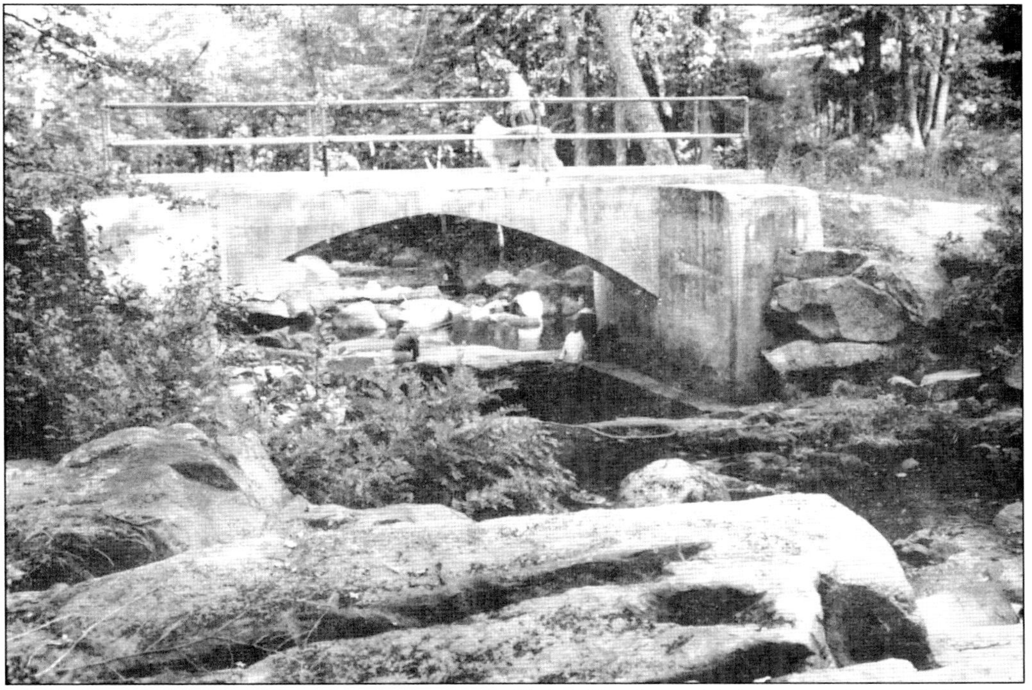

TWIN BRIDGE PARK. Dedicated to Reverend John Wright and John Pirog, this park, located on Route 3, is named for the two identical bridges within the park that span Baboosic Brook.

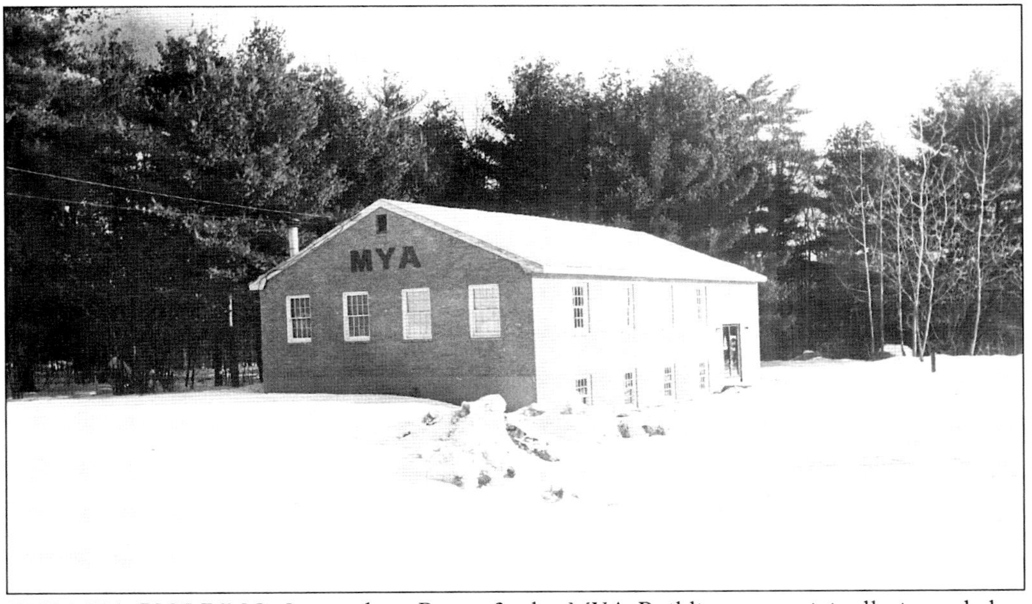

THE MYA BUILDING. Located on Route 3, the MYA Building was originally intended as a teen center. The teen center did not work out and the building became the home of the Merrimack Youth Association. This is a volunteer organization that provides sports programs for some twenty-two hundred Merrimack children.

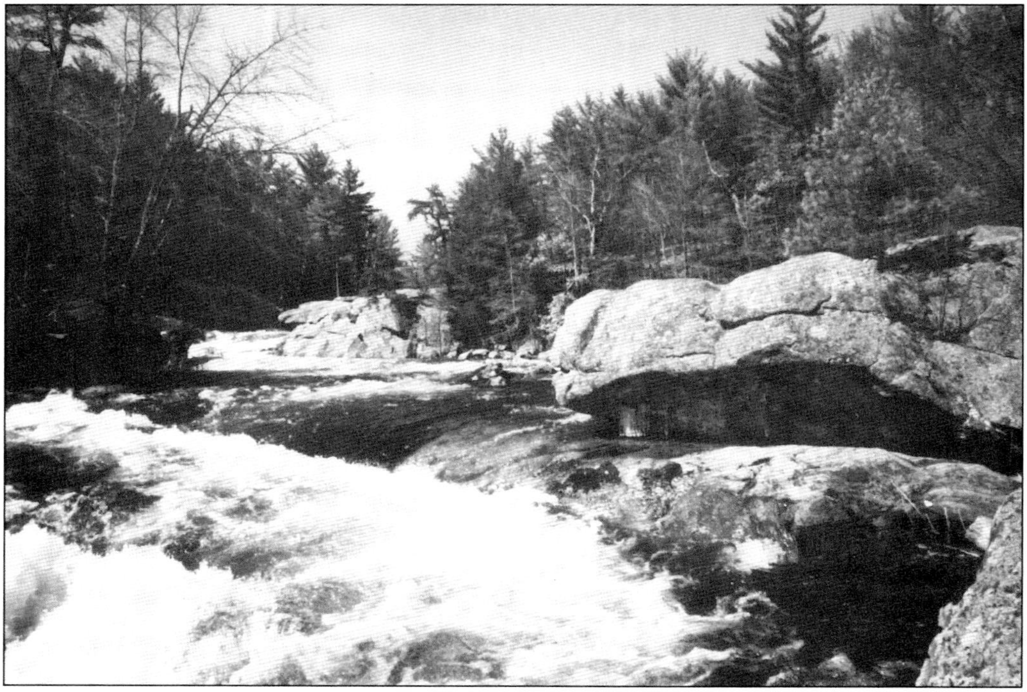

WILD CAT FALLS. Originally known as Atherton Falls, this beautiful but very dangerous section of the Souhegan River has been the site of many rescues by the fire and police departments. It is part of the Eighty Acres Town Park, located off Currier Road, and also part of the Heritage Trail.

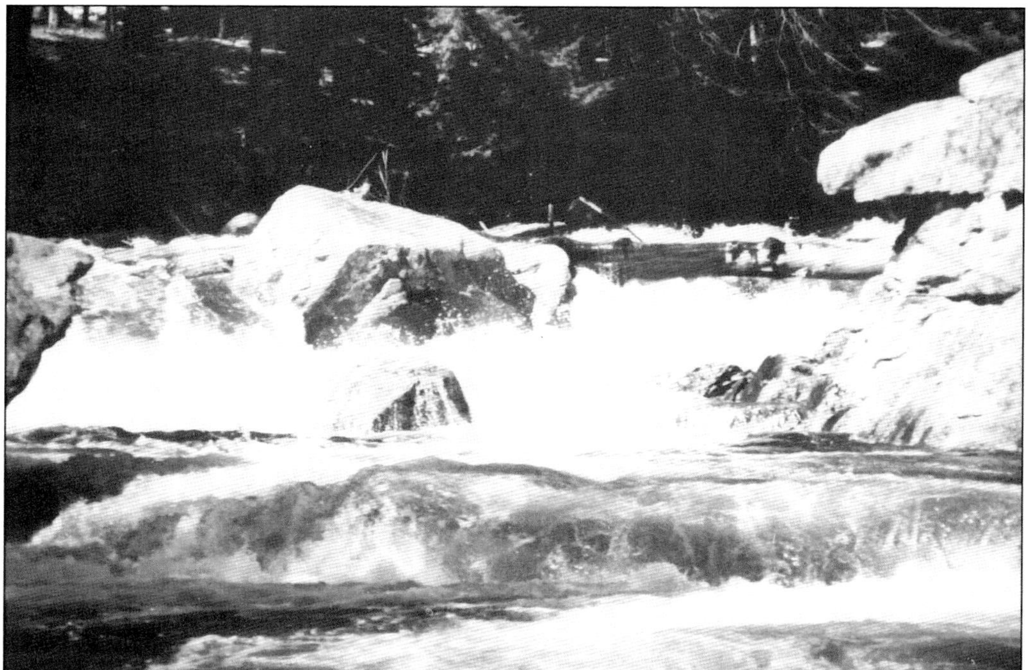

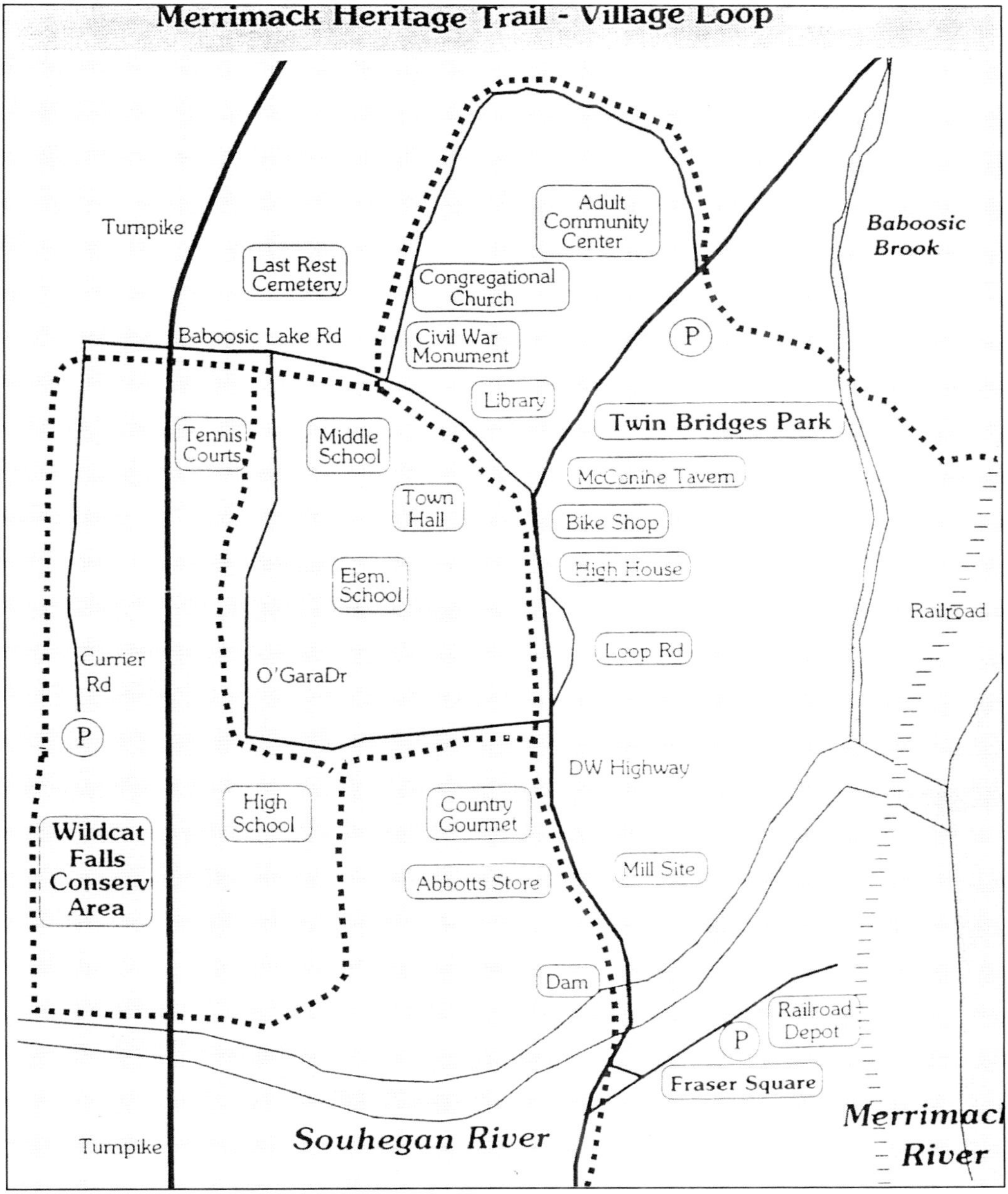

THE MERRIMACK HERITAGE TRAIL. The Merrimack section of the New Hampshire Heritage Trail begins at Fraser Square, goes north of Route 3 to Baboosic Lake Road, proceeds west to Currier Road and makes the loop back down Baboosic Lake Road to Church Street. The trail then follows Church Street to Route 3 and through Twin Bridge Park to the Merrimack River.

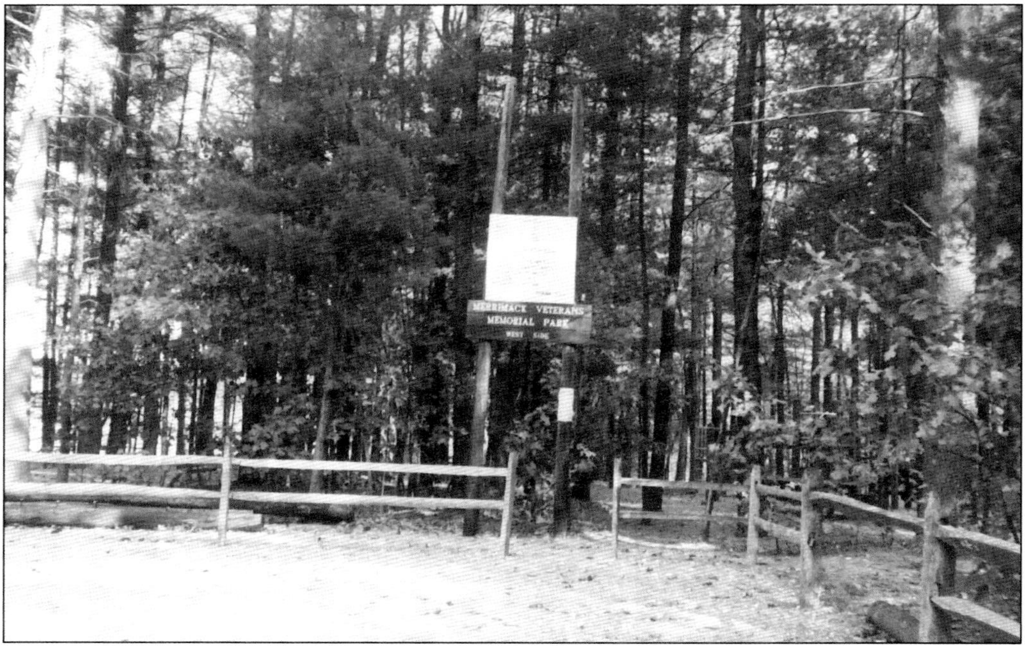

VETERANS' MEMORIAL PARK. The 25 acres along the shore of Naticook Lake seemed like a dream come true for Selectman Robert Brundige when he first walked the property ten years ago. Due to his efforts and at no cost to the taxpayers, the park is now a memorial to the Korean and Vietnam veterans of Merrimack.

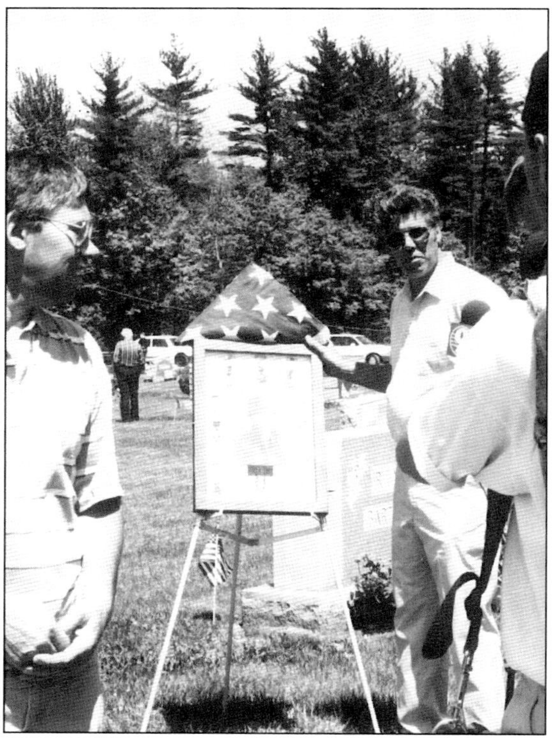

THE RIVARD MEMORIAL BALL FIELD. The major league ball field at Veterans' Memorial Park was dedicated in memory of Army Spec 4 Richard N. Rivard, the town's only casualty of the Vietnam War. On Memorial Day, 1994, various members of the Rivard family were present for the dedication.

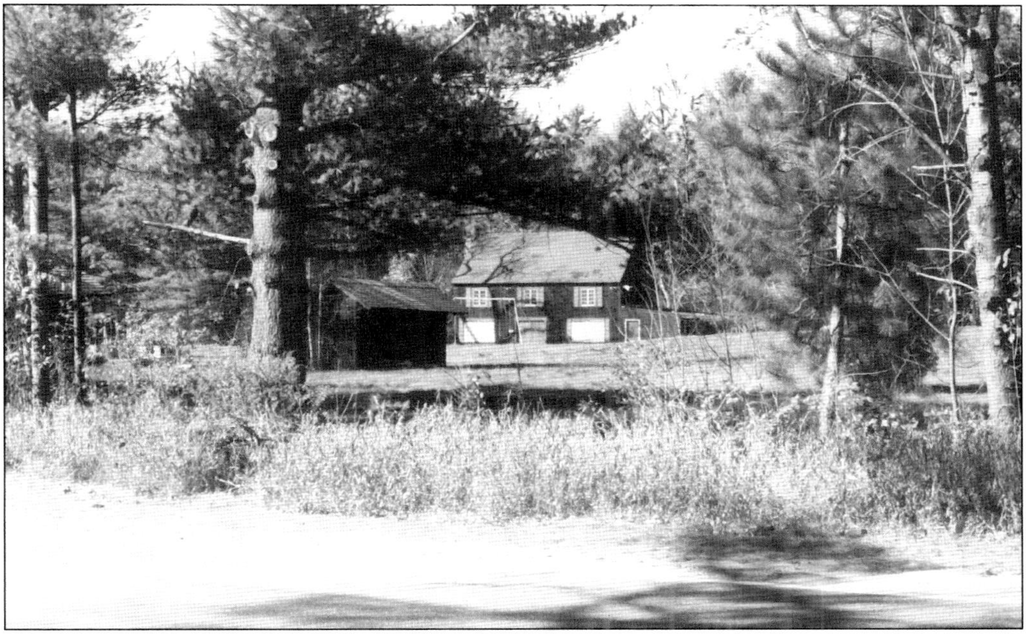

CAMP SARGENT. The YMCA facility known as Camp Sargent has been located on Camp Sargent Road for many years. It is used for many of the YMCA's activities and as a day-care camp in the summer.

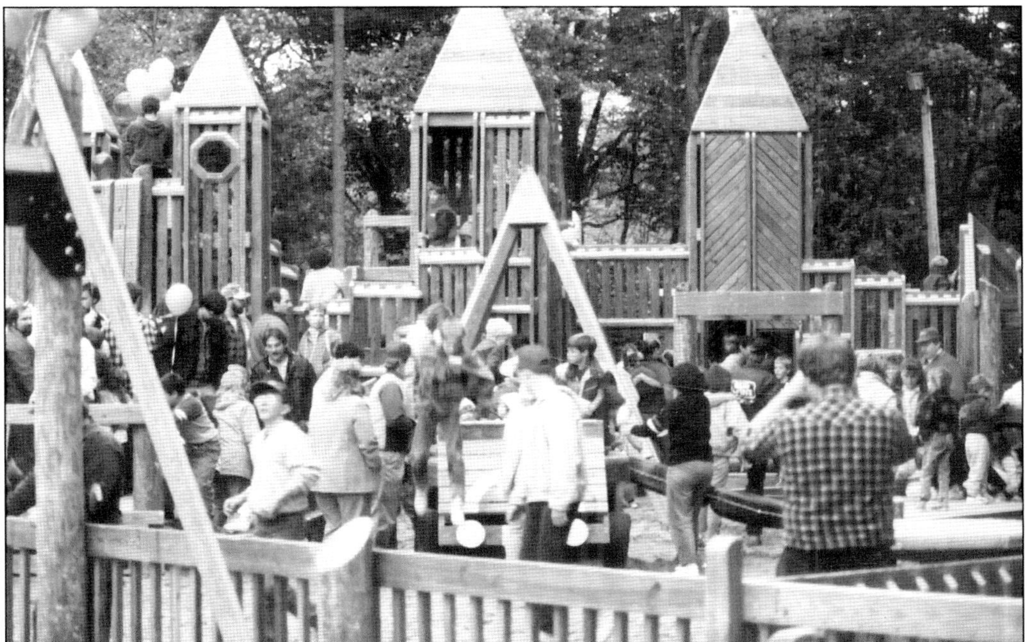

THE KIDS KOVE PLAYGROUND. This playground was built by volunteers in 1989. It is located at Twin Bridge Park on Route 3. Approximately fifty volunteers, working in four-hour shifts, built this playground in five days. Meals for the workers were provided as well as day care for children under the age of nine. Older children were allowed to help with the construction.

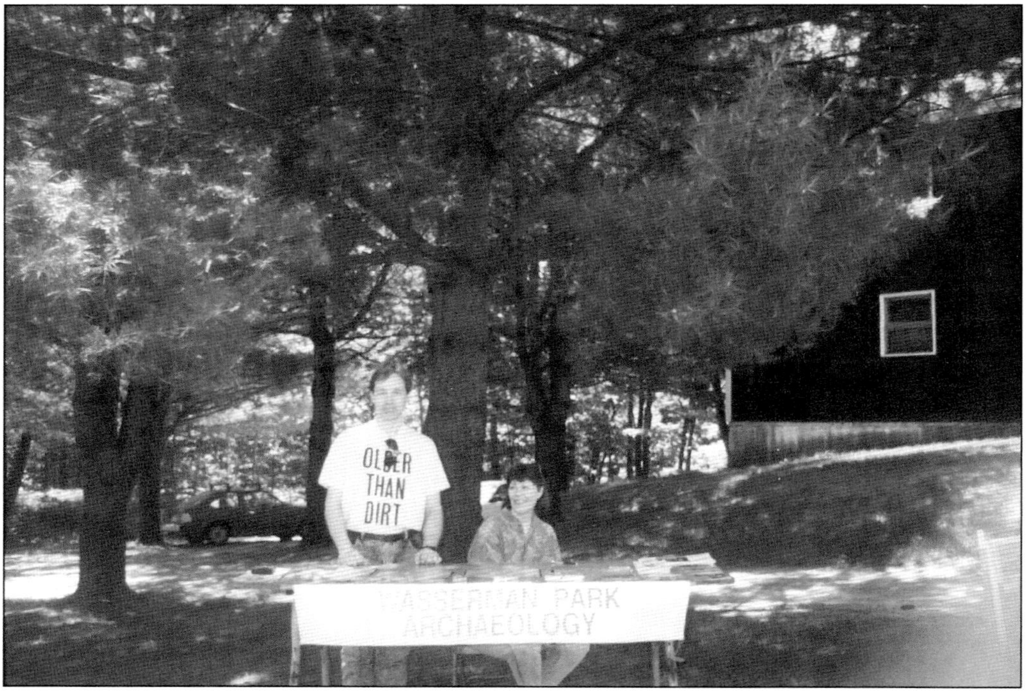

ARCHEOLOGY—WASSERMAN PARK. Under the direction of Doug Dickinson, archeological digs are being conducted at Wasserman Park. Evidence of early Indian settlements and prehistoric man has been uncovered. Several of these digs have involved students from the middle and high schools.

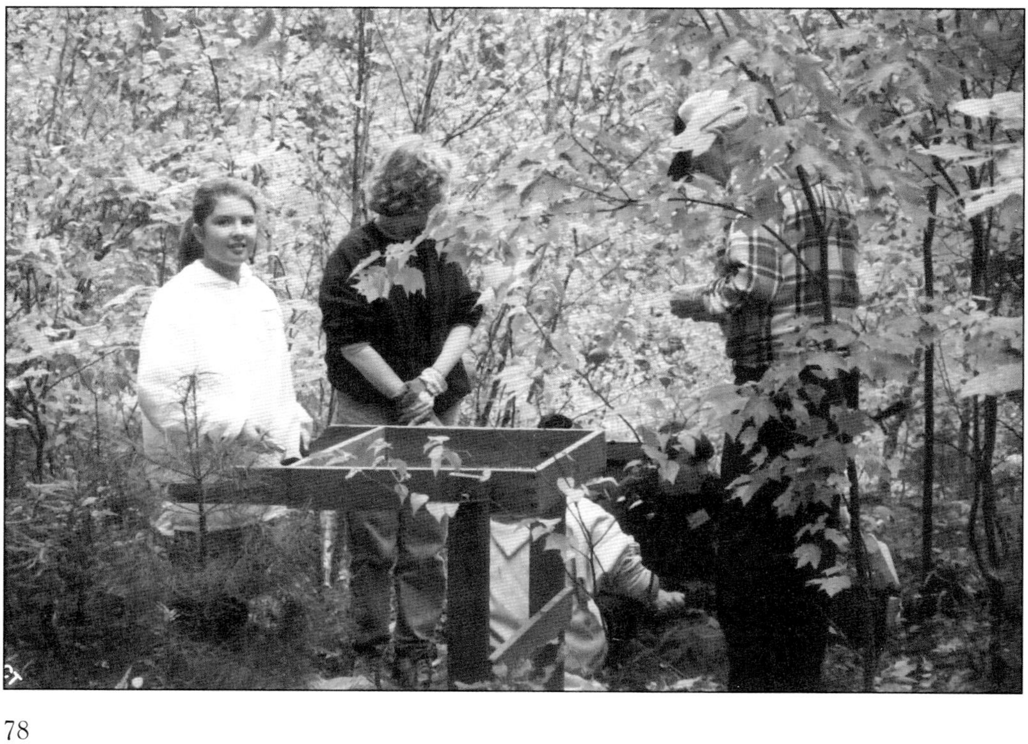

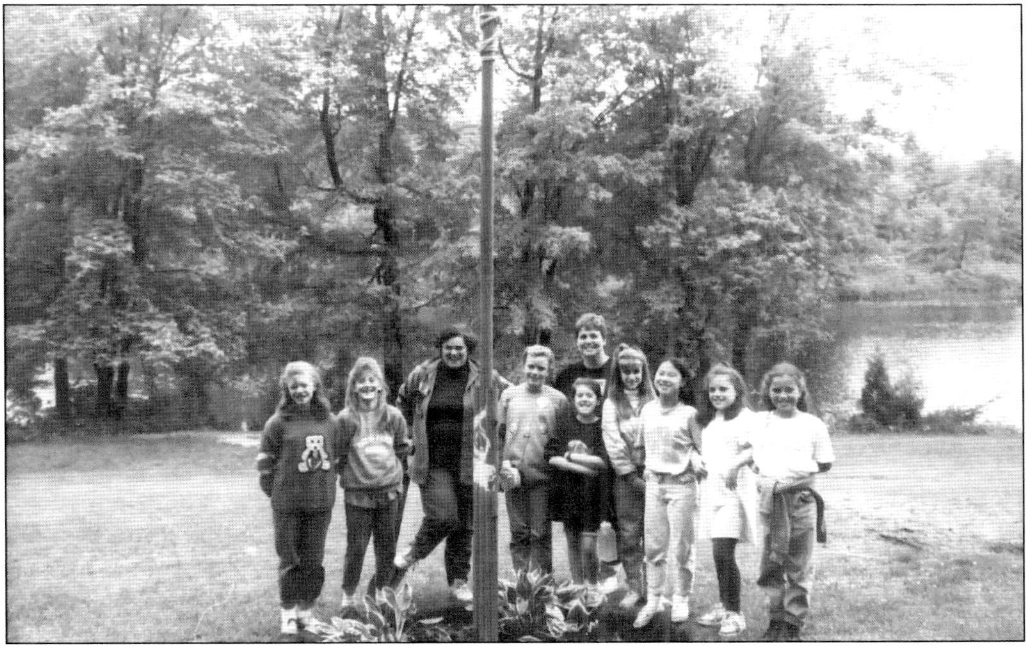

A GIRL SCOUT CAMPOREE. On one weekend in June, the Merrimack Girl Scouts hold their camporee, which includes approximately two hundred girls from all levels of scouting, and their leaders. Prior to 1991, the camporees were held in Bedford. With the town's purchase of Wasserman Park, the girls are now able to hold them in Merrimack.

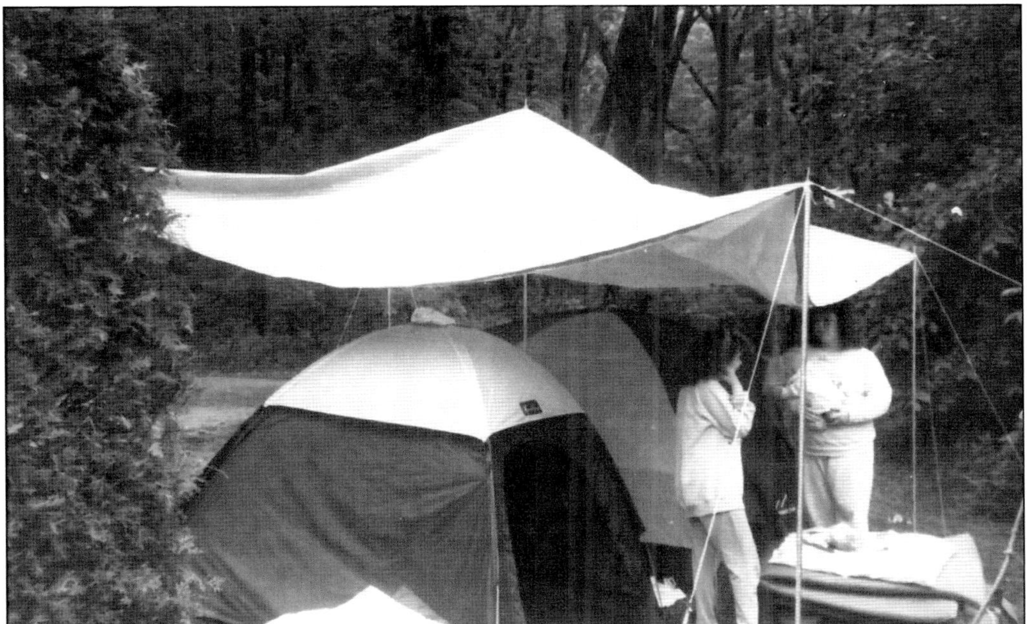

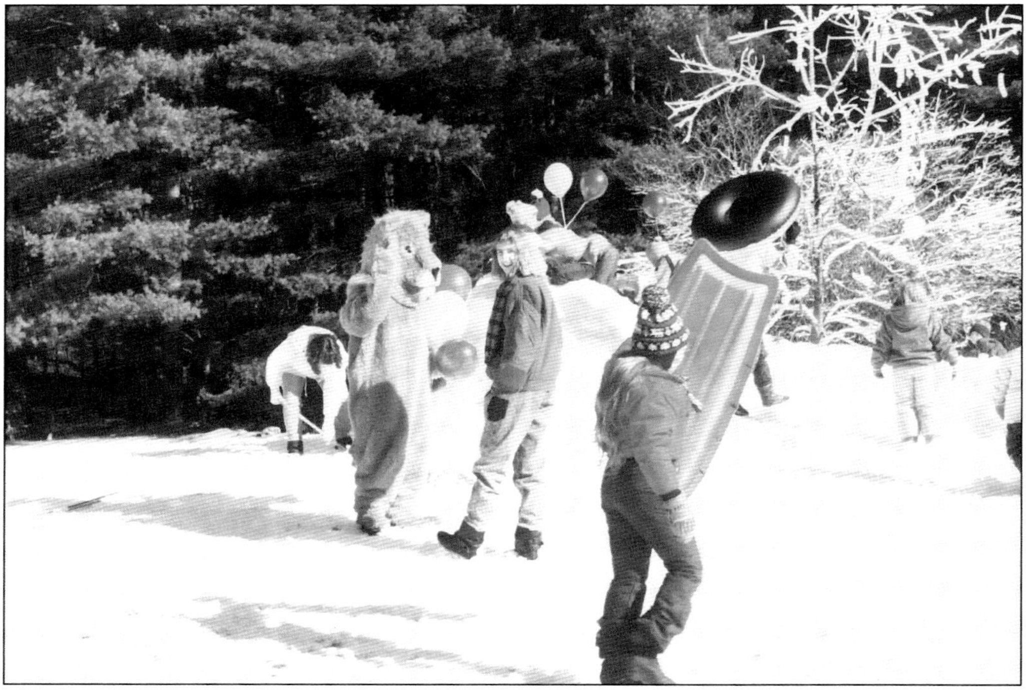

THE WINTER CARNIVAL. One of the annual events sponsored by the Merrimack Parks and Recreation Department is the Winter Carnival, held at Wasserman Park. There is sliding and ice skating as well as refreshments and exhibits for all to enjoy.

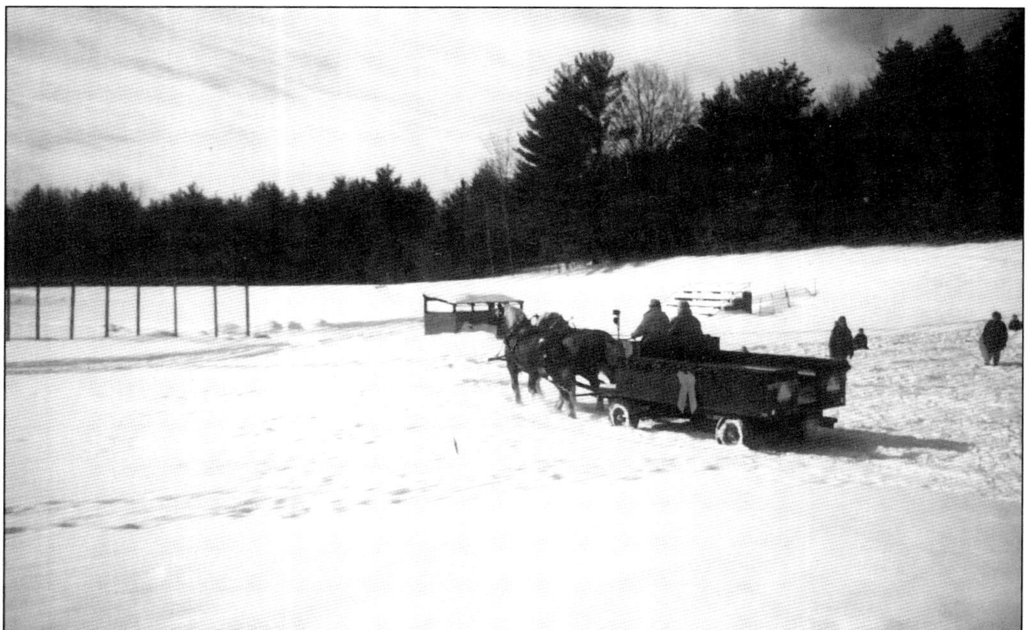

SLEIGH RIDES. Even though it is a wagon, not a sleigh, this is one of the most popular attractions of the Winter Carnival.

Seven

Business

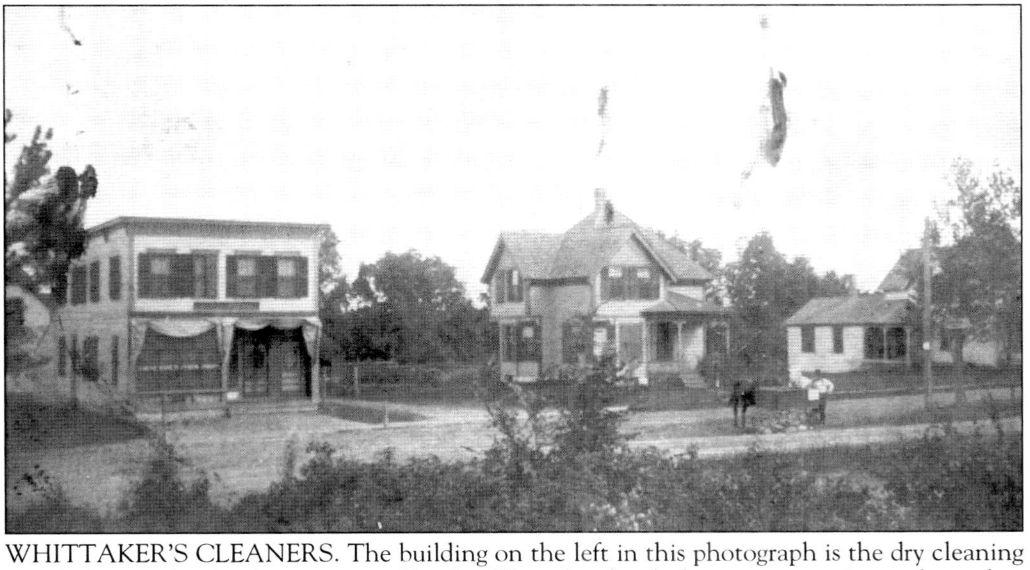

WHITTAKER'S CLEANERS. The building on the left in this photograph is the dry cleaning establishment that has been operated by the Whittaker family for many years. It was formerly a grocery store. The building on the right is the Merrimack Flower Shop.

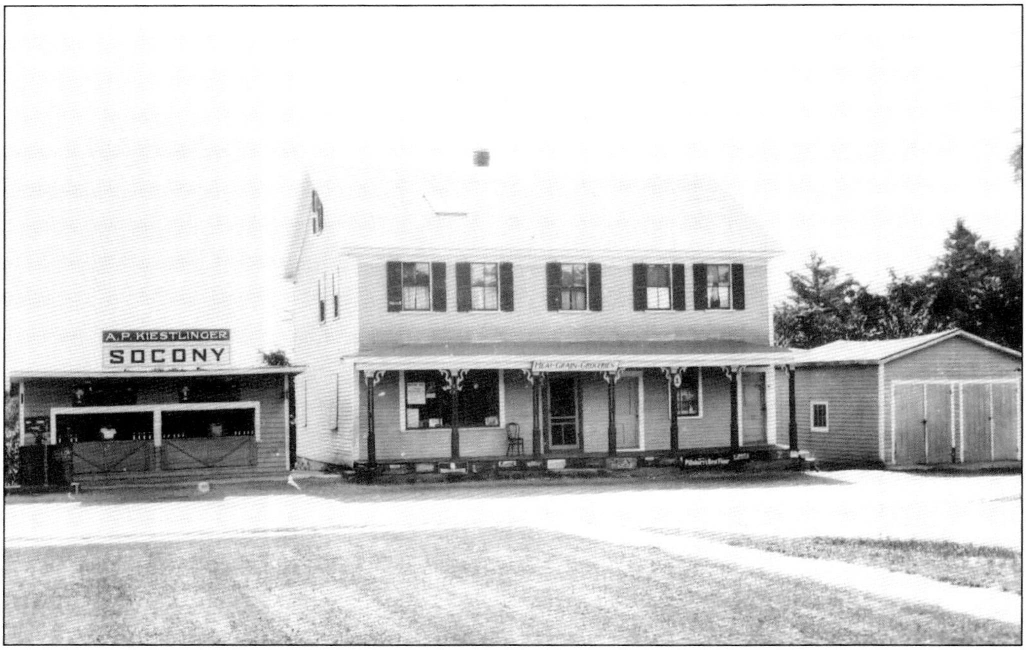

KIESTLINGER'S STORE. Ayer's Hall, where meetings and social gatherings were held, was located in the upper level of this store on Daniel Webster Highway. A.P. Kiestlinger purchased it in 1920 and his family operated it for many years.

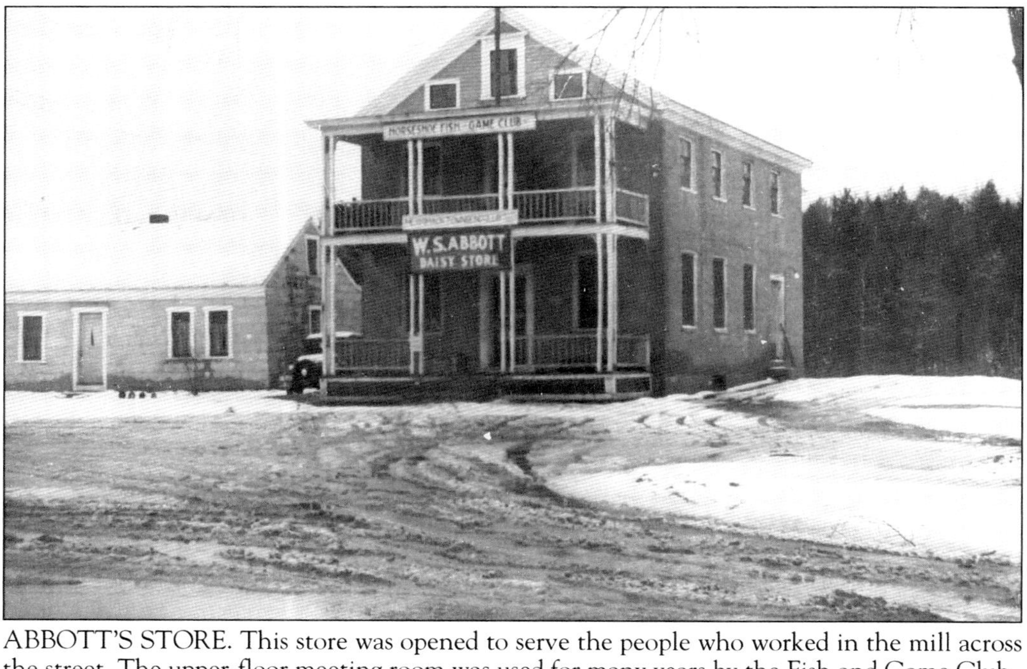

ABBOTT'S STORE. This store was opened to serve the people who worked in the mill across the street. The upper-floor meeting room was used for many years by the Fish and Game Club.

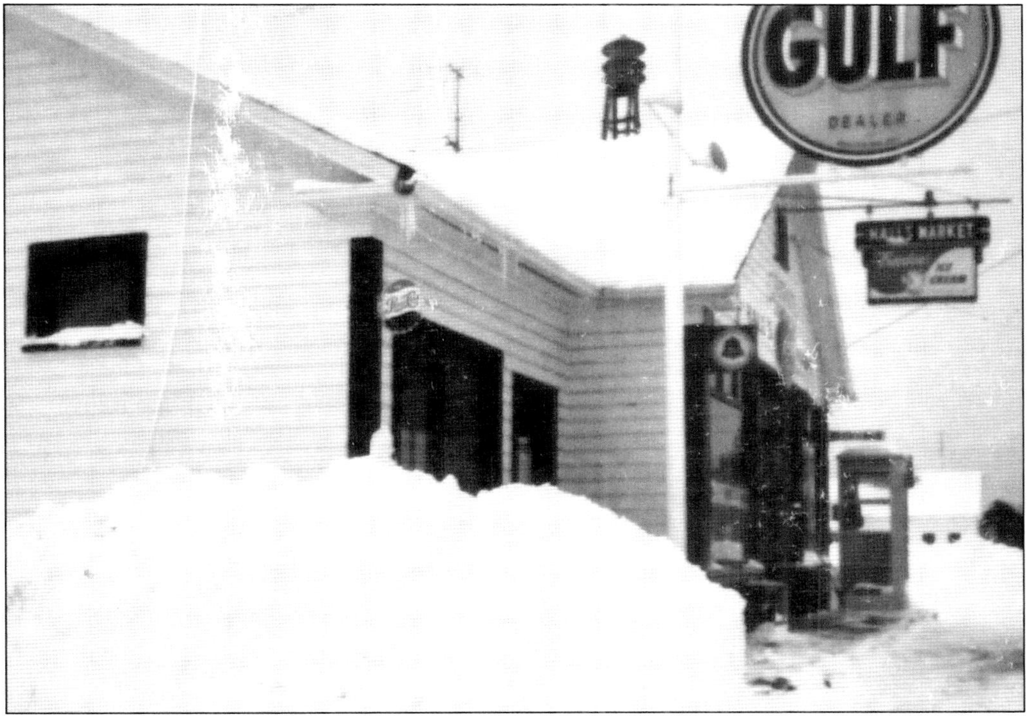

HALL'S STORE. This store on Craftsmen Lane was bought in 1937 by Carroll Hall. The South Merrimack Post Office was located in the store, with Mr. Hall as the post master, until 1960. After being operated by the Hall family for many years, the building was sold to a building supply company. In the 1980s it was destroyed by arsonists.

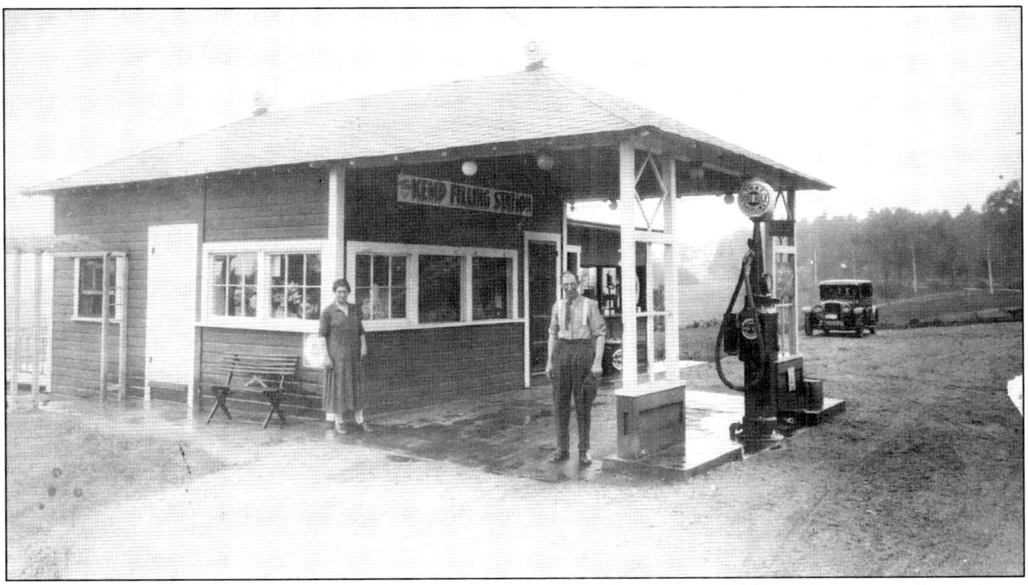

COX'S STORE AND SERVICE STATION. Formerly Kemp's Filling Station, this place, located on Daniel Webster Highway, is best remembered as Cox's Store. Operated by Lorraine and Hershel Cox, it was a very popular variety store and gas station.

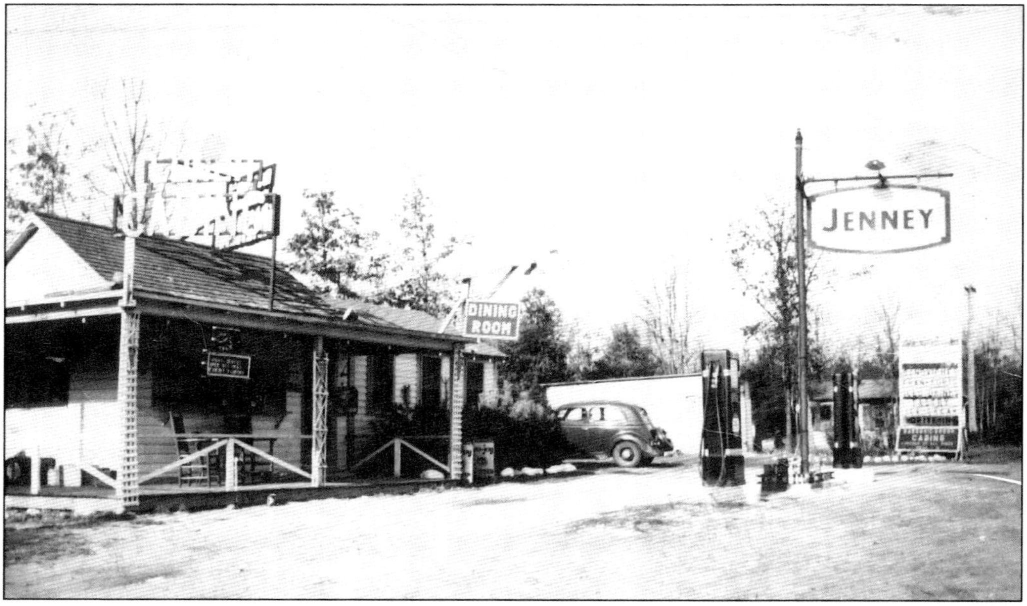

PYNENBURG'S CITGO STATION. This business, started by Helen and Joseph Pynenburg, was a Jenny gas station and store located on Route 3. There were also cabins for rent. The cabins and store are gone, and a garage and car wash have been added. Now operated by Joseph Pynenburg Jr. and his sons as a Citgo service station, it is Merrimack's oldest gas station still in operation.

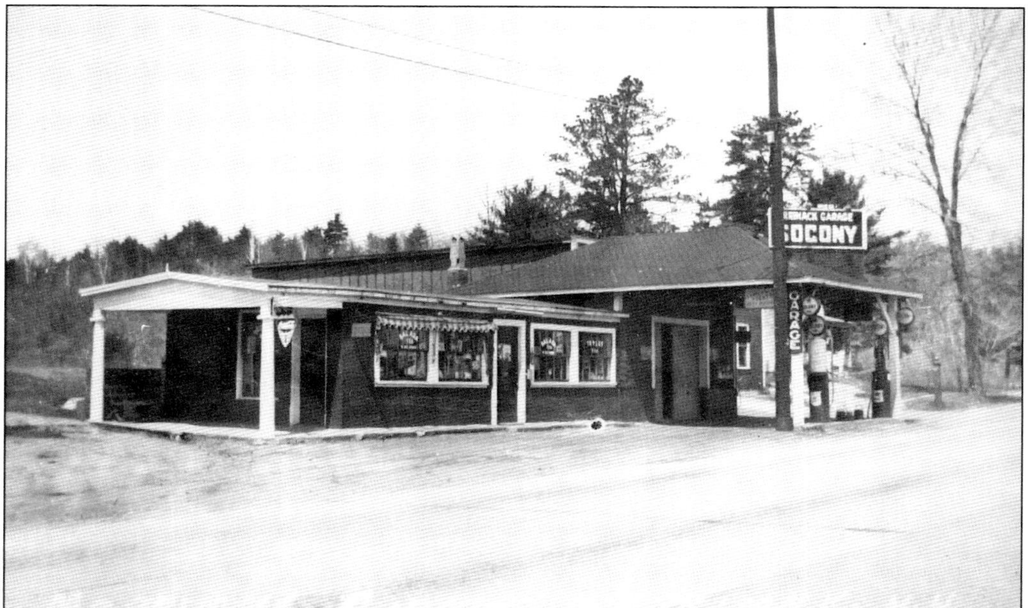

THE MERRIMACK GARAGE. Many long-time Merrimack residents still remember Greenleaf's Store and Station as Grammie Ames'. It stood for many years in the center of town, before being replaced by Connell's Shopping Mall on Route 3. It is another Merrimack landmark that no longer exists.

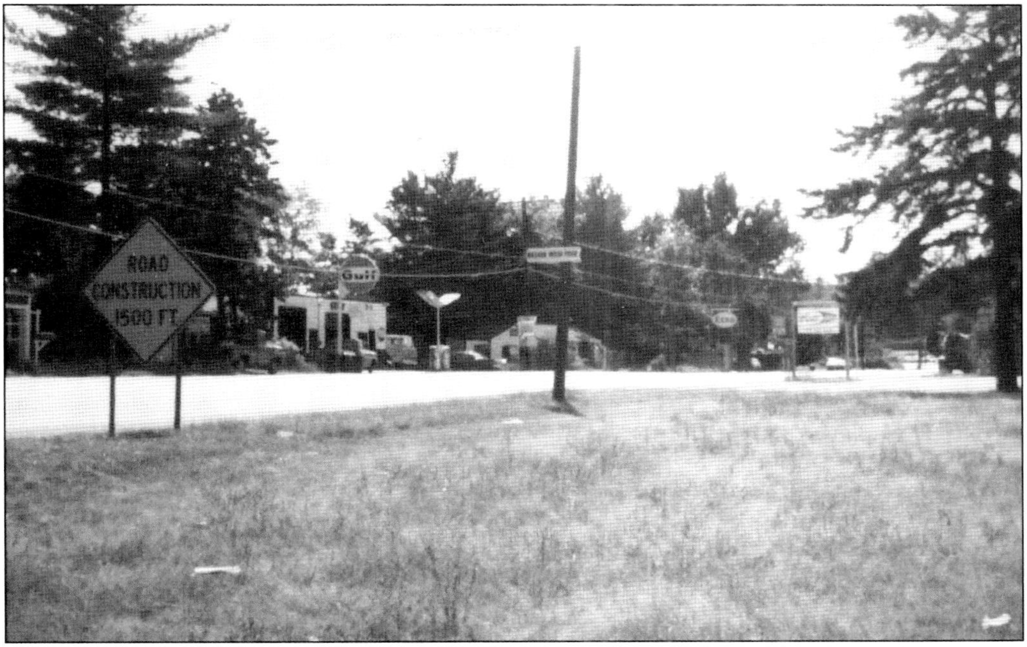

OLD ROUTE 3. Route 3, prior to the 1960s, consisted of a two-lane road with a few gas stations, other small family businesses, and private homes. This section shows Russell's Gulf Station and garage in what was then referred to as Thornton's Ferry.

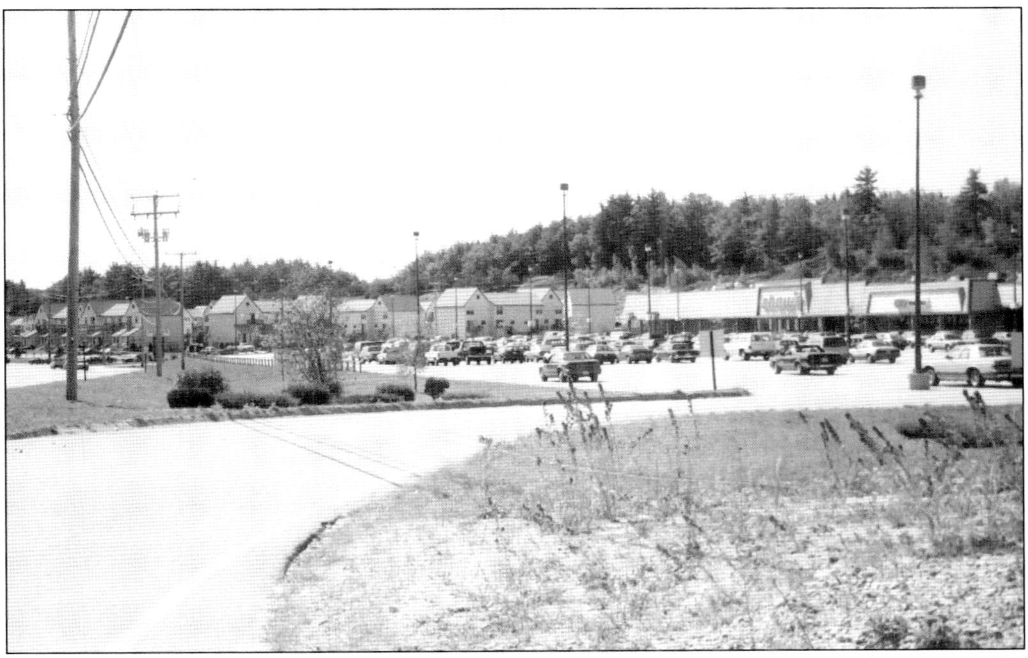

SHAW'S PLAZA. Small stores and businesses along Route 3 have given way to shopping malls. In a 6-mile stretch of road, there are ten malls. At Shaw's Plaza there is a grocery store, a pharmacy, a state liquor store, a music store, a restaurant, a laundry, and a beauty parlor.

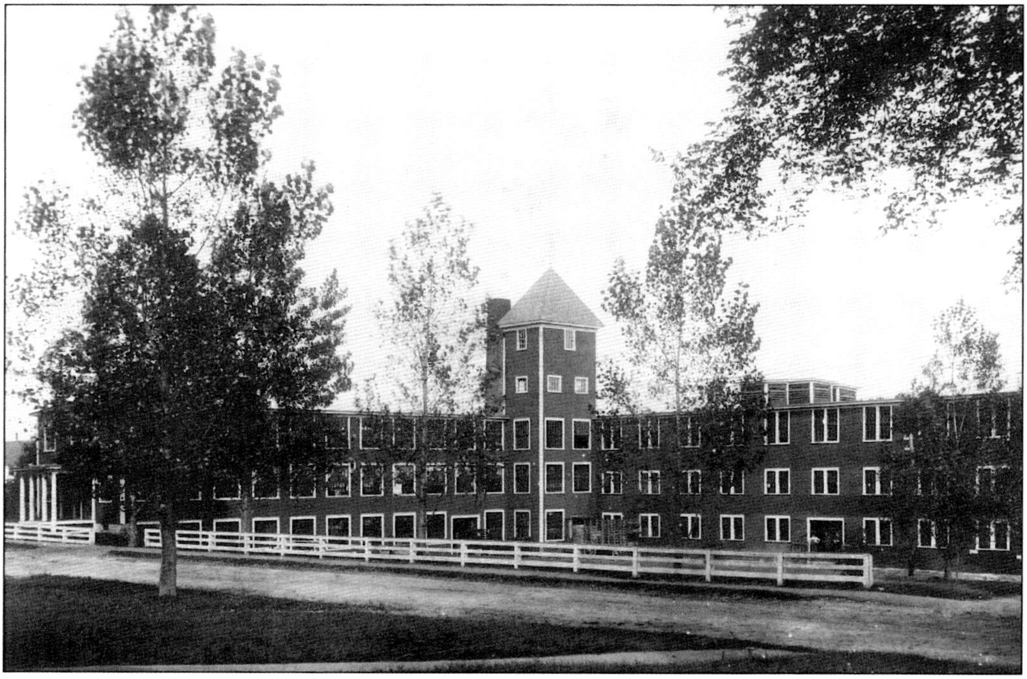

THE OLD WHITE MILL. After Riddle's mills were destroyed by a fire, they were replaced by the Old White Mill. In 1906 the mill was bought by the McElwain Shoe Company and soles for military boots began being manufactured here. The building now houses a chemical company.

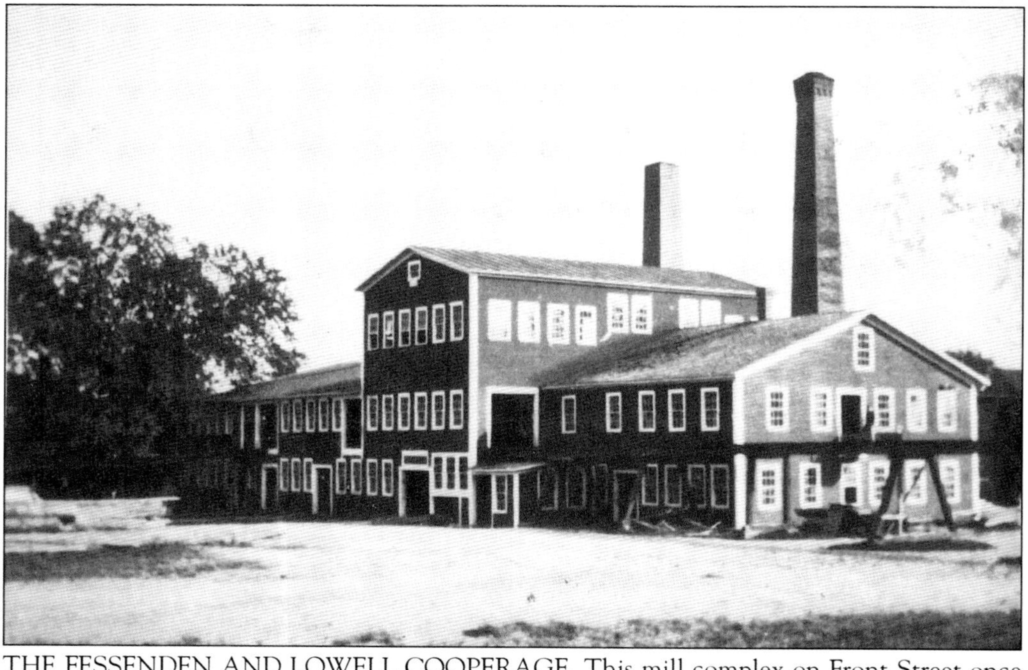

THE FESSENDEN AND LOWELL COOPERAGE. This mill complex on Front Street once manufactured wooden containers and pails. At one time these mills were owned by the Haseltine family and were used to make wood products.

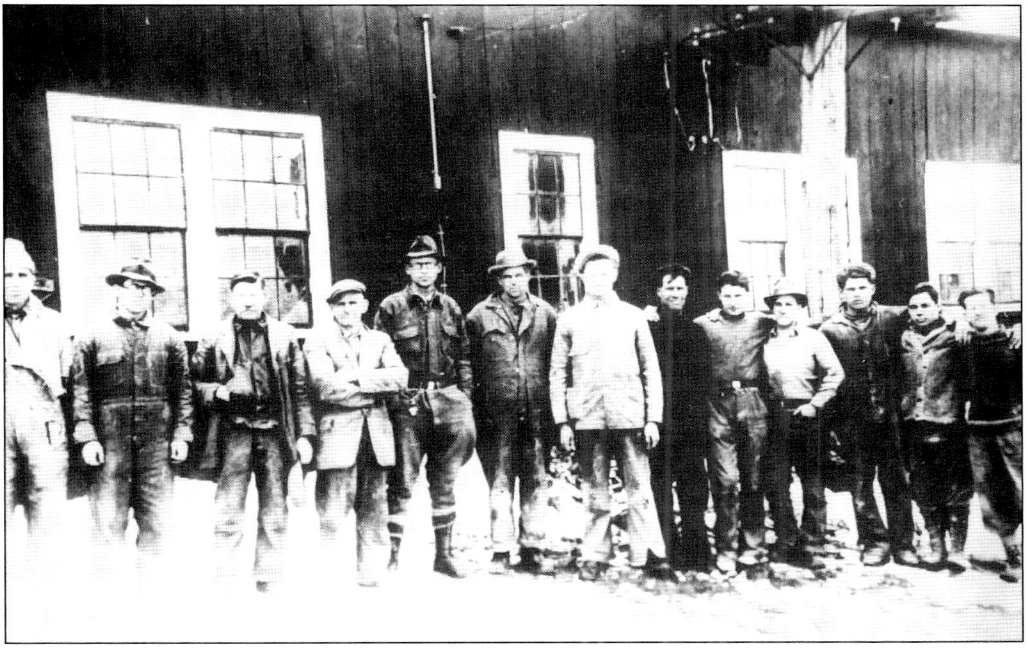

THE MERRIMACK LEATHER COMPANY. One of Merrimack's largest employers in the 1930s was located on Railroad Avenue. The company processed hides for leather goods.

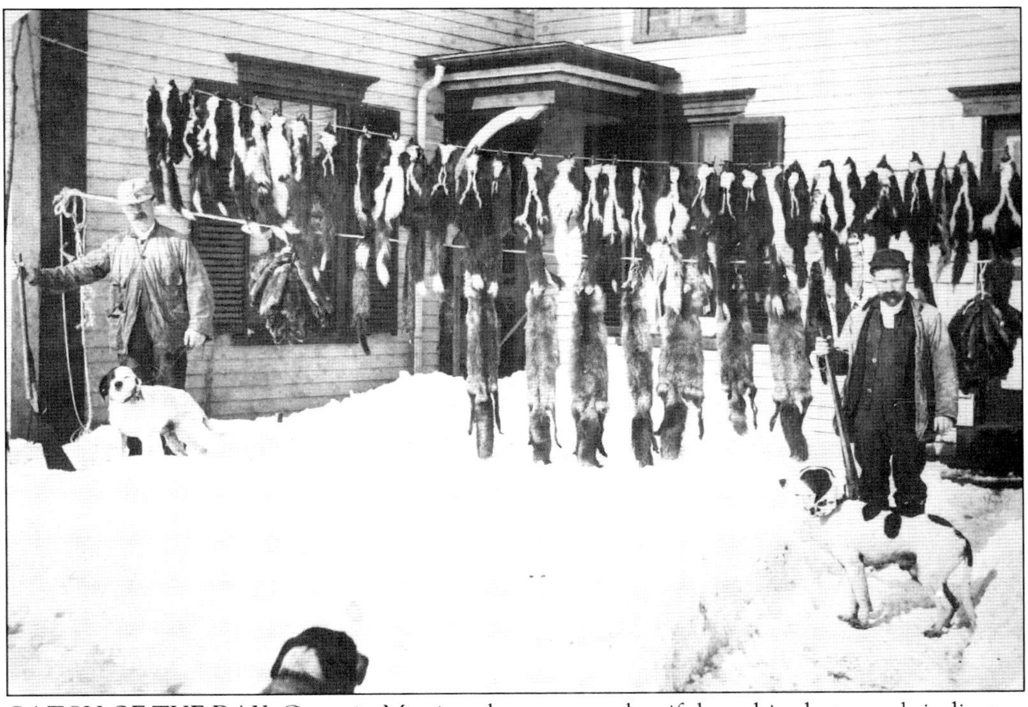

CATCH OF THE DAY. Game in Merrimack was once plentiful, as this photograph indicates. These two enterprising gentlemen pose with their catch in front of their home on Patten Road. Game was hunted for food as well as the pelts.

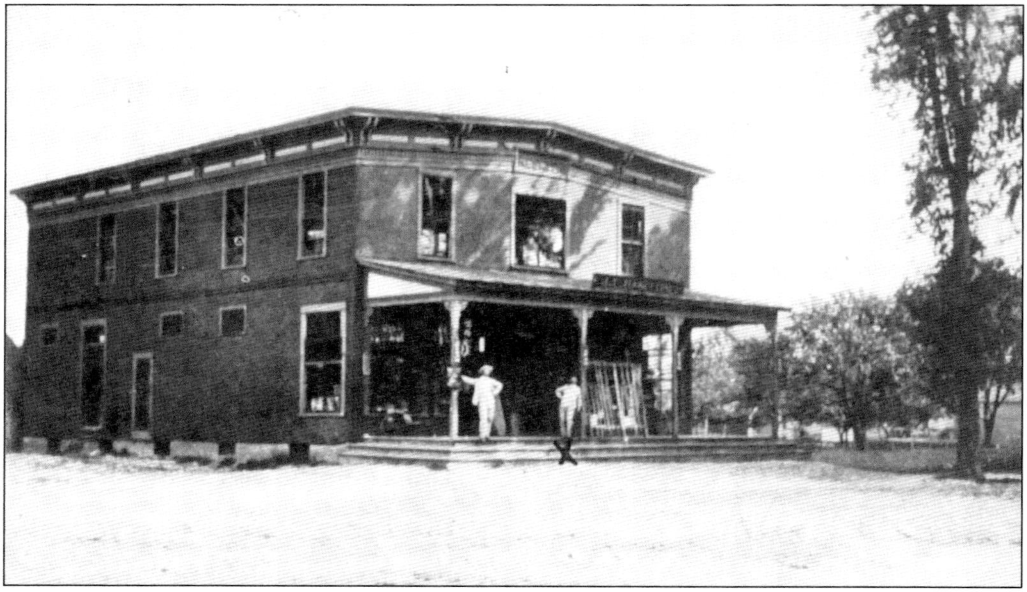

THE FESSENDEN AND LOWELL STORE. This was your typical company store. Located on the corner of Depot Street and Route 3, it was a general store built for the convenience of the employees of the cooper shop, and it sold everything you could possibly need. Charles Nesmith, an associate of Fessenden and Lowell, operated the store for a time.

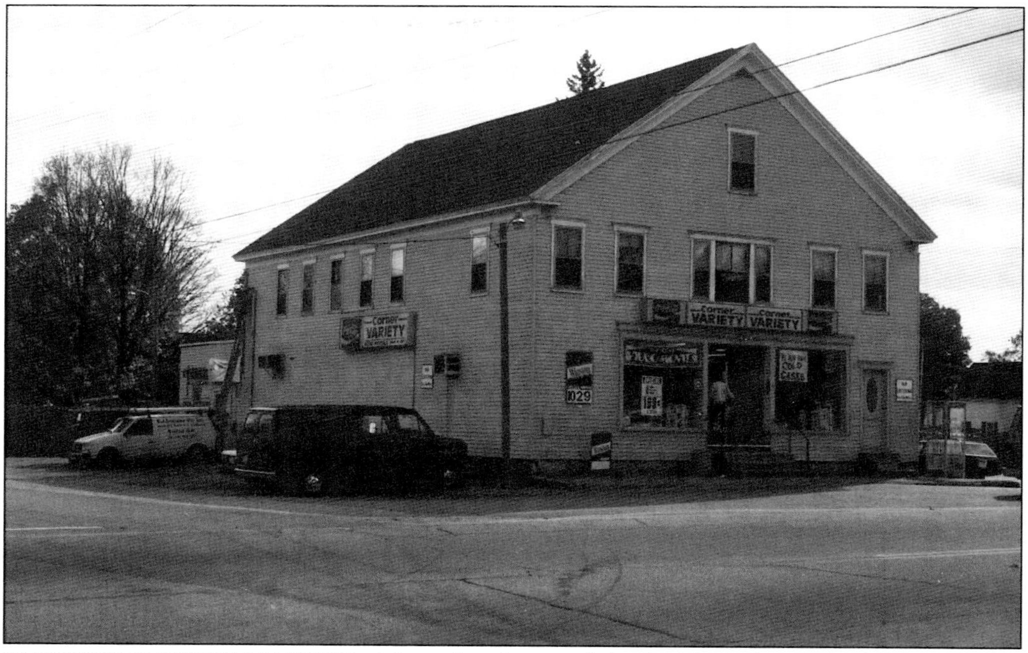

THE REED'S FERRY MARKET. After a fire destroyed the building, the Fessenden and Lowell Store was rebuilt and became the property of the Jenkins family, who operated a variety store for two generations. The post office was located in this building with Raymond Jenkins as postmaster. Stanley and Millie Green operated the store when it became known as the Reed's Ferry Market.

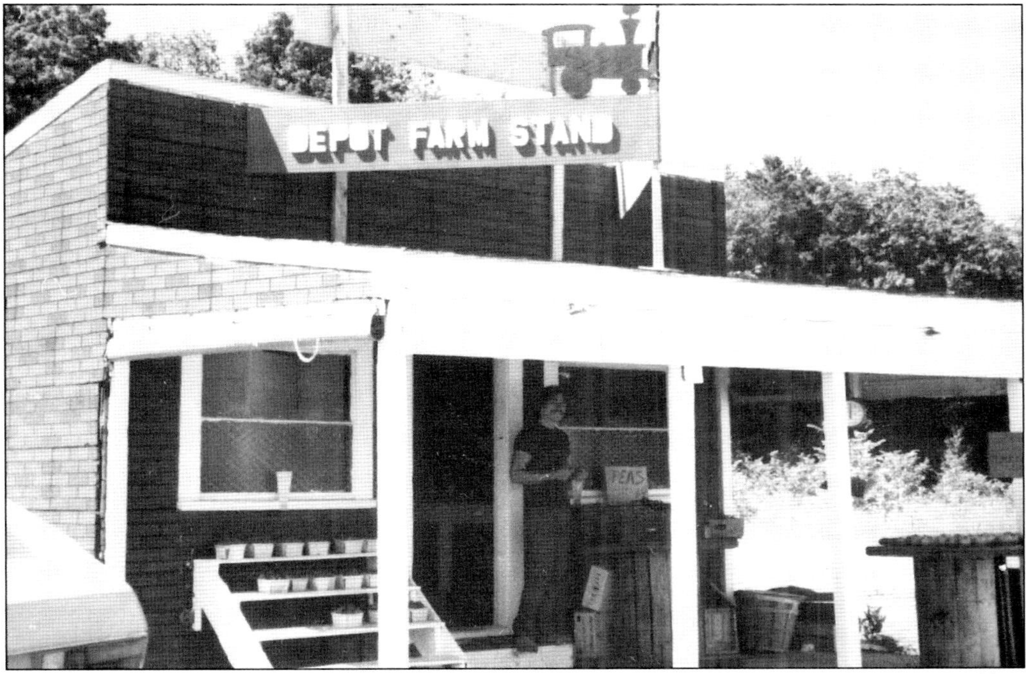

THE DEPOT FARM STAND. A small backyard stand that sold mostly home-grown vegetables, this business began on Depot Street. Presently located on Route 3, the stand now sells a variety of fruits and vegetables as well as trees, plants, decorative arrangements, and Christmas trees.

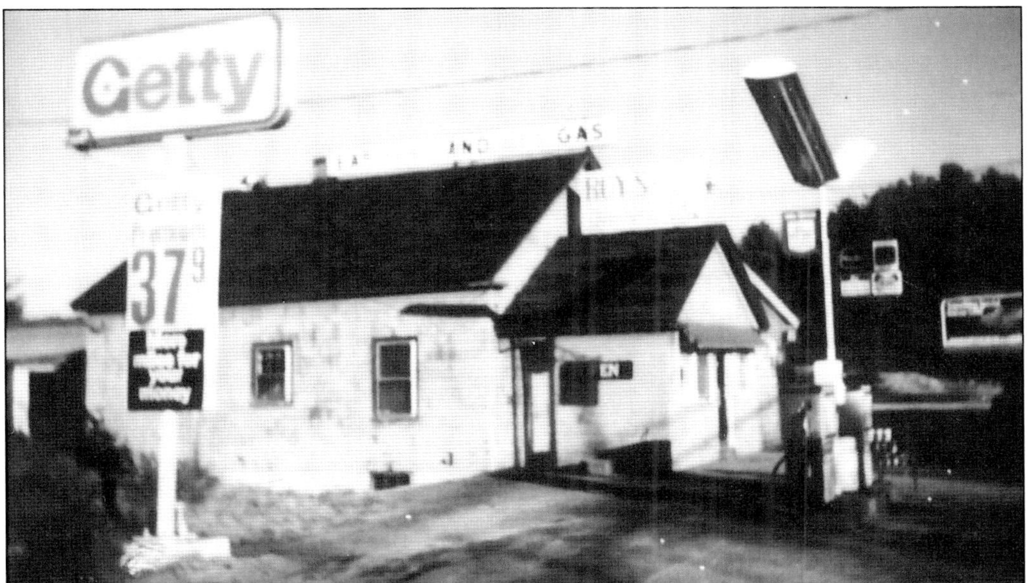

"EAT HERE AND GET GAS." One of the most talked about eating places in Merrimack was located on Route 101A. A restaurant and gas station, owned by the Levesques and then the Roy family, it had a sign stating that you could "Eat Here and Get Gas. However, this did not stop people from eating here. It is now Pennichuck Square.

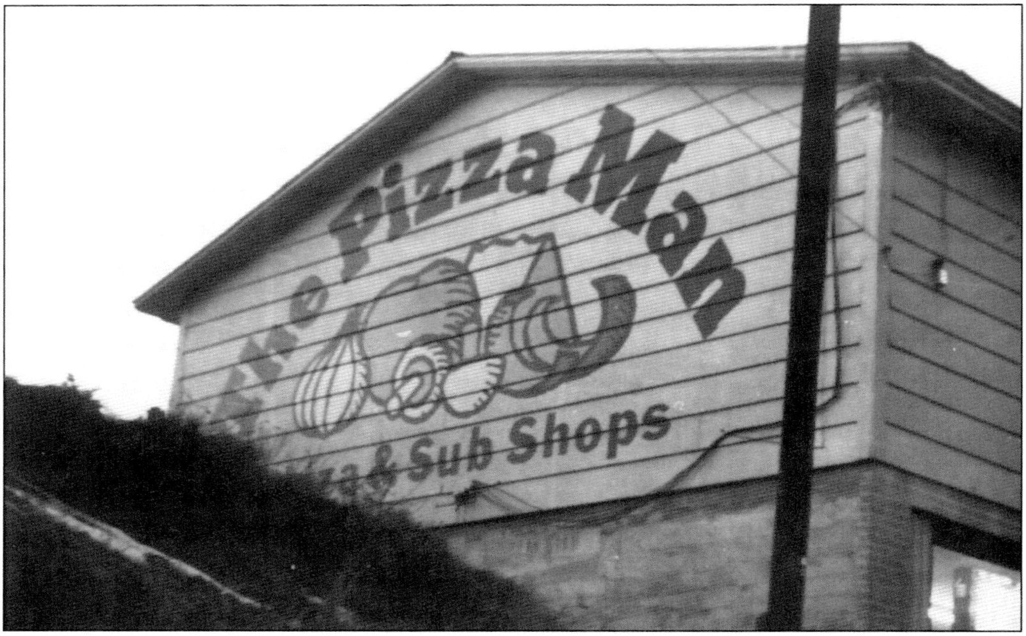

THE PIZZA MAN. Merrimack's first pizza parlor opened in 1972 on Daniel Webster Highway. A very popular place after any sports event, you could usually find both officials and players there discussing the game. The building now houses a sports card store.

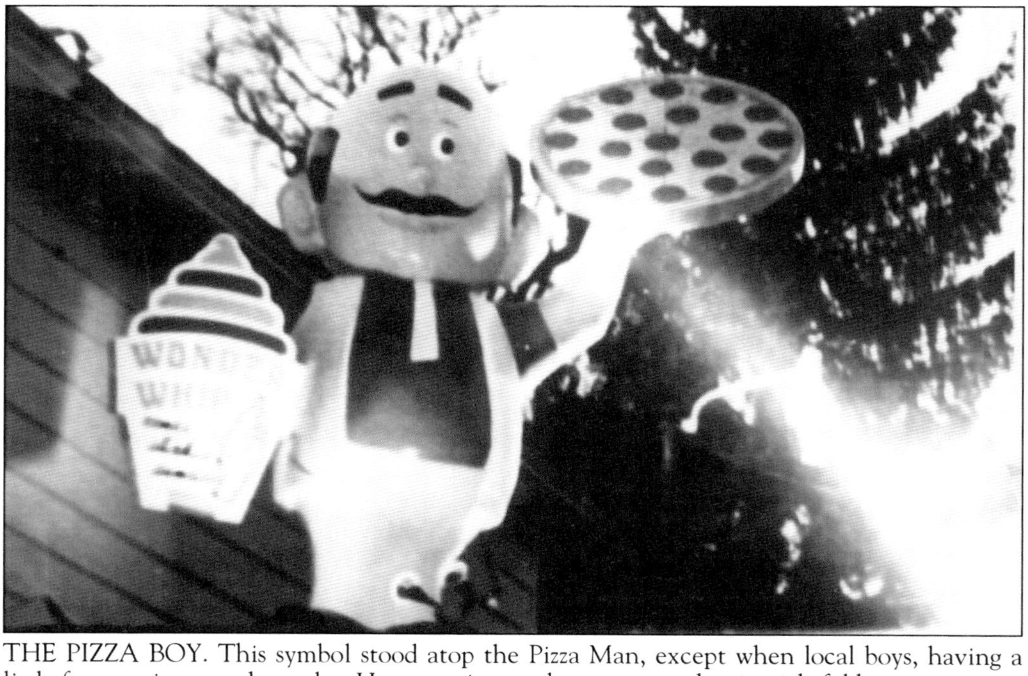

THE PIZZA BOY. This symbol stood atop the Pizza Man, except when local boys, having a little fun, put it somewhere else. However, it was always returned to its rightful home.

Nine

Rivers, Lakes, and Streams

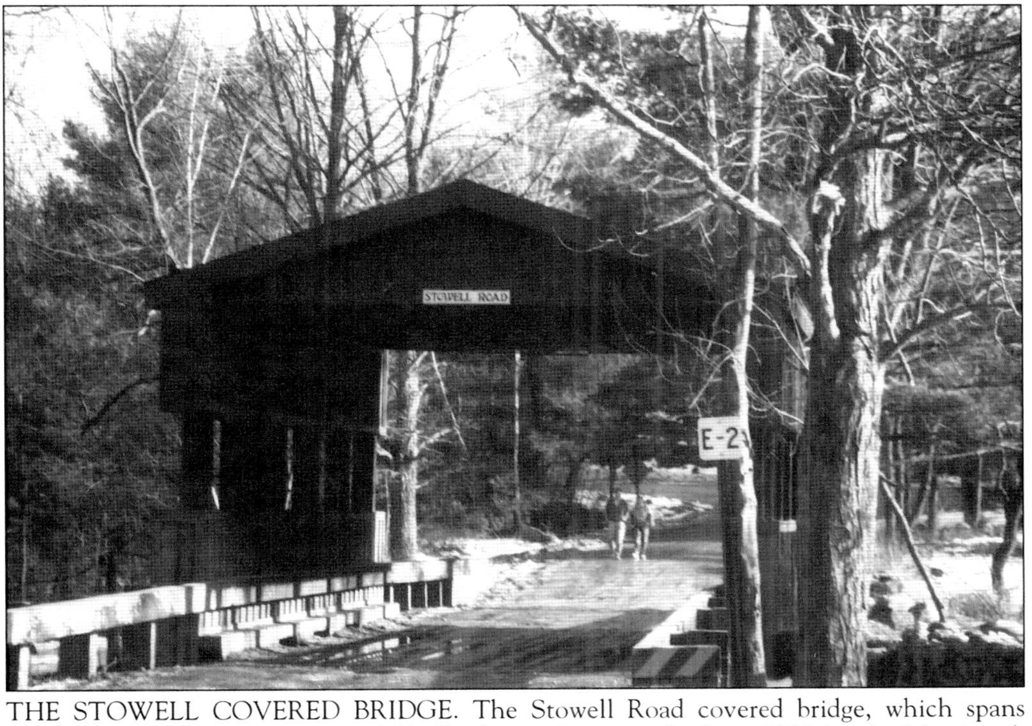

THE STOWELL COVERED BRIDGE. The Stowell Road covered bridge, which spans Baboosic Brook on the Merrimack/Bedford town line, was built in 1990 by the Merrimack Department of Public Works. A video made during its construction is used by the University of New Hampshire and sent to towns across the country that are considering building timber bridges.

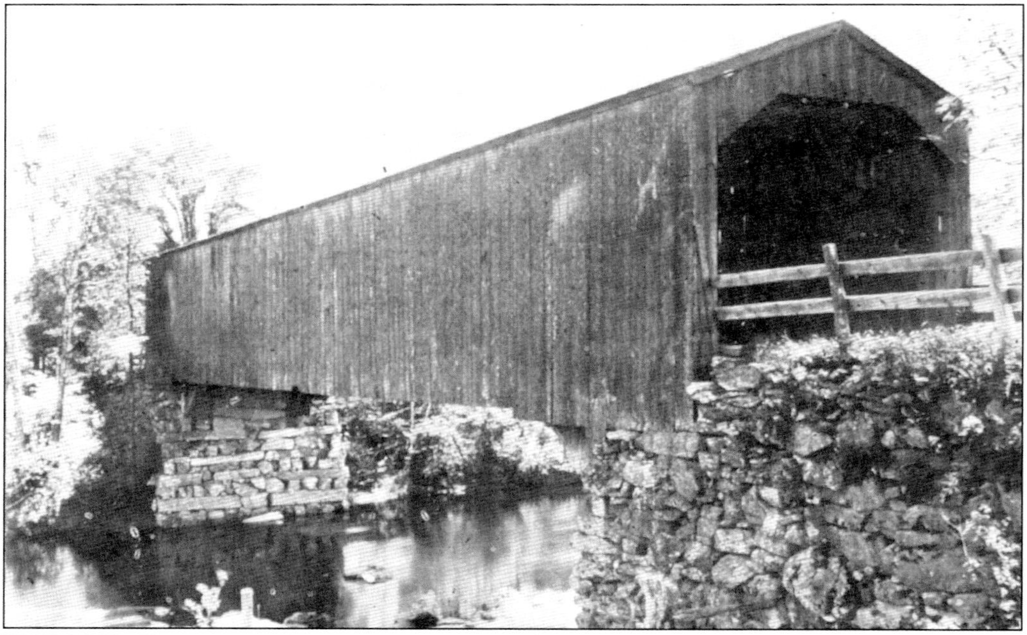

THE TURKEY HILL COVERED BRIDGE. This was Merrimack's first covered bridge to span the Souhegan River. It was a Town Lattice design with an added arch, and was one of New Hampshire's oldest covered bridges when arsonists destroyed it. Once again, Merrimack lost a landmark.

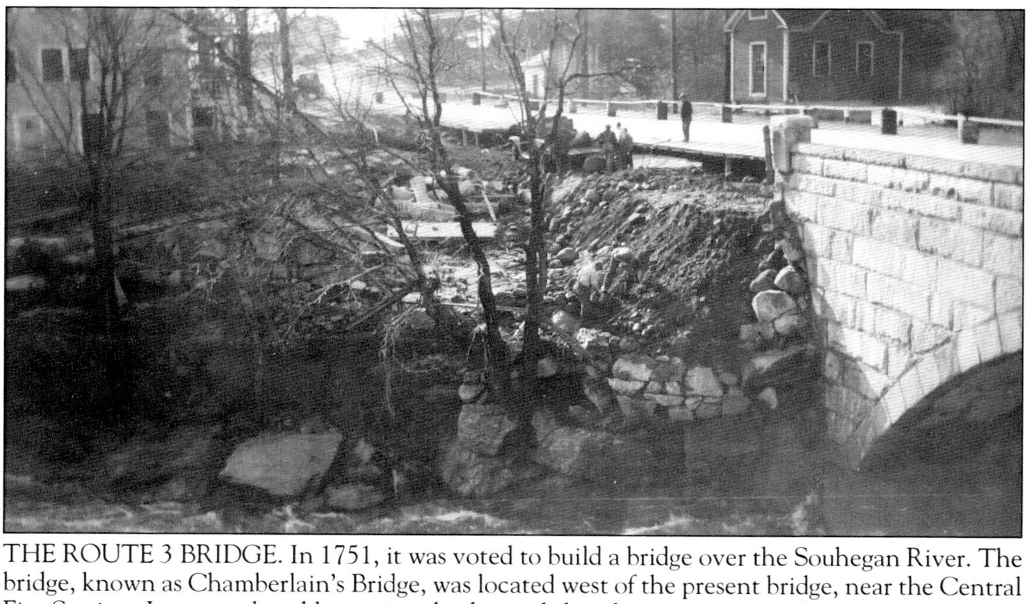

THE ROUTE 3 BRIDGE. In 1751, it was voted to build a bridge over the Souhegan River. The bridge, known as Chamberlain's Bridge, was located west of the present bridge, near the Central Fire Station. It was replaced by an iron bridge and then by a granite one. Major repairs had to be made to the bridge after the 1936 Flood.

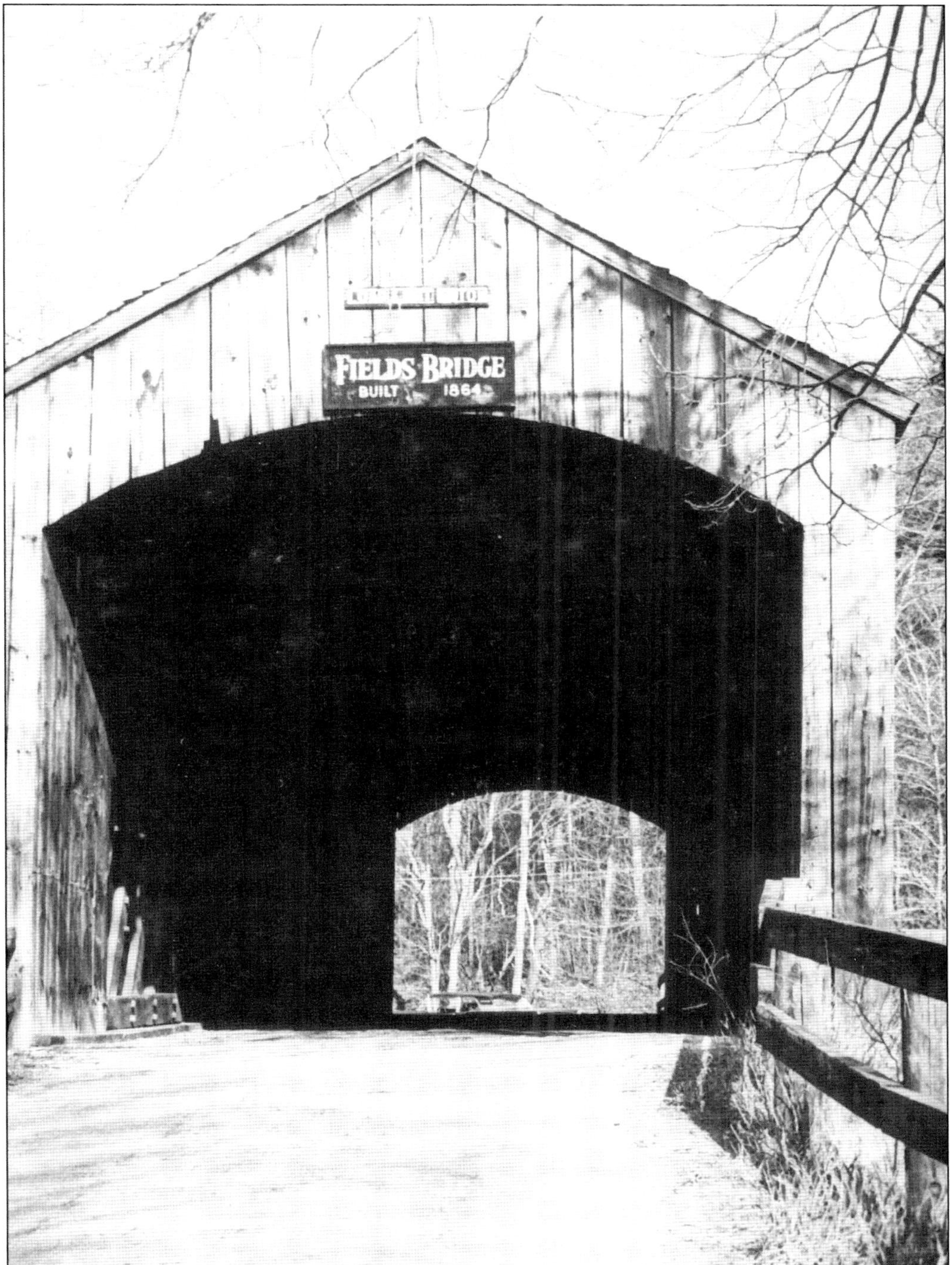

FIELD'S COVERED BRIDGE. The upper bridge over the Souhegan River was also known as Severn's Bridge. Field's Bridge was a single span of Town Lattice design with round portals. An advertising sign for D.F. Runnels, a clothing store that closed around 1905, was found in the bridge.

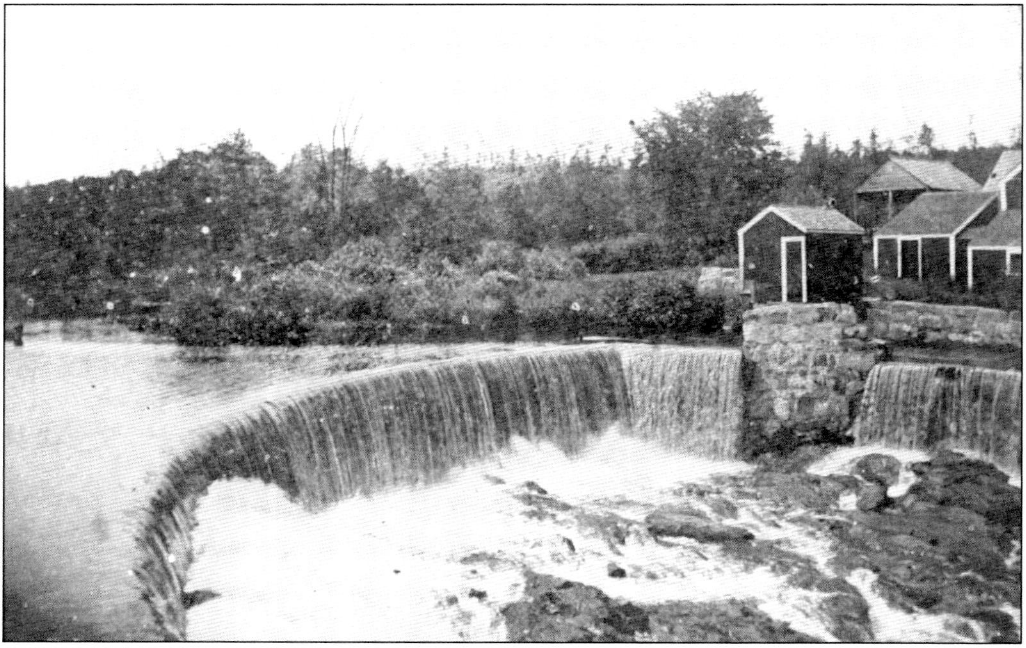

SOUHEGAN DAM. This dam on the Souhegan River, next to the Central Fire Station, was built to provide hydropower for the mills that were located where the chemical company is now.

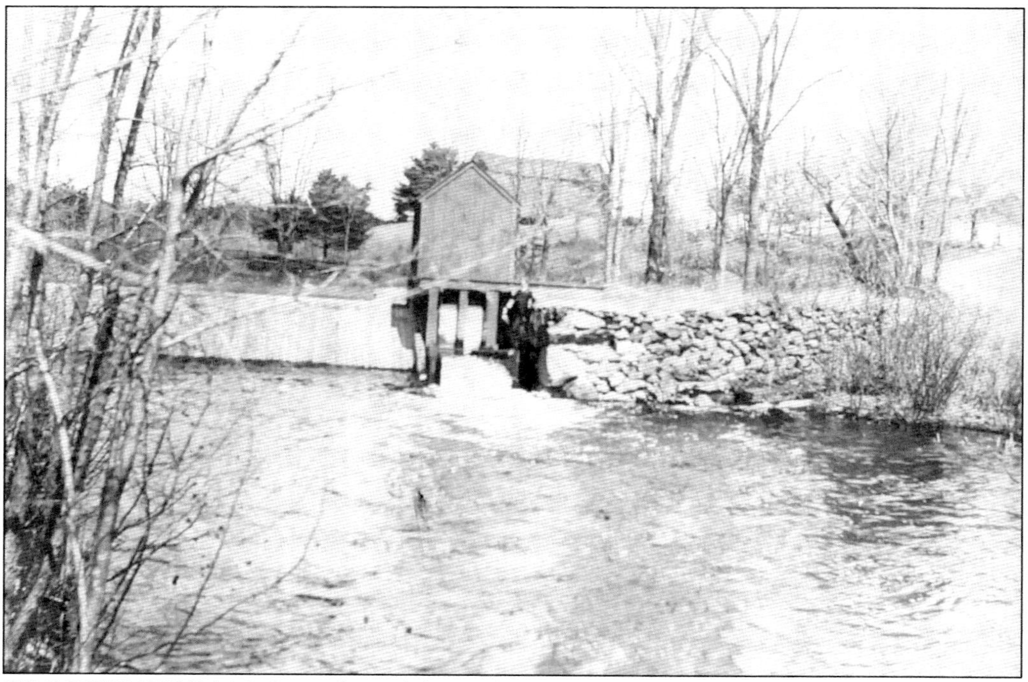

PENNICHUCK DAM. Several ponds located on the Nashua/Merrimack town line, known as the Pennichuck Ponds, provide the water supply for the city of Nashua. This dam on Thornton Road regulates the flow from one pond to the other.

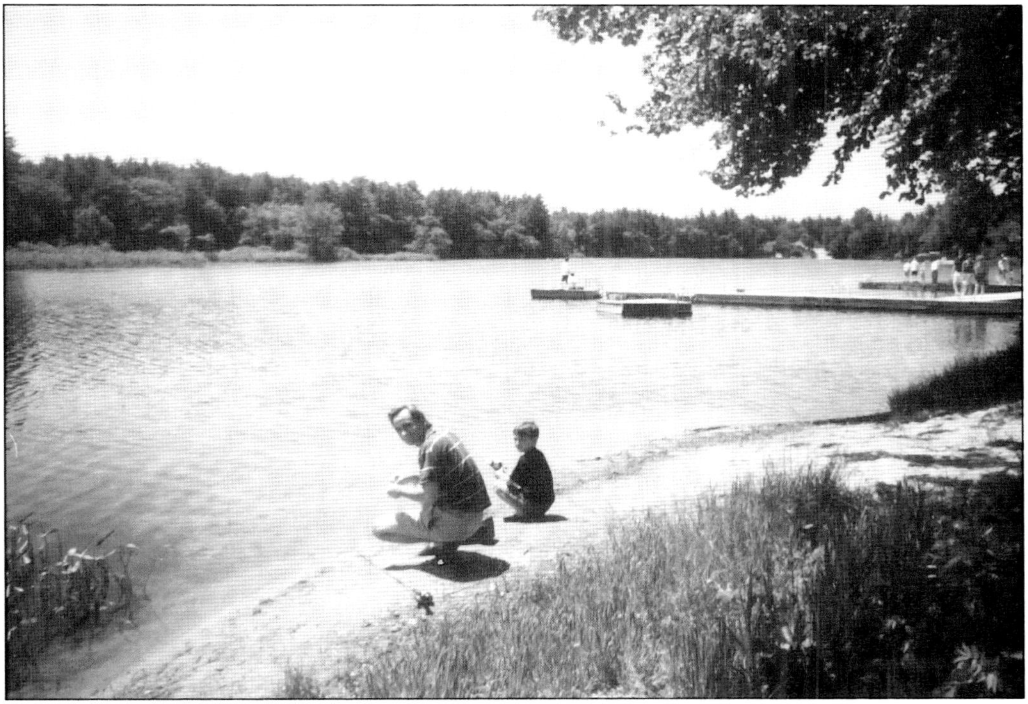

NATICOOK LAKE. Merrimack has two rivers, many brooks, and several lakes and ponds. All are used for recreation. Naticook Lake, on the corner of Naticook and Camp Sargent Roads, has always been a popular fishing place.

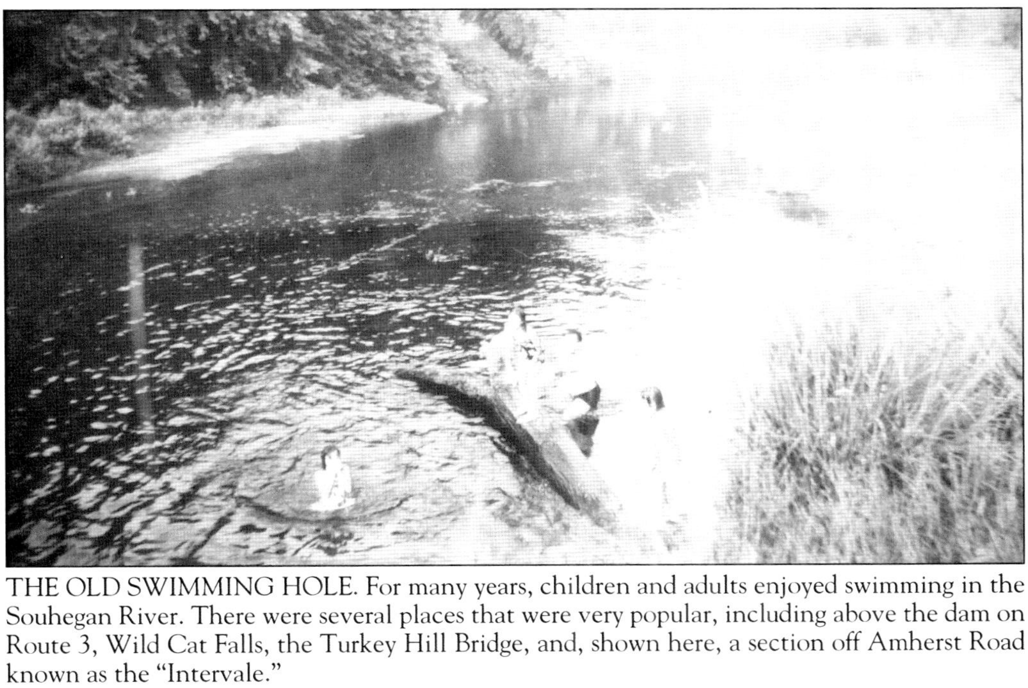

THE OLD SWIMMING HOLE. For many years, children and adults enjoyed swimming in the Souhegan River. There were several places that were very popular, including above the dam on Route 3, Wild Cat Falls, the Turkey Hill Bridge, and, shown here, a section off Amherst Road known as the "Intervale."

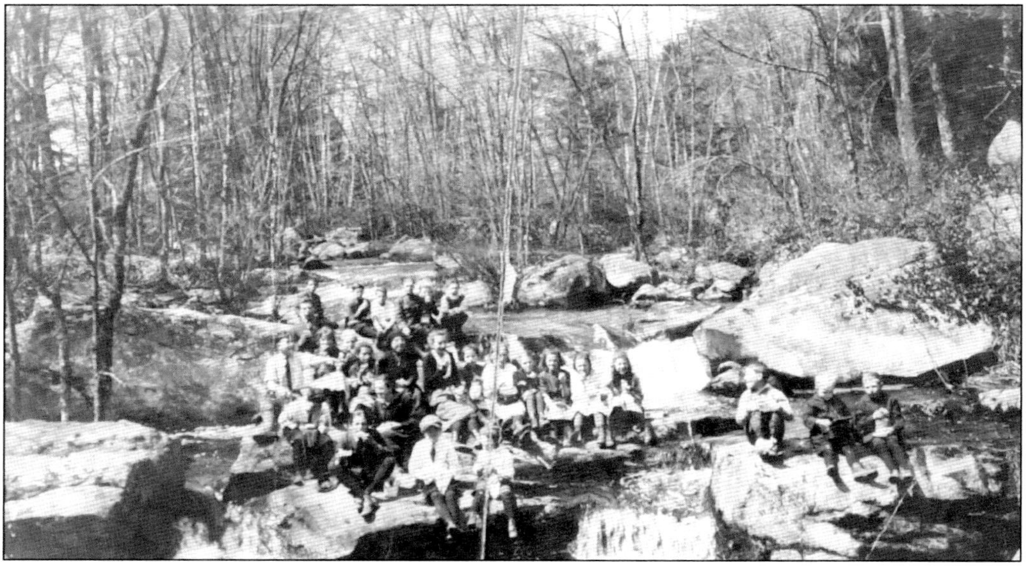

PICNIC IN THE PARK. Many school and church outings have been held along Baboosic Brook in Twin Bridge Park. There are rocks to climb on, water to wade in, hiking trails, and picnic areas to enjoy.

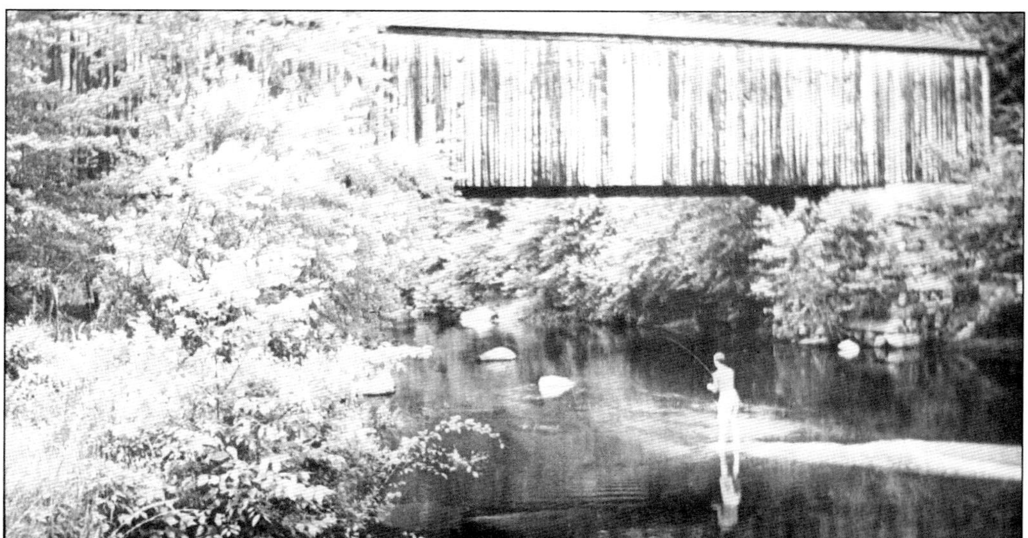

FISHING. A person could almost always catch a fish under the Turkey Hill Bridge. If the fish were not biting, you could go for a swim, so the trip was never wasted.

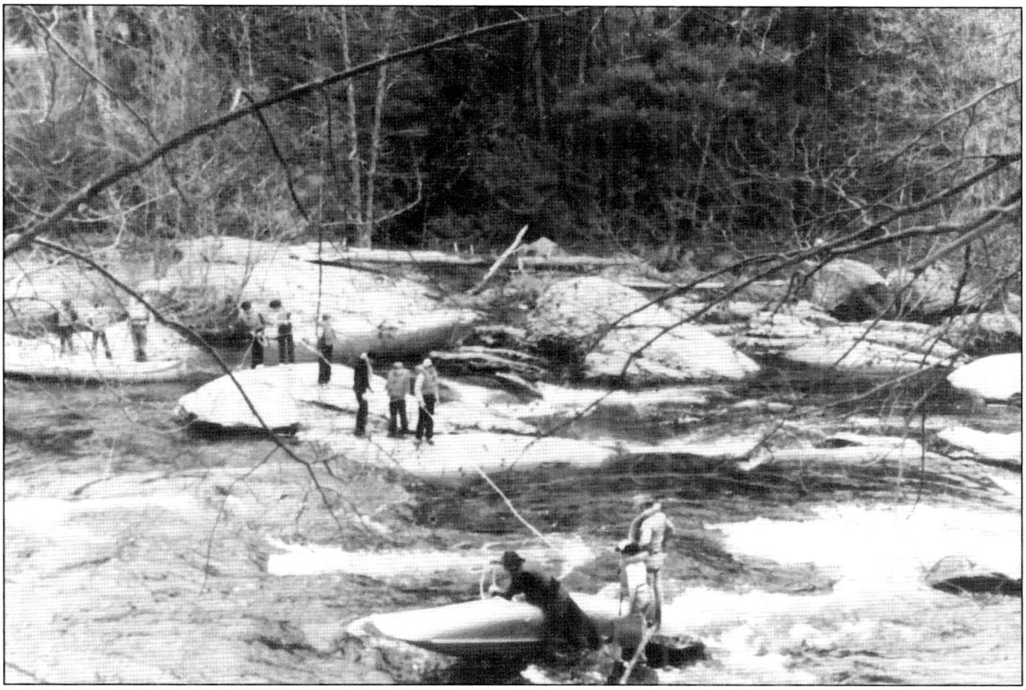

CANOE TRIPS. The Souhegan and Merrimack Rivers are used by many canoeists during the year. In April, high water conceals the rocks in the Souhegan River near the Tomasian Farm. As a result, many capsized canoeists have to be rescued from the raging waters.

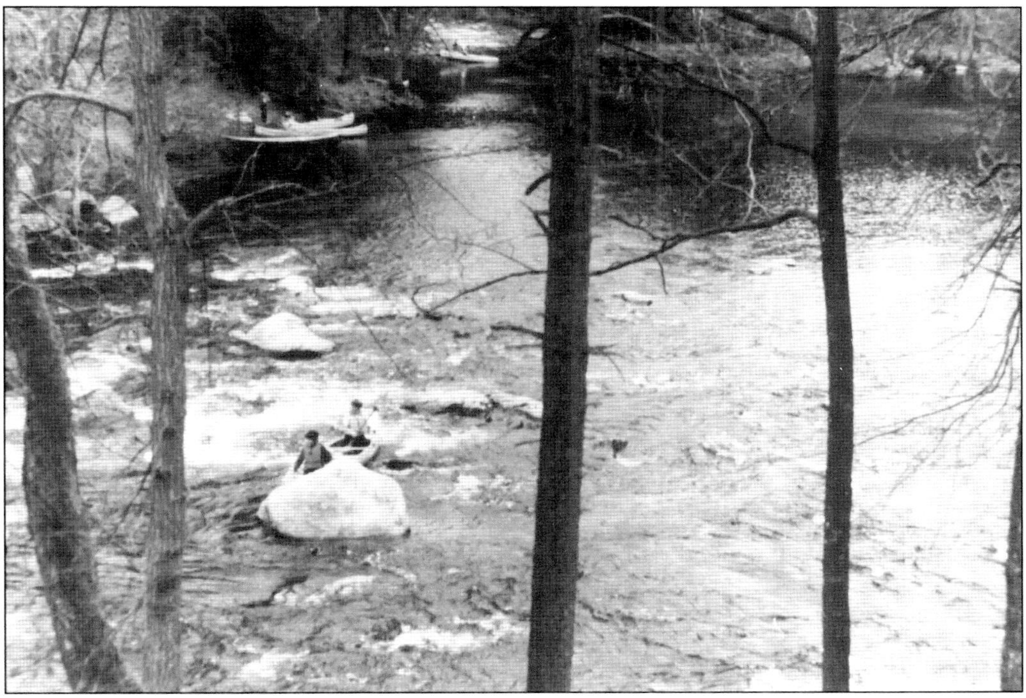

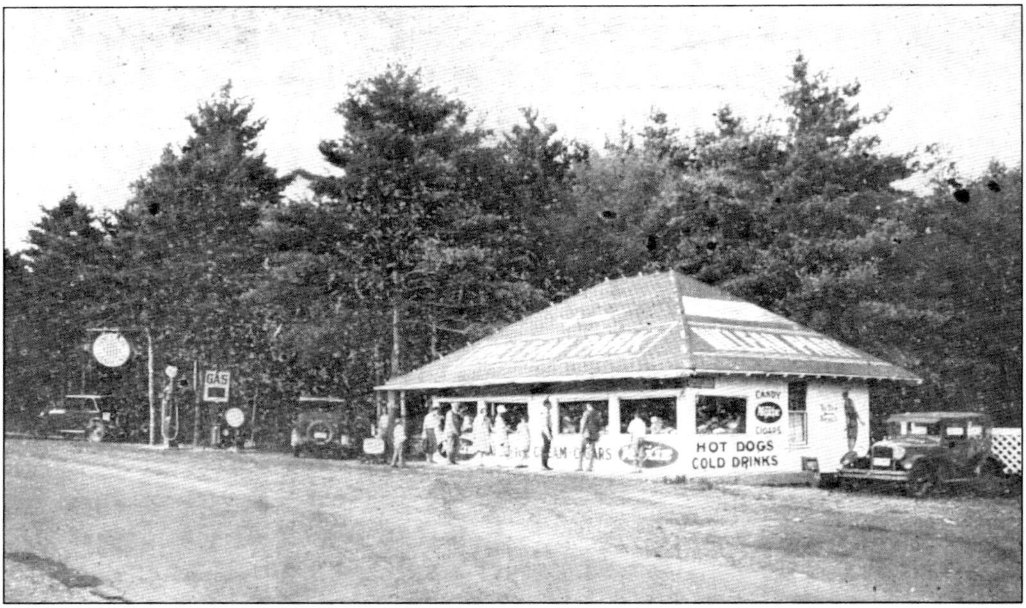

HILLEAH PARK. You would never know it today but Horseshoe Pond was once a well-known summer retreat. Many people came from Boston and New York to enjoy the summer in the country. Located on Daniel Webster Highway, Hilleah Park, later known as Sheila's Grove, boasted the best spring water in the USA.

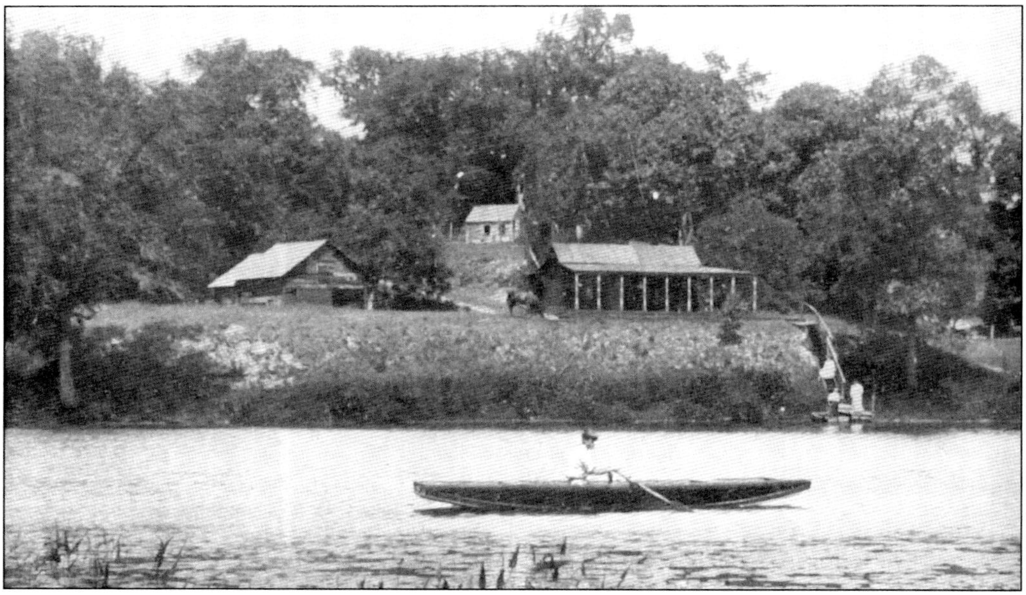

HORSESHOE POND. During the early 1900s, many privately-owned summer camps were located along the shore of Horseshoe Pond. People from many other places owned the buildings but rented the land. When many of the leases ran out they were not renewed, and the buildings were torn down or moved. The property was then sold and redeveloped.

Ten

Organizations

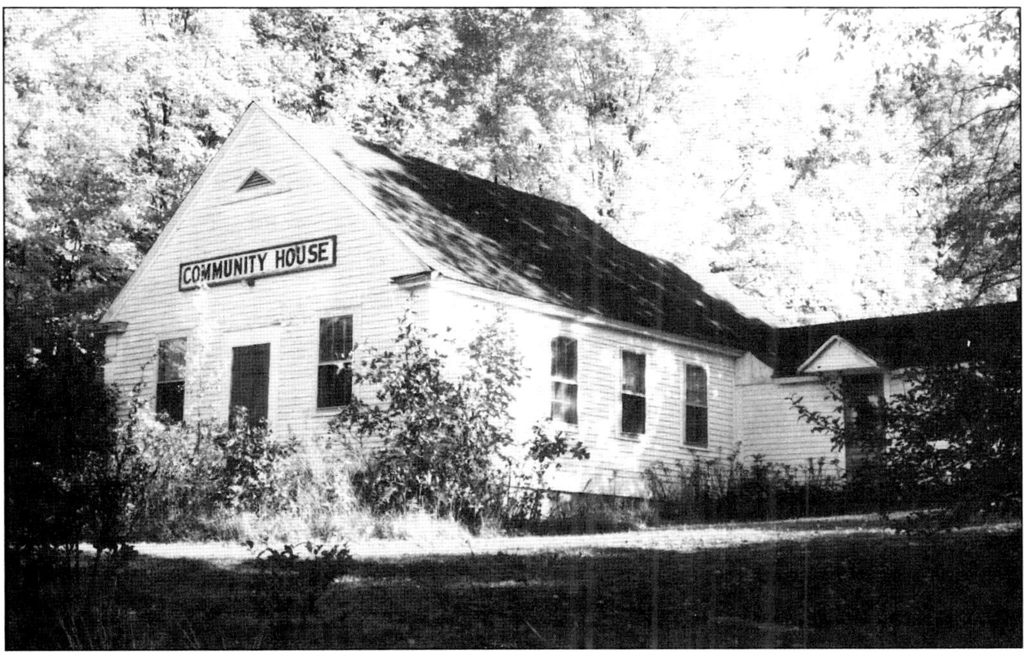

THE SOUTH MERRIMACK COMMUNITY CLUB. In 1948 the South Merrimack Community Club purchased the vacant 1847 one-room schoolhouse on Boston Post Road. A kitchen addition was added and suppers, whist parties, and meetings were held. The building served the community as a social center, and is now the home of the Merrimack Historical Society.

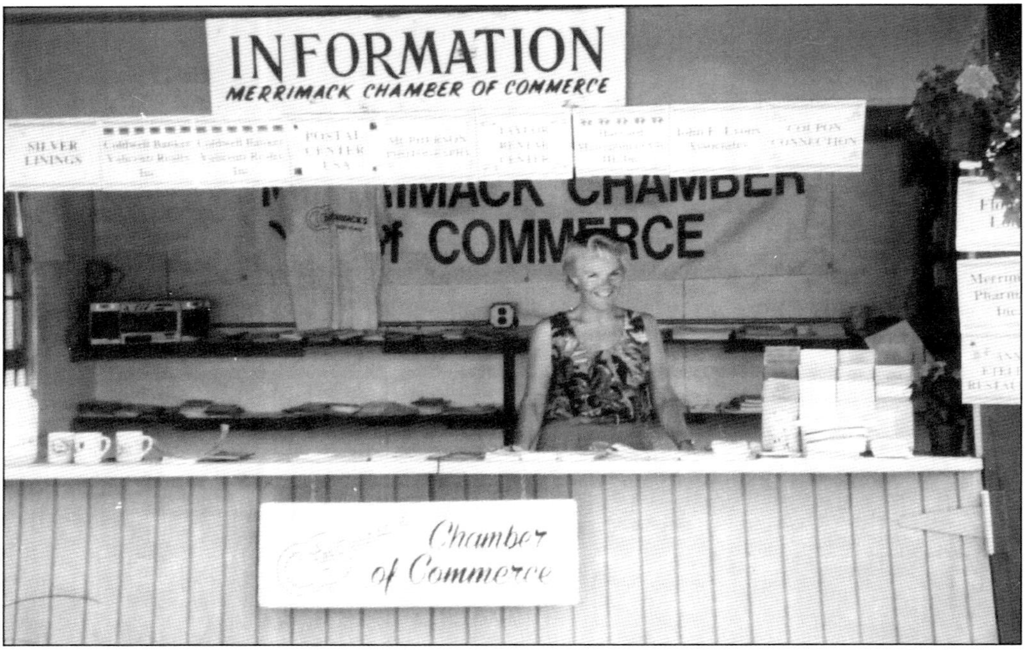

THE INFORMATION BOOTH. State and local brochures and maps are available from the Information Booth at Fraser Square on Route 3. Owned and operated by the Merrimack Chamber of Commerce since 1982, it is open from July 1 until September 1.

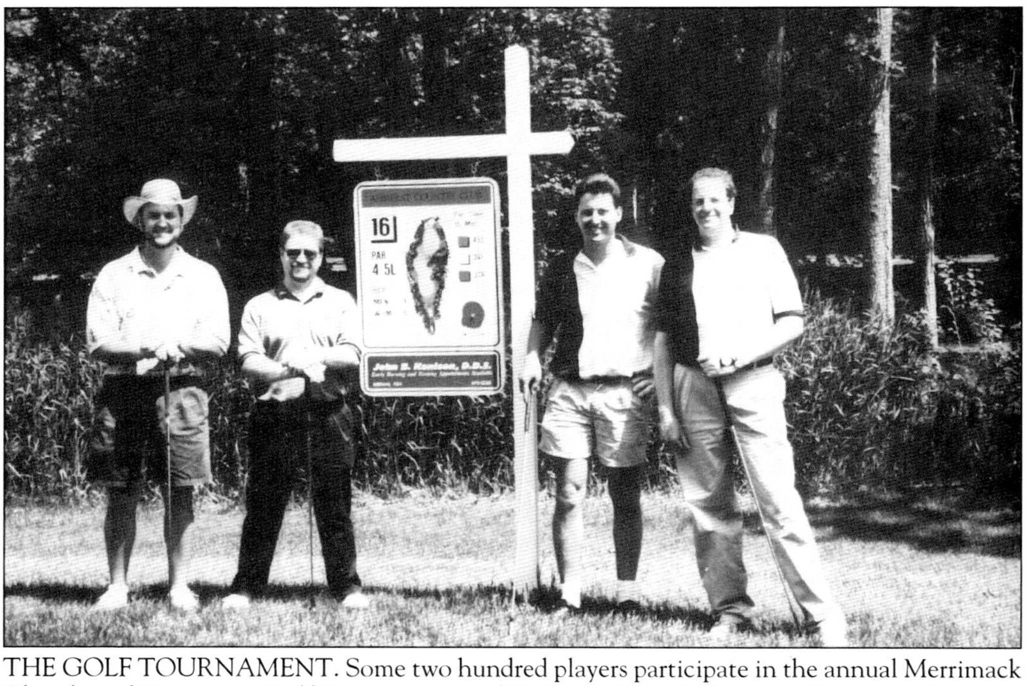

THE GOLF TOURNAMENT. Some two hundred players participate in the annual Merrimack Chamber of Commerce Golf Tournament and Barbecue. Now in its seventh season, the event is held at the Amherst Country Club. Proceeds are used for the operating expenses of the Chamber's office.

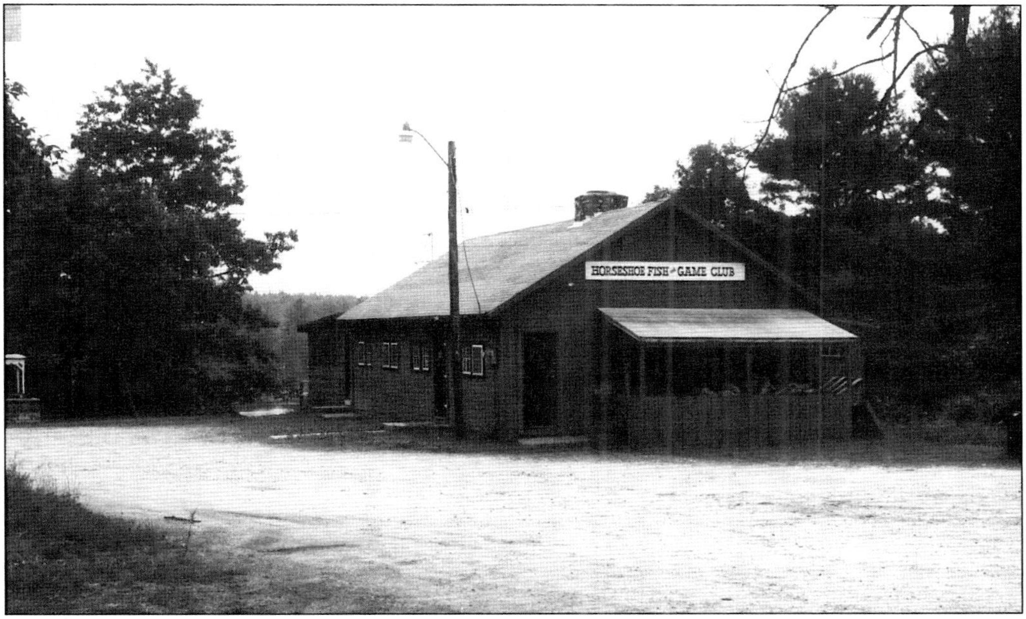

THE MERRIMACK FISH AND GAME CLUB. The Fish and Game Club is located at Green's Pond on Green's Pond Road. For many years, Saturday night dances, wild game suppers, and an annual fishing derby were held here. The pond is now a watershed under the direction of the Merrimack Village district, but the clubhouse is still used by the Fish and Game Club.

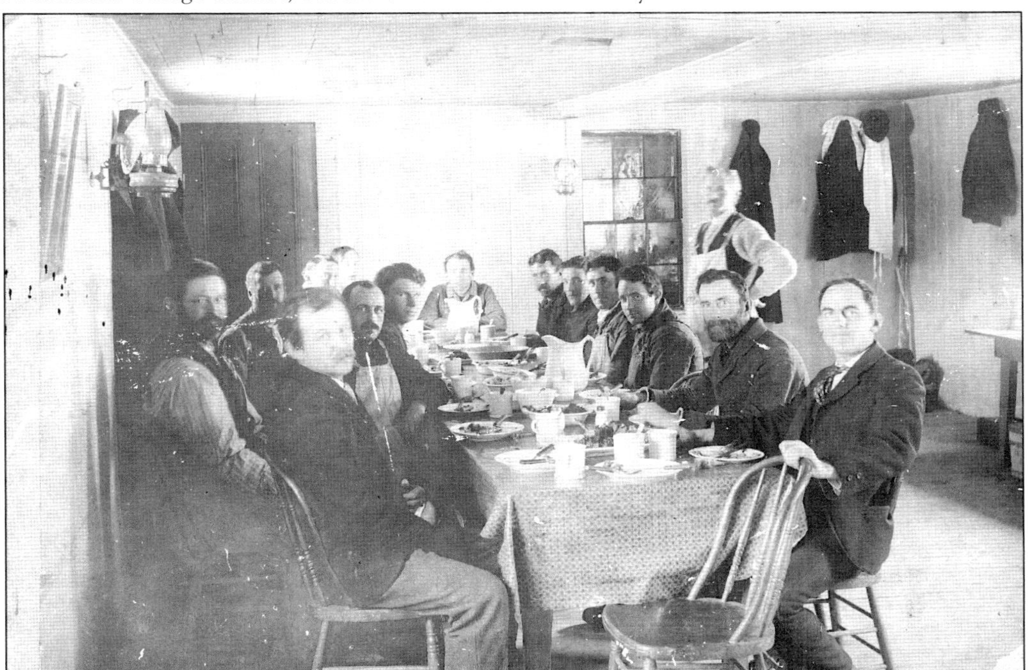

FISH AND GAME SUPPERS. Prior to the building of their clubhouse on Green's Pond Road, the Fish and Game Club held their meetings in the upper level of Abbott's Store. Many meetings were preceded by a supper.

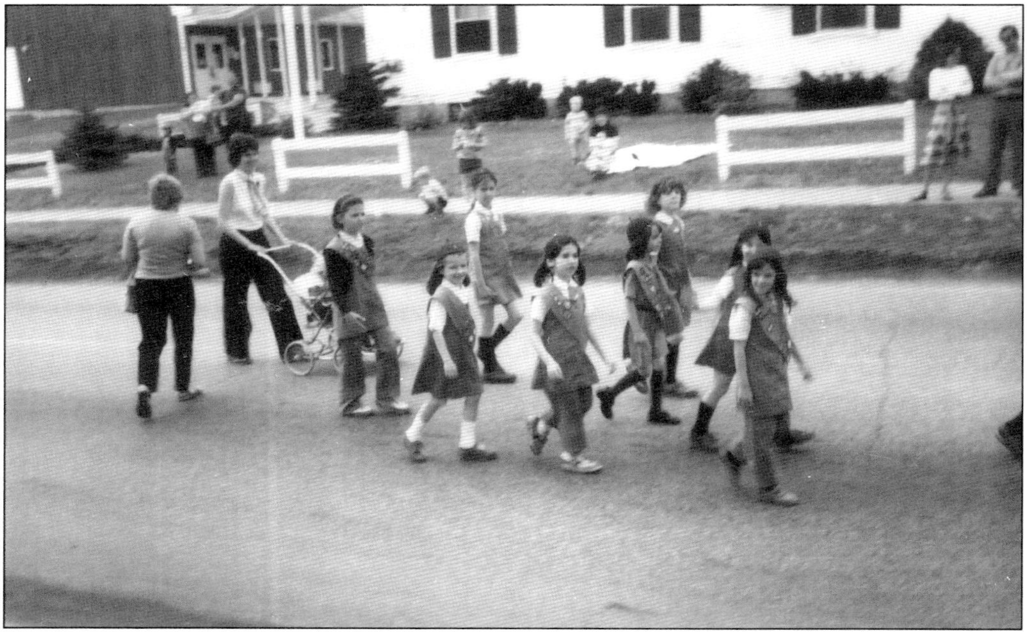

SCOUTING. Scouting was one of the first organizations for girls and boys in Merrimack. Starting as Brownies and Cub Scouts, many would go on to become Senior Scouts and leaders.

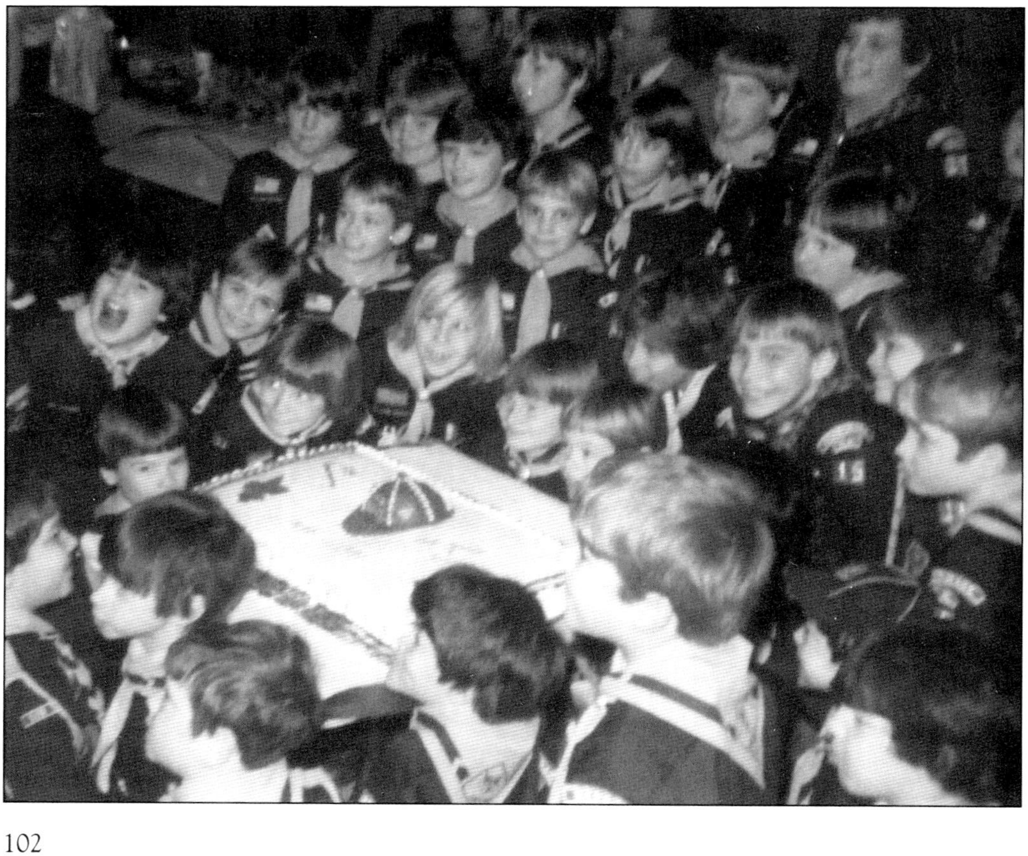

Eleven

Around the Town

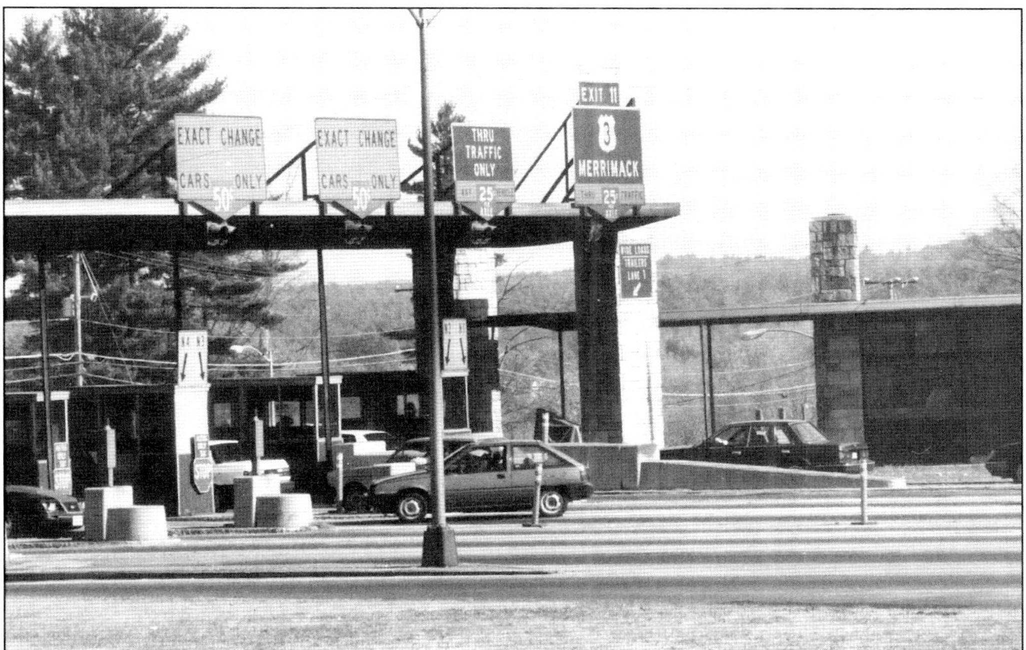

THE F.E. EVERETT TURNPIKE. The turnpike, a toll road, was built in 1956. Merrimack had one toll plaza for collecting tolls, whether passing through, entering, or exiting. These booths were moved to Bedford, and Merrimack now has three access points, requiring tolls for entering and exiting the road.

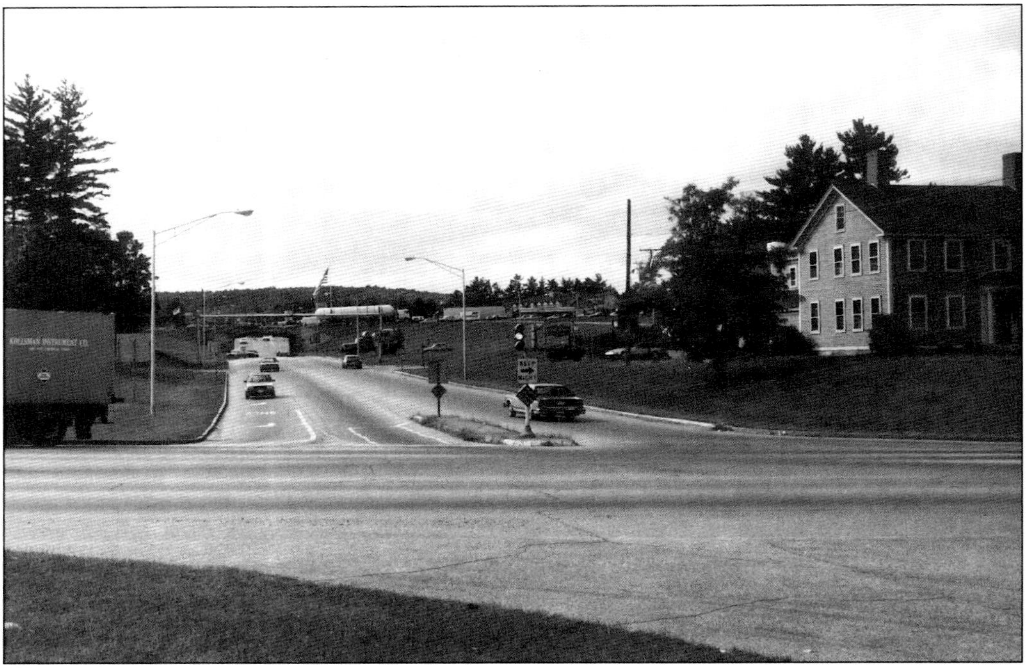

AMHERST ROAD. This road is so named because it was the only road from Merrimack to Amherst. It was relocated at the time the F.E. Everett Turnpike was built. Originally it was on the north side of the Hannah Jack Tavern and was only two lanes wide.

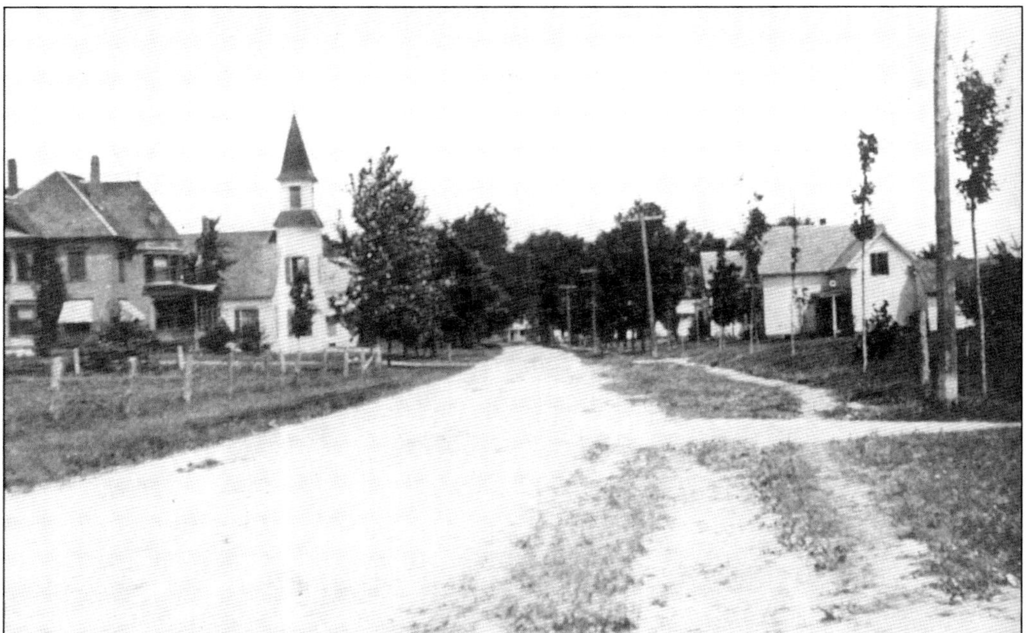

ROUTE 3 NORTH. Passing through a quiet little country town on a two-lane dirt road is just a memory. This section of town, with its stately old homes and quaint chapel, was known as Reed's Ferry.

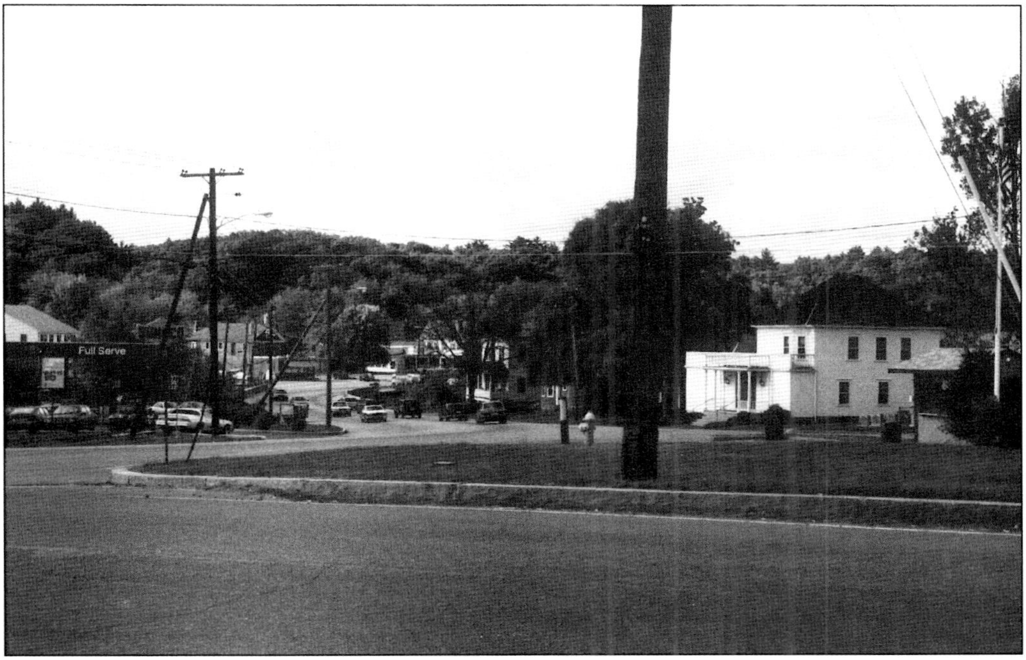

MAIN STREET. This section of Route 3 is often referred to as Main Street. The top photograph is looking north from Fraser Square; the bottom one is looking south toward the Central Fire Station. Loop Road, just out of sight in this view, was once part of Route 3.

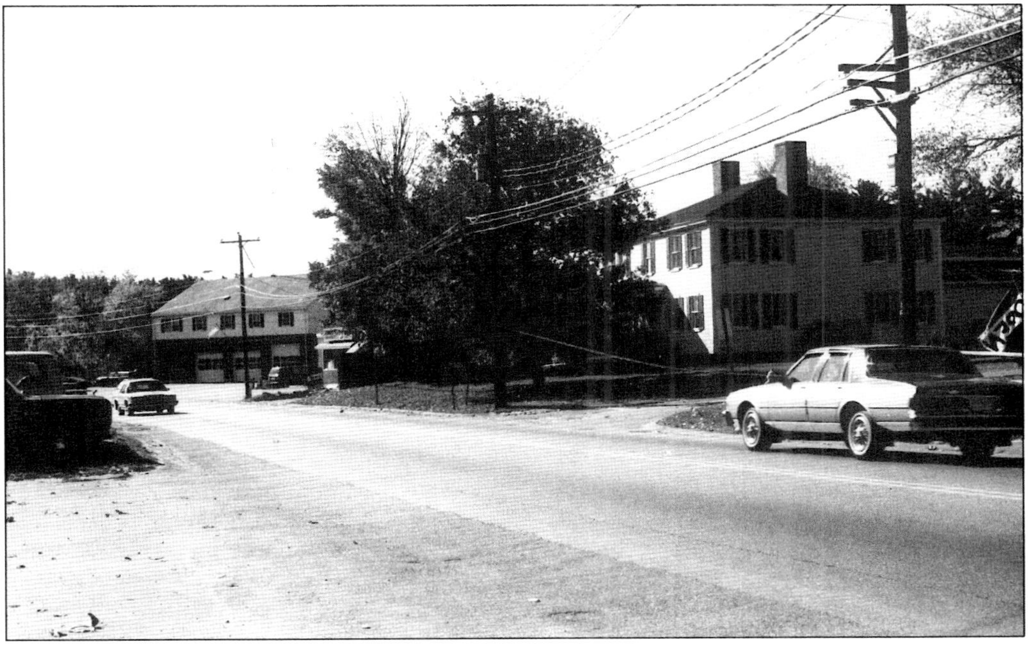

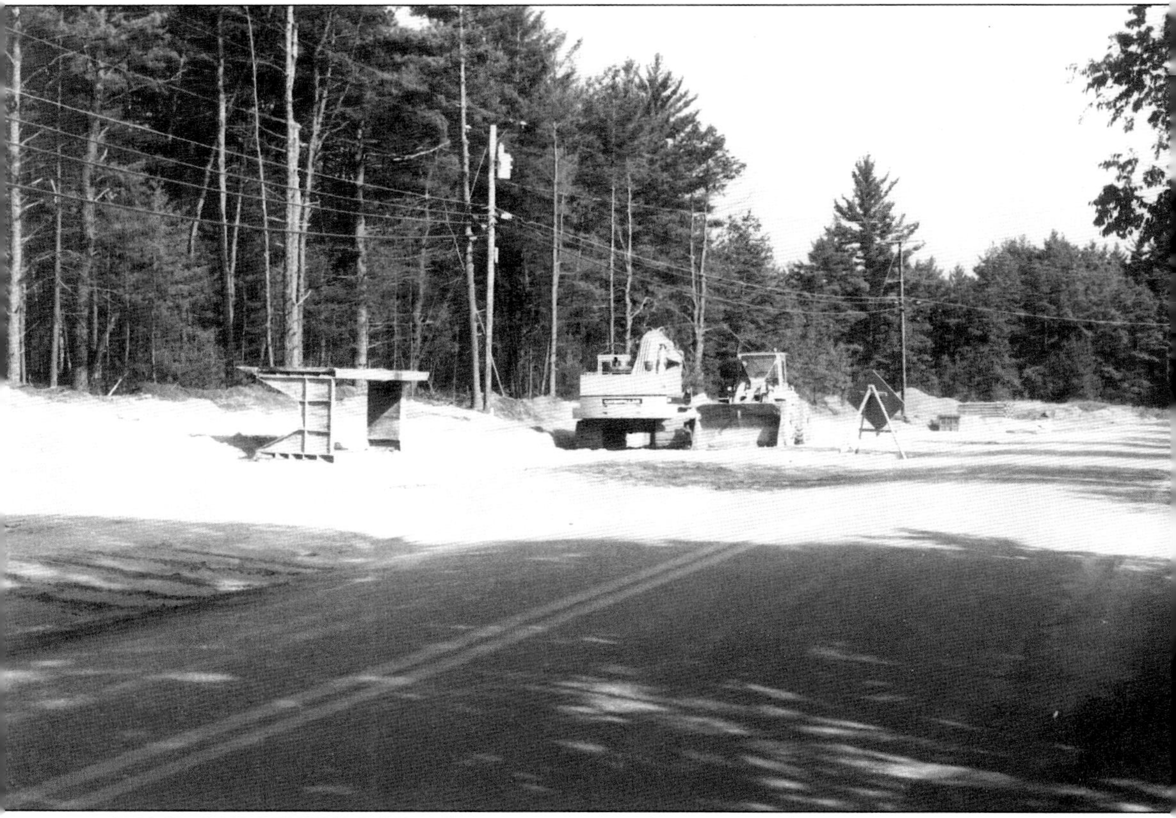

CAMP SARGENT ROAD. The construction of Continental Boulevard, and the arrival of additional businesses on Route 101A, created heavy traffic on Camp Sargent Road. With many homes and a school off this road, safety became an issue. As a result, the Camp Sargent Road Bypass was built and opened in 1994.

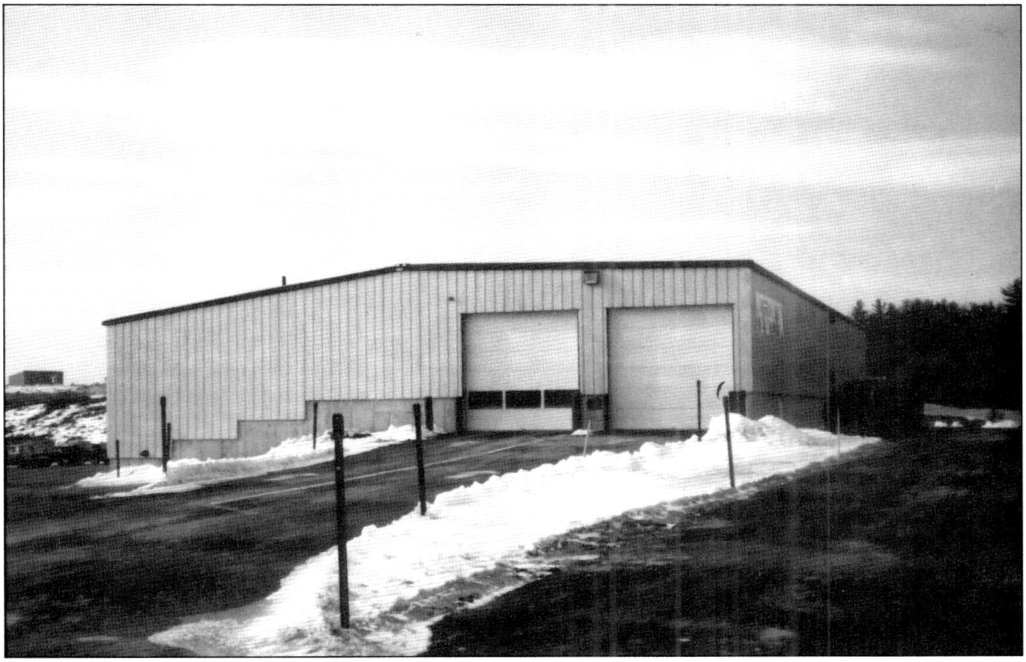

THE RECYCLING FACILITY. Ground was broken with salvaged junk shovels and a recycled cornerstone was laid to begin construction of the Merrimack Landfill Recycling Building, located off Lawrence Road. Opened for operation on February 5, 1990, the building is heated with a waste oil-burning furnace. The recycling center was built and is run free of tax dollars.

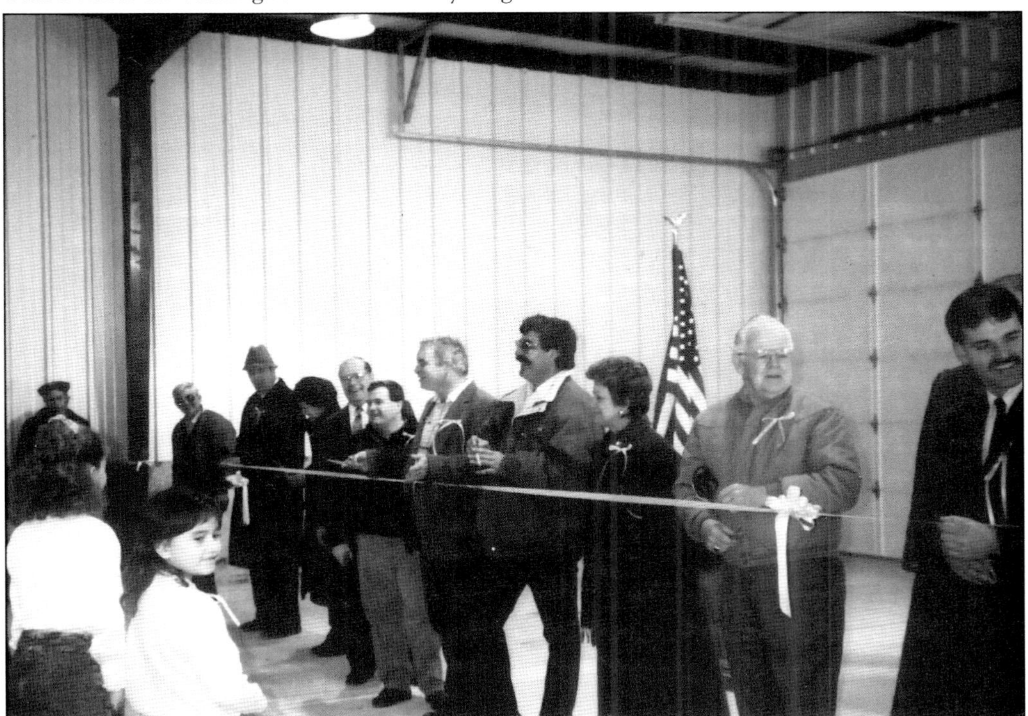

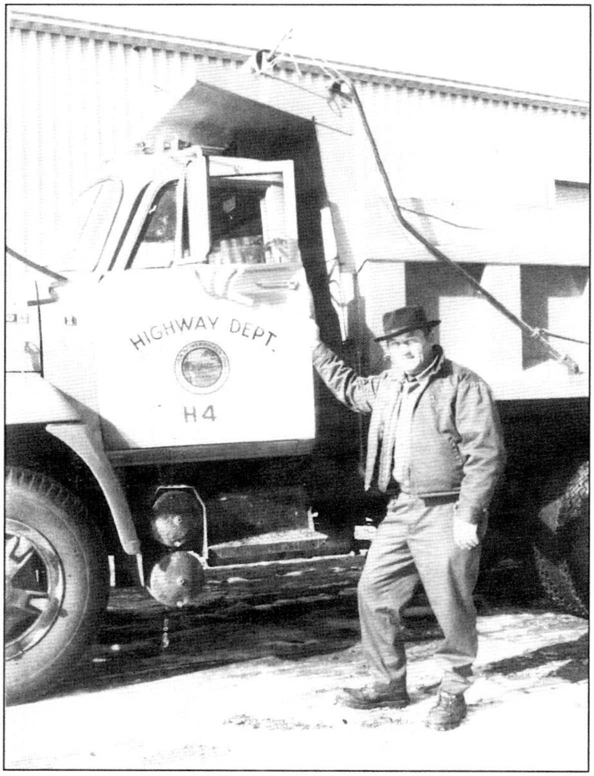

ROAD AGENTS. Road, bridge, and snow-plowing problems came under the jurisdiction of the road agent before the department of public works was formed. Trucks were privately-owned and serviced. For many years Edgar Thibodeau was the road agent and when he retired, his son saw to the care of the roads.

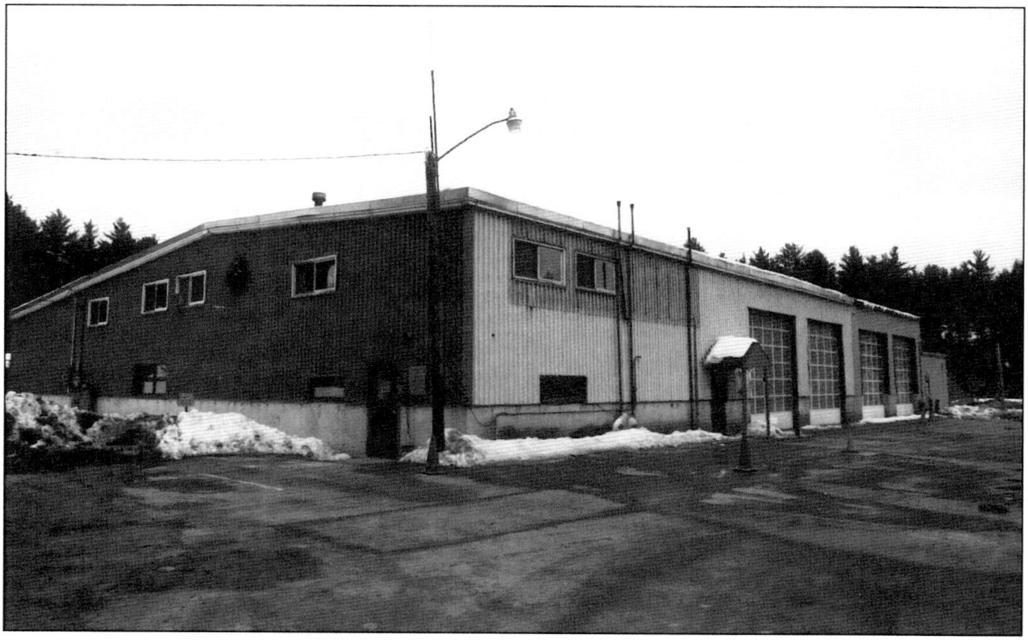

THE DEPARTMENT OF PUBLIC WORKS. With the formation of the Merrimack Department of Public Works, Merrimack had its own trucks and equipment. Maintenance is done at the Town Garage on Turkey Hill Road.

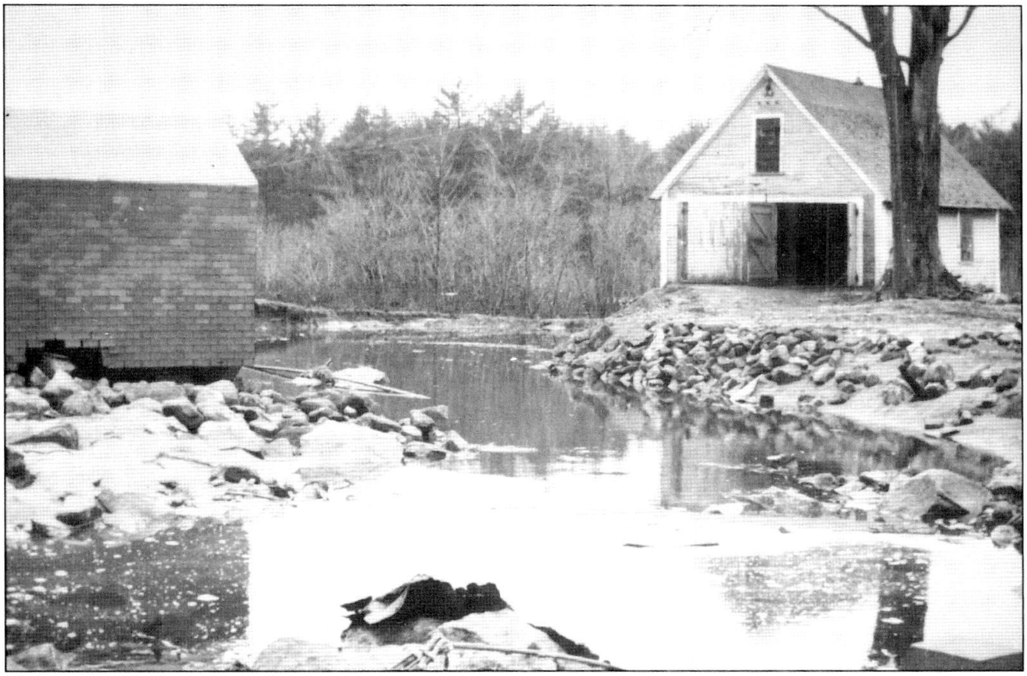

THE FIRE STATION. Merrimack's first fire station was a carpenter shop and stable that was moved from the mills across the street to the land next to the bridge on Route 3. It served the town for many years until the Arthur Gordon Memorial Station was built in 1959.

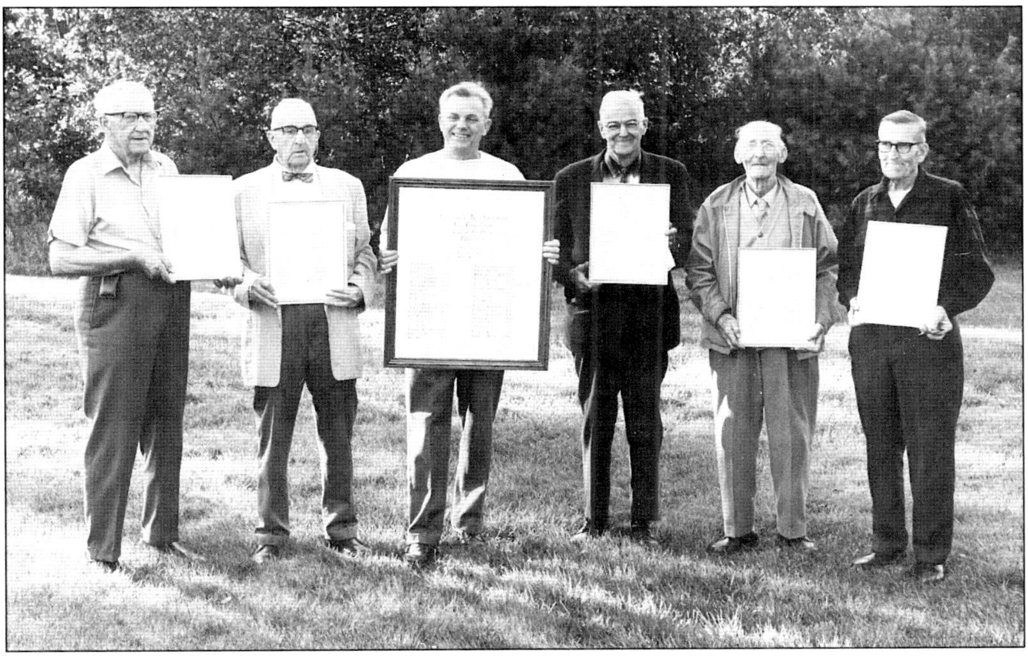

THE MERRIMACK FIRE DEPARTMENT. From a carpenter shop/stable and a volunteer fire department, the fire department has grown into a full-time force plus volunteers. Shown here are the charter members of the fire department.

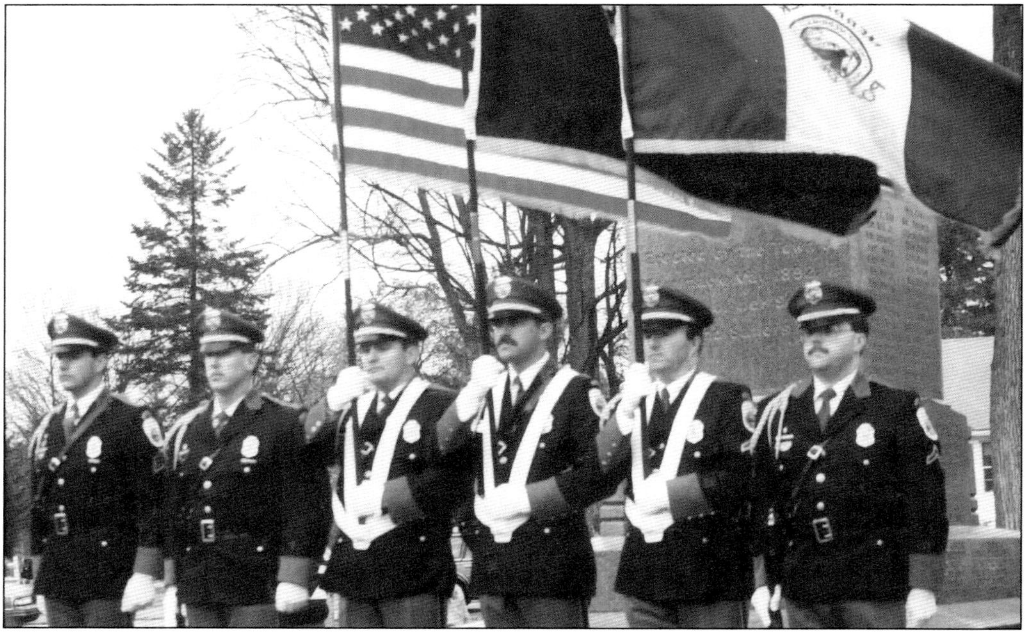

THE HONOR GUARD. The Merrimack Police Department Honor Guard was formed in 1989 and has seven members. It represents the police department at the wakes and funerals of policemen, and also performs at parades and competitions.

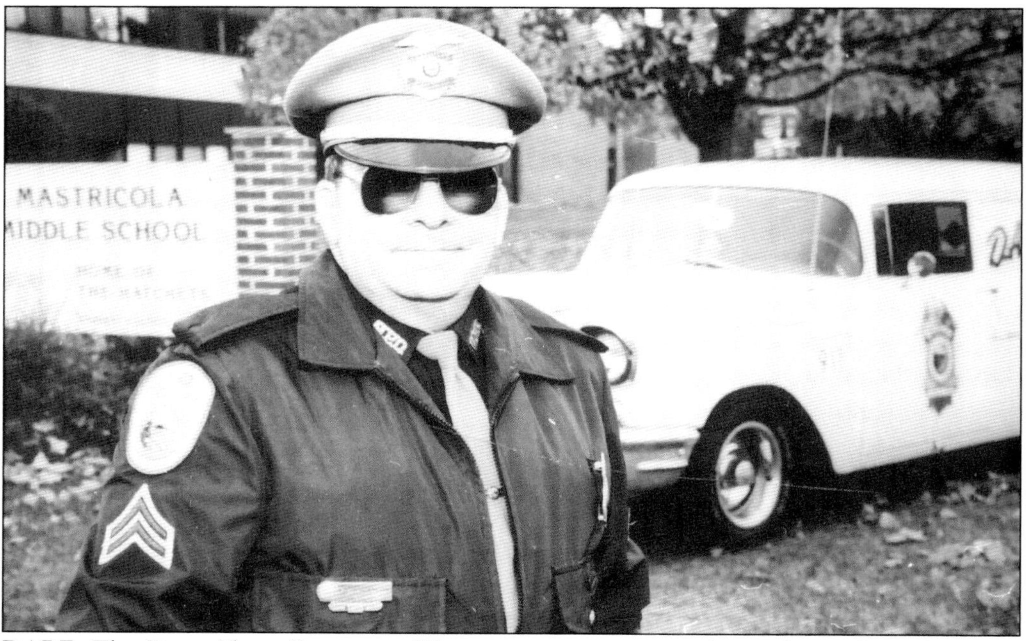

DARE. The Drug Abuse Resistance Education program is taught in the sixth grade of the Merrimack school system by Detective Ronald W. Ketchie. Shown here with the "DARE mobile" is the most recognizable person to Merrimack's children. Detective Ketchie speaks to civic groups as well as schoolchildren about the dangers of drug and alcohol abuse.

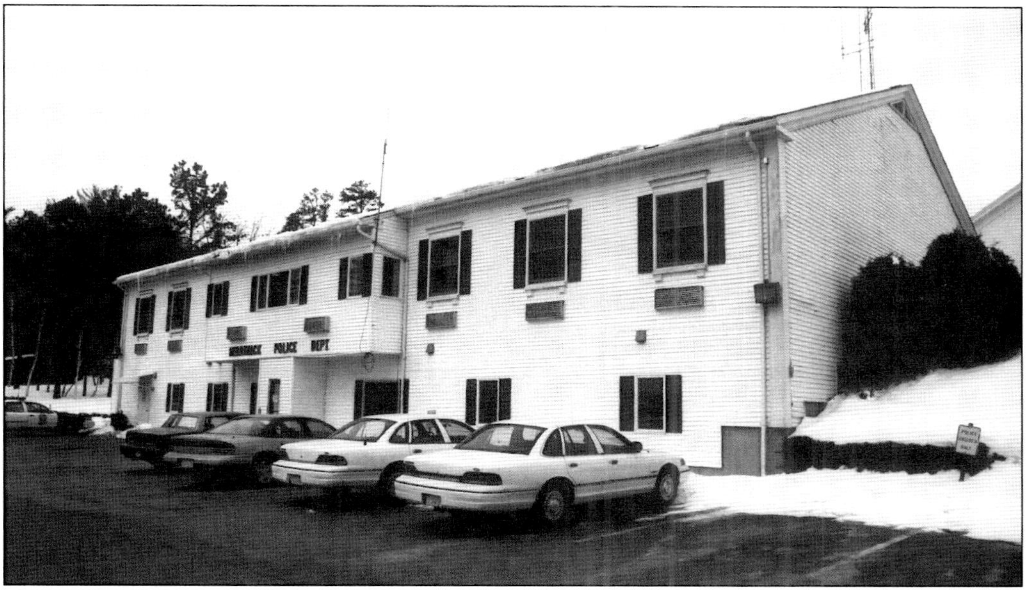

THE POLICE DEPARTMENT. Until Frank Flanders was appointed chief in 1963, police chiefs were elected officials. The first police station was a small room in the Town Hall. Members of the force renovated and remodeled the vacant Schoolhouse #9 in the 1970s to be used as a police station. In 1981 the police department moved to the lower level of the east wing of the Town Hall.

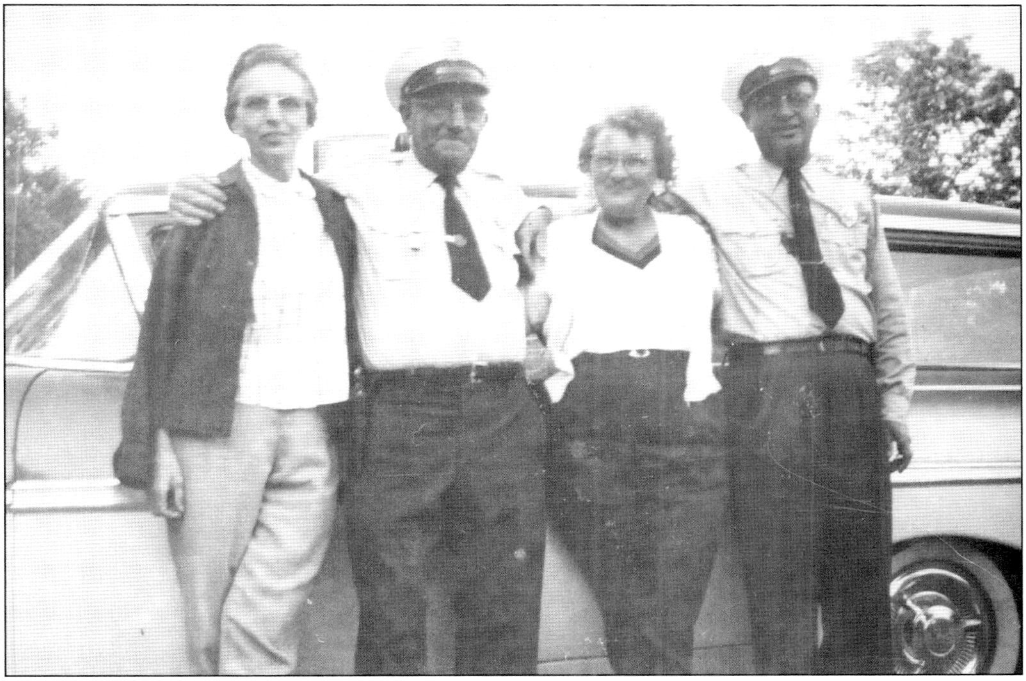

THE POLICE FORCE. In the 1950s, Merrimack's police force had not yet been established. There was only a chief, deputy, and clerk. Shown here is former Chief Joseph Pynenburg and his staff.

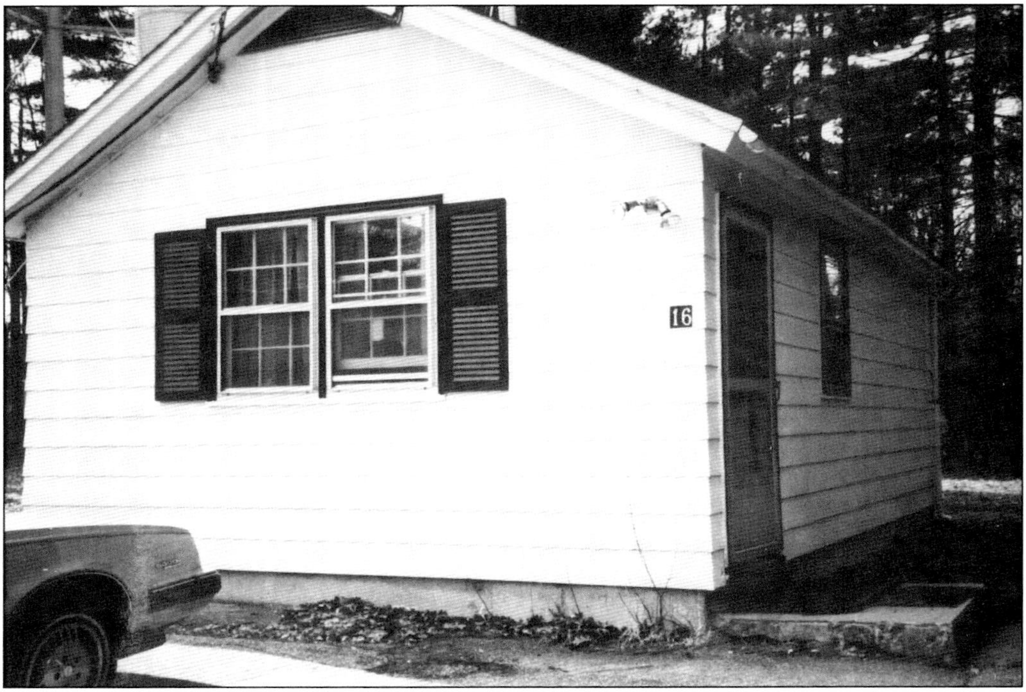

THE REED'S FERRY WATER DEPARTMENT. This office on Harris Avenue was open mornings daily. After the present water department merged with the Reed's Ferry Department, the Harris Avenue office was used by the superintendent, until the new office building on Green's Pond Road was built.

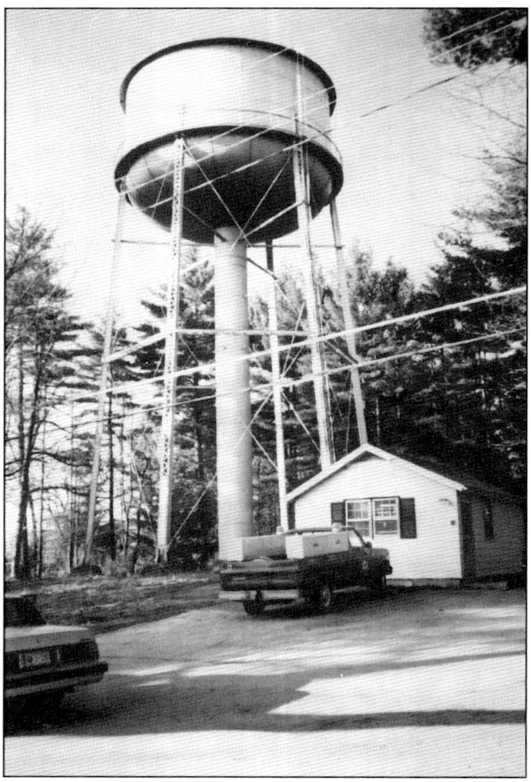

WATER TANKS. One of the town's first water tanks was the Reed's Ferry tank. Built in the early 1930s, it was a riveted tank that held 200,000 gallons of water. Located on Harris Avenue, it was demolished when the Bedford Road tollbooth was built.

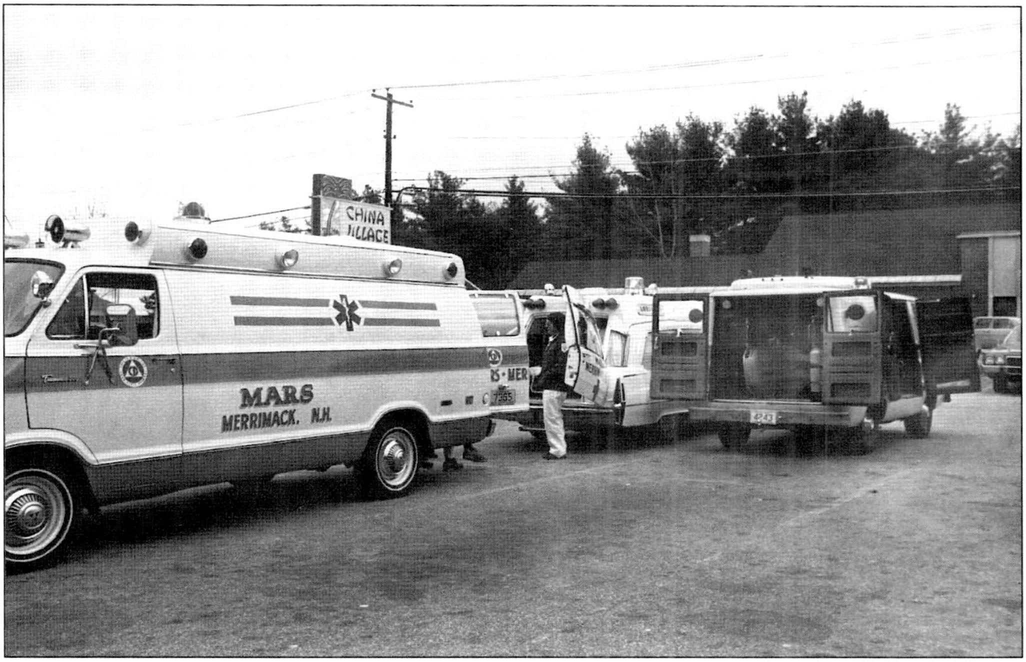

MARS. The Merrimack Ambulance Rescue Squad was started by volunteers and has provided service to the town for many years. Now a full-time plus volunteer organization, it is housed in its own facility behind Town Hall. Various training sessions are part of the services provided.

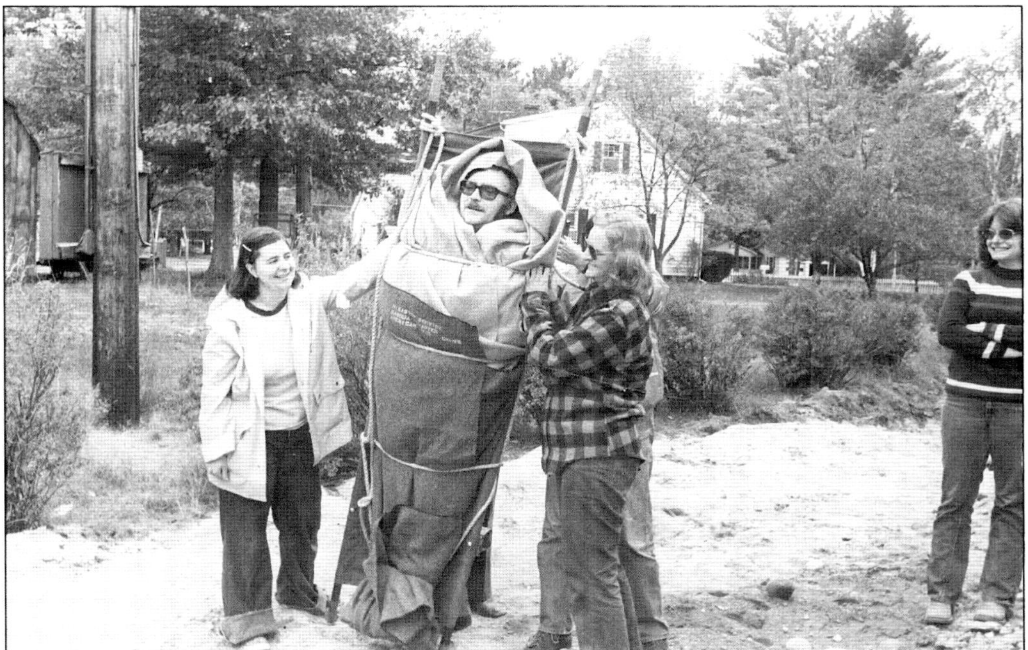

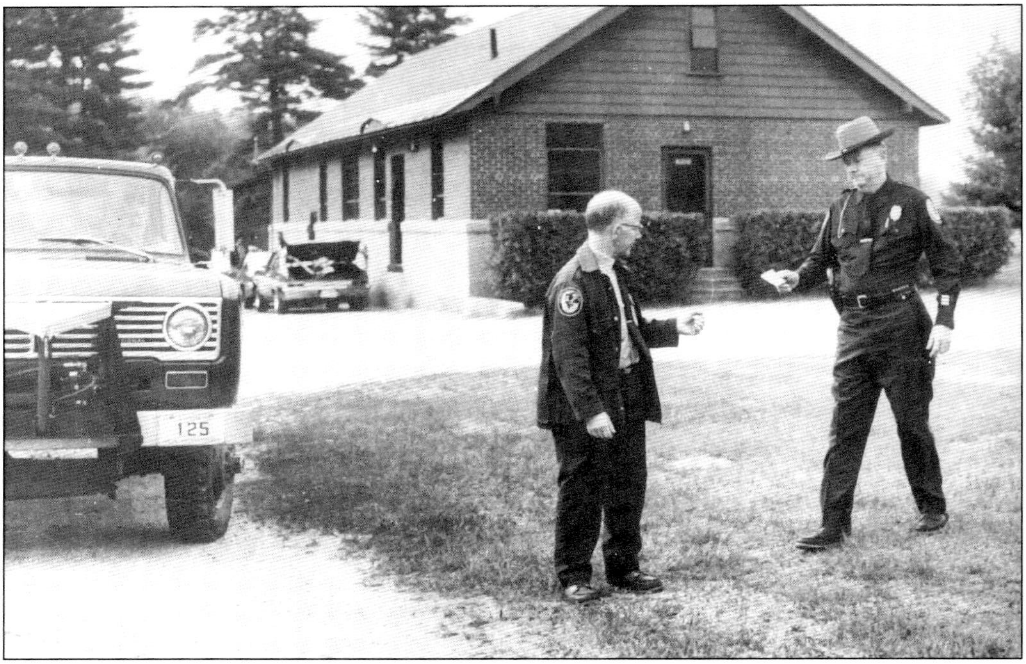

THE MERRIMACK FISH REARING STATION. Opened in 1948, this hatchery produced about 15,000 pounds of fish annually to stock local brooks and ponds. Located on Route 3, the station boasted fourteen pools and was a popular visiting place during the summer months.

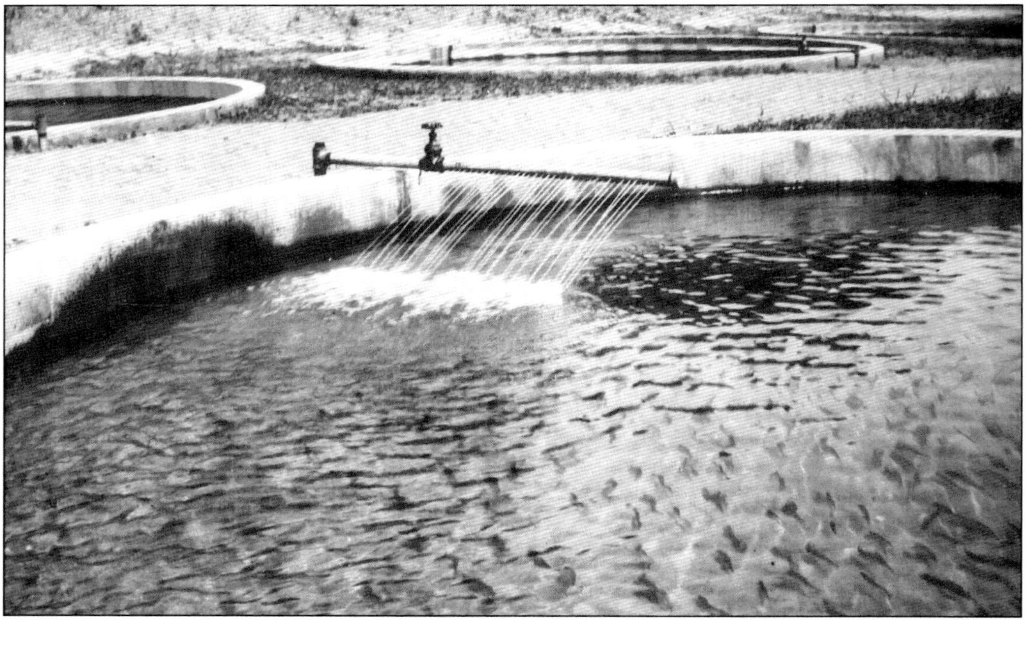

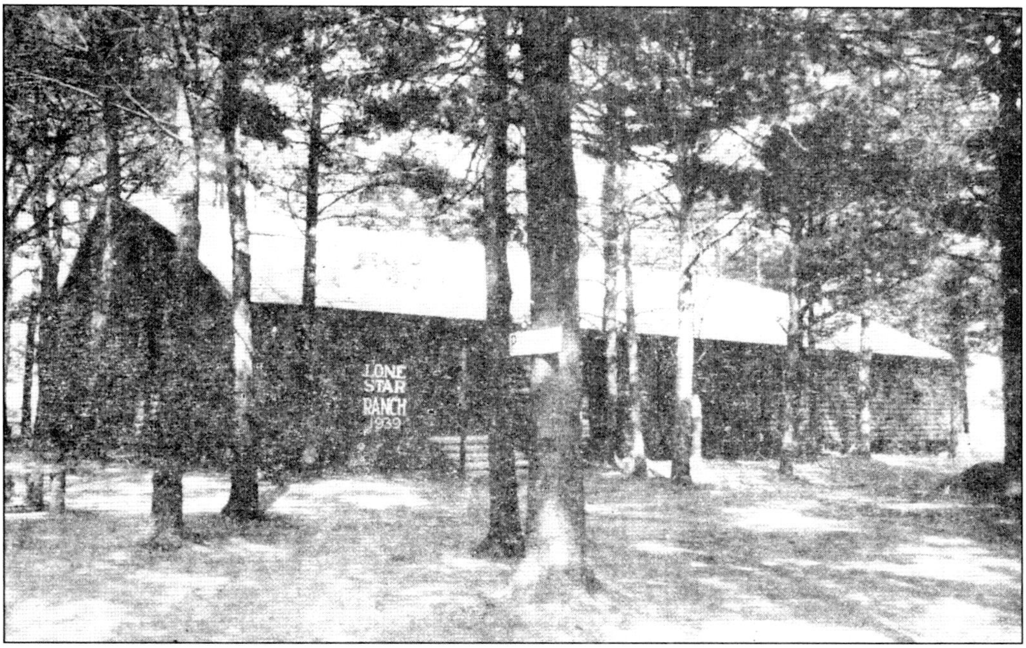

THE LONE STAR RANCH. Pine groves and campfire smoke conjure up memories of this country/western ranch, the first of its kind in New England. Located on Route 3, it was started by Baron West in 1938 and was, for many years, hosted by Grammy and Dad Bell. It was known nationwide.

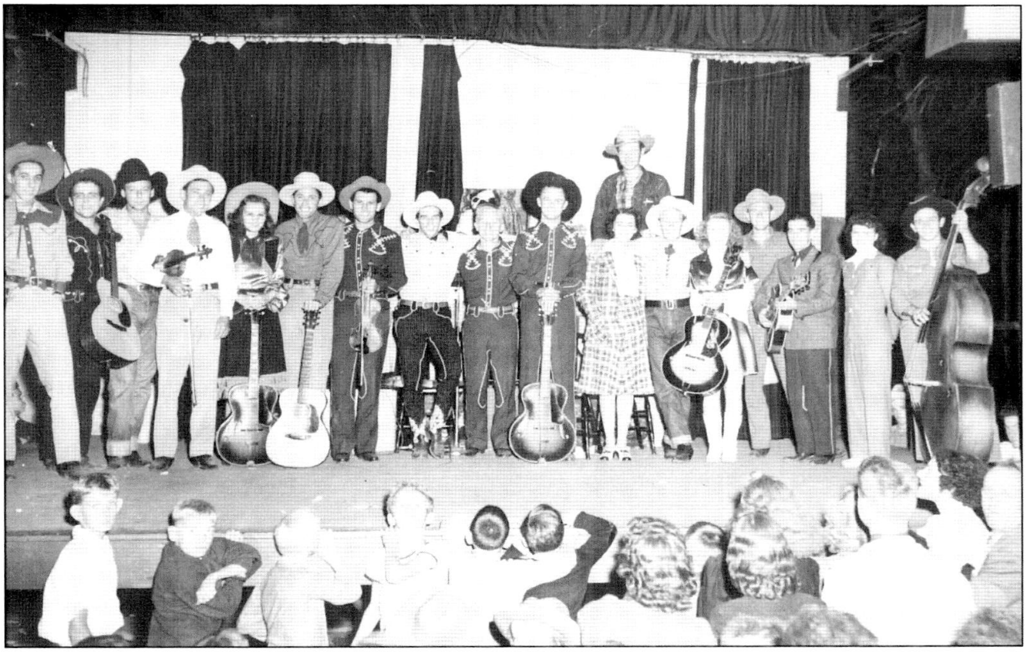

LONE STAR RANCH SHOWS. Singing cowboys and variety acts from Merrimack and around the country, both professional and amateur, have been featured at the Lone Star Ranch. On any given Sunday as many as sixty-five hundred people were entertained here.

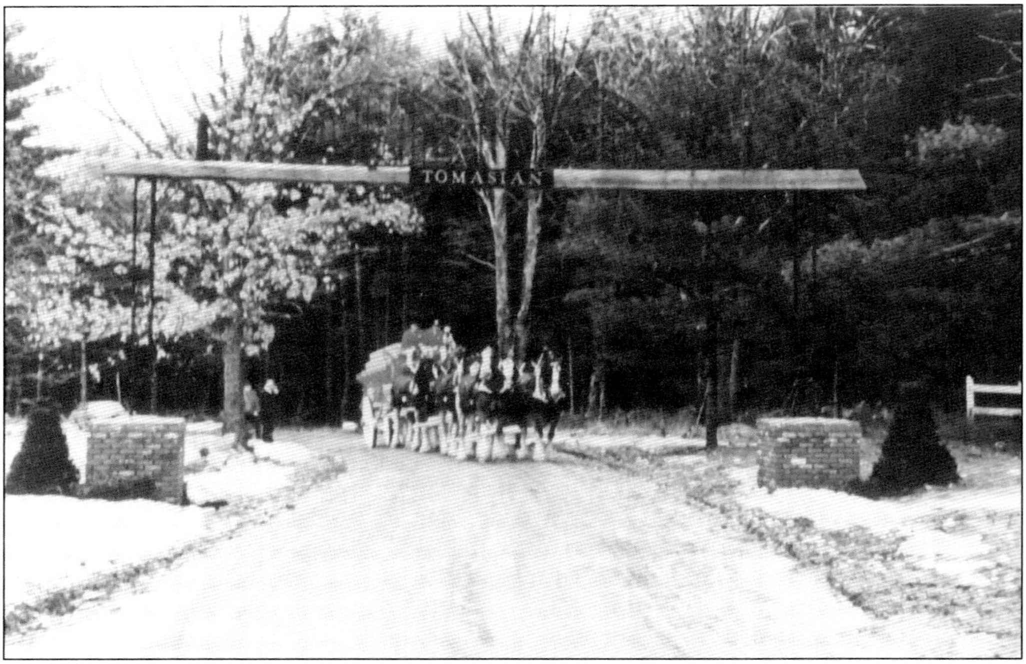

THE CLYDESDALES. When Anheuser Busch built the brewery in Merrimack, they decided Merrimack was not a suitable place for a theme park, so they decided to house the Clydesdale horses here instead. While the hamlet was being constructed at the brewery on Route 3, the horses were housed at the Tomasian Farm on Fuller Mill Road (now Tomasian Road).

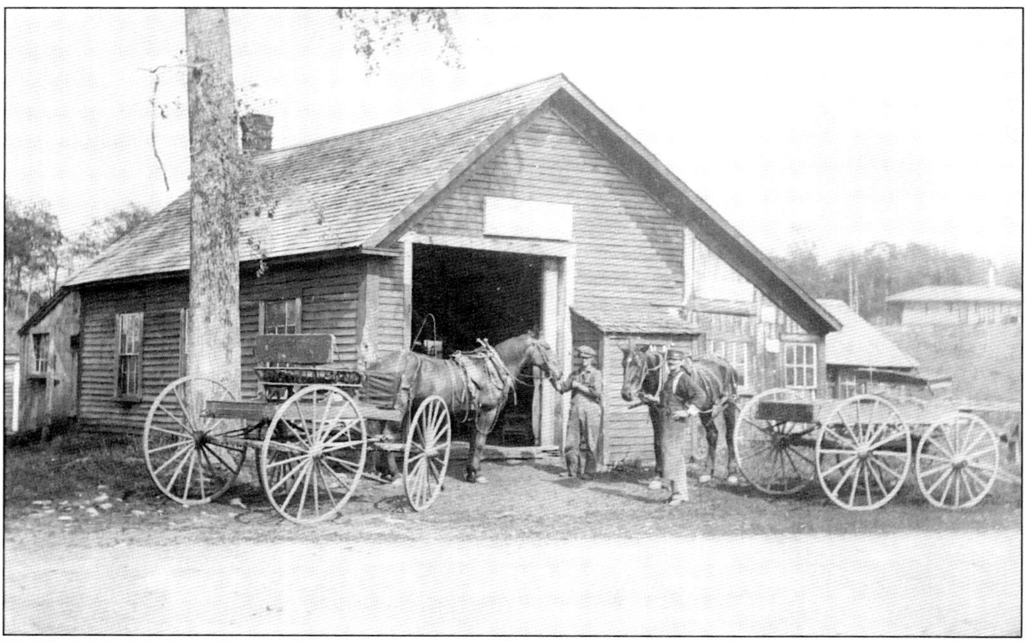

THE OLD BLACKSMITH SHOP. Many still remember the old blacksmith shop in Reed's Ferry. It was not, however, under the spreading chestnut tree. As horses gave way to automobiles, garages soon replaced the blacksmith shops in Merrimack.

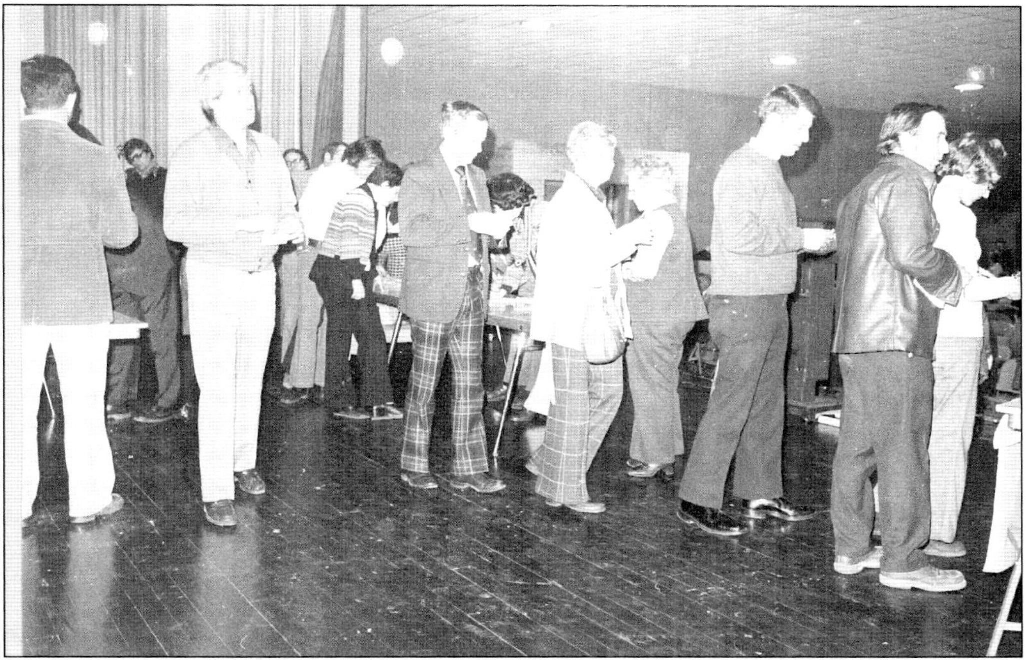

TOWN MEETINGS. Merrimack holds the school and water district meetings in March and a town meeting in May to elect officials and conduct any business that needs to come before the voters. Anyone wishing to vote must have their names checked against the list of registered voters.

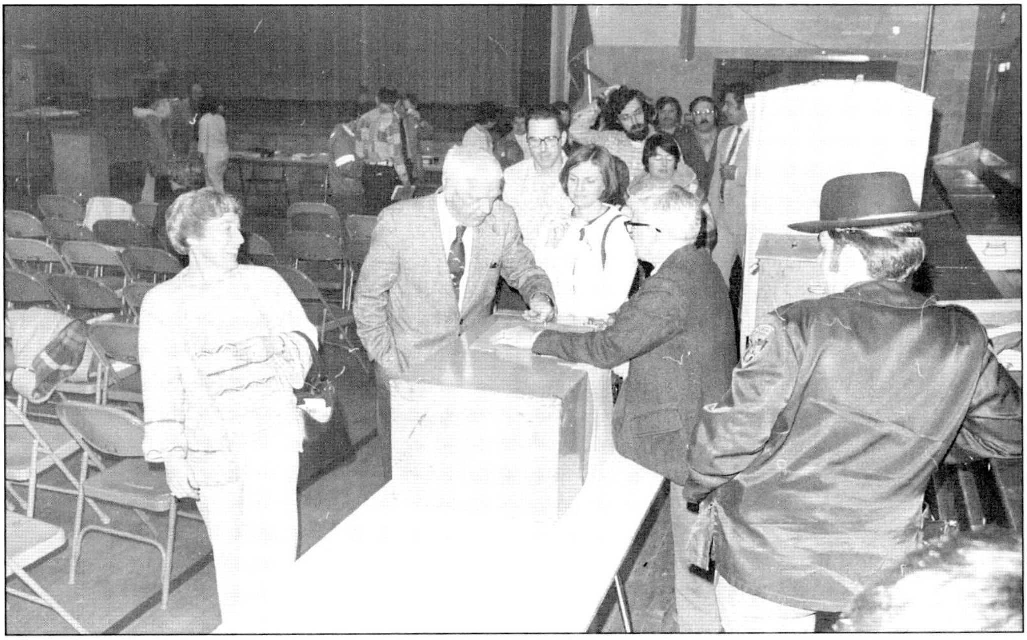

VOTING. Ballot boxes and paper ballots were used in Merrimack until 1988 and votes were hand-counted. A vote-counting machine is now used, which eliminates the many hours spent counting ballots.

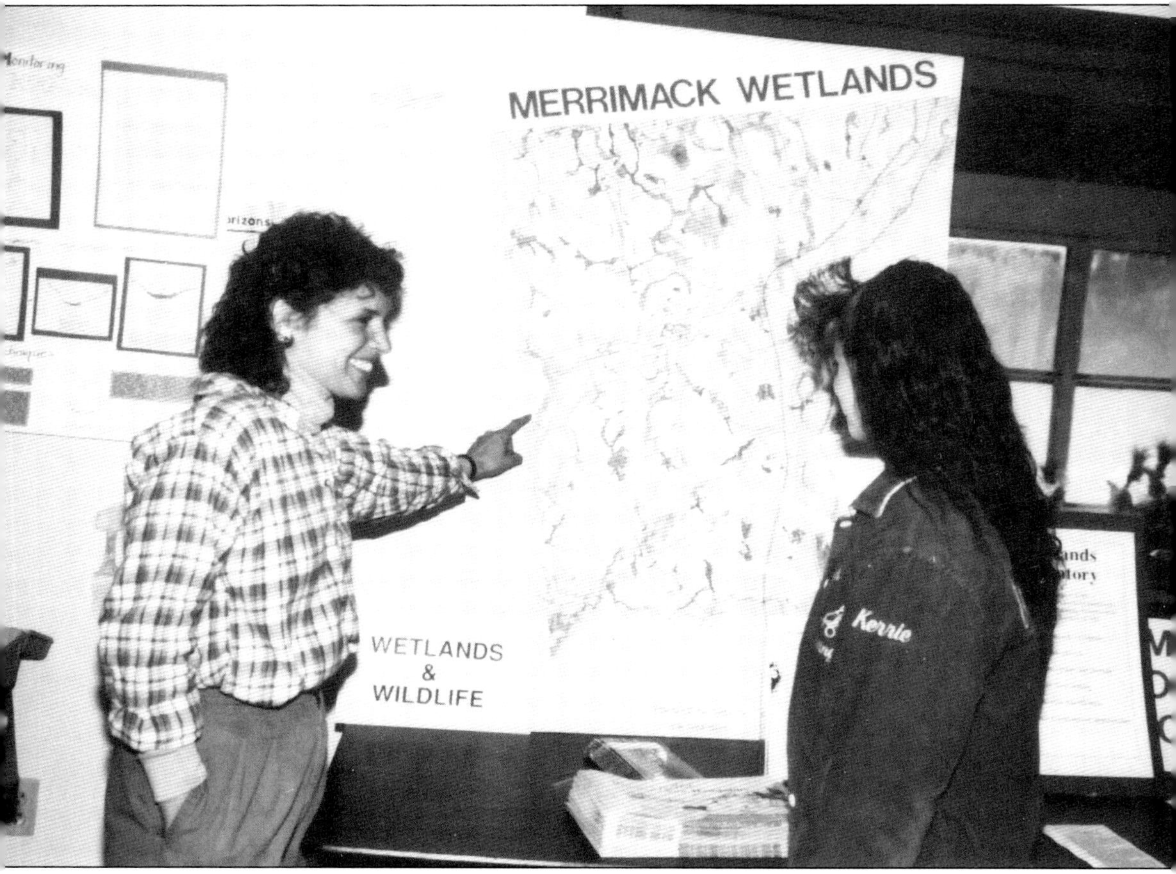

EARTH DAY. Earth Day is a town-wide festival devoted to recognizing the importance of our environment and how each of us can make a difference in our community. It is held annually at Wasserman Park with various organizations presenting informational displays and nature walks.

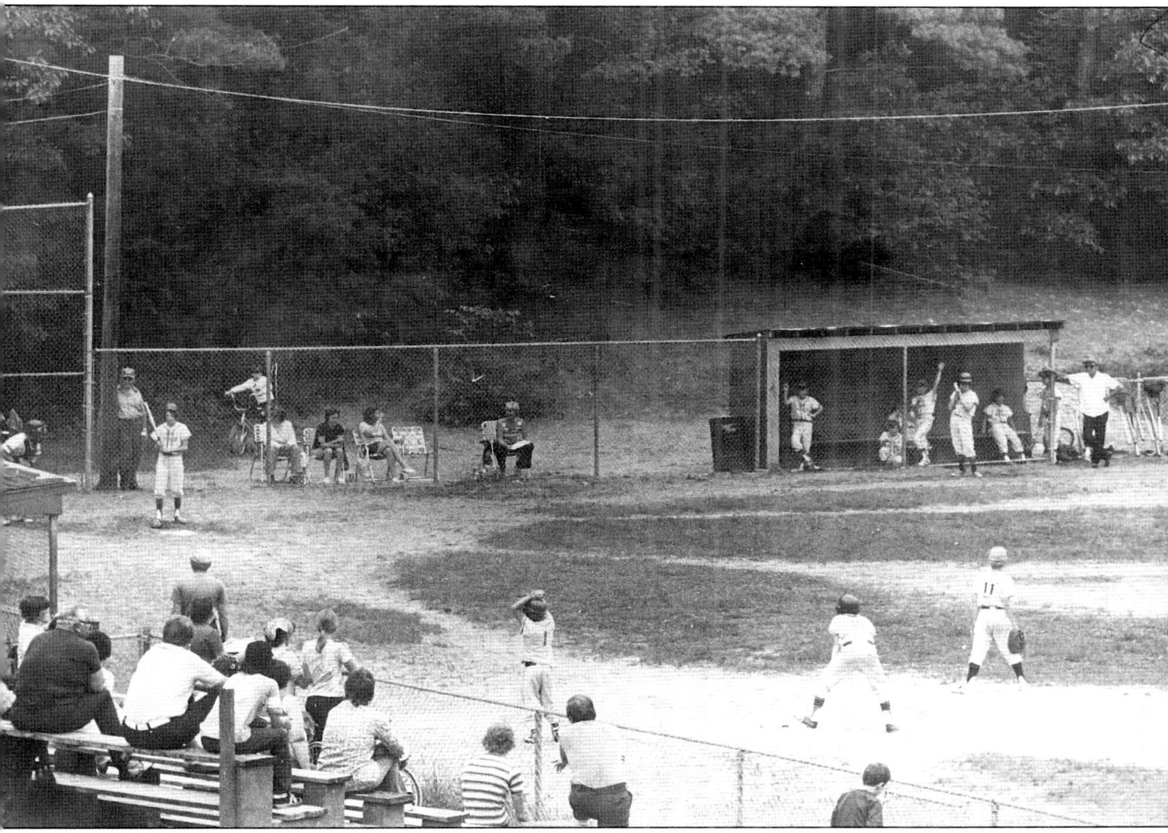

LITTLE LEAGUE. Baseball has been played in Merrimack since the 1800s. The tradition continues today with leagues available for all ages. Bise Field, located at Twin Bridge Park, is shown here.

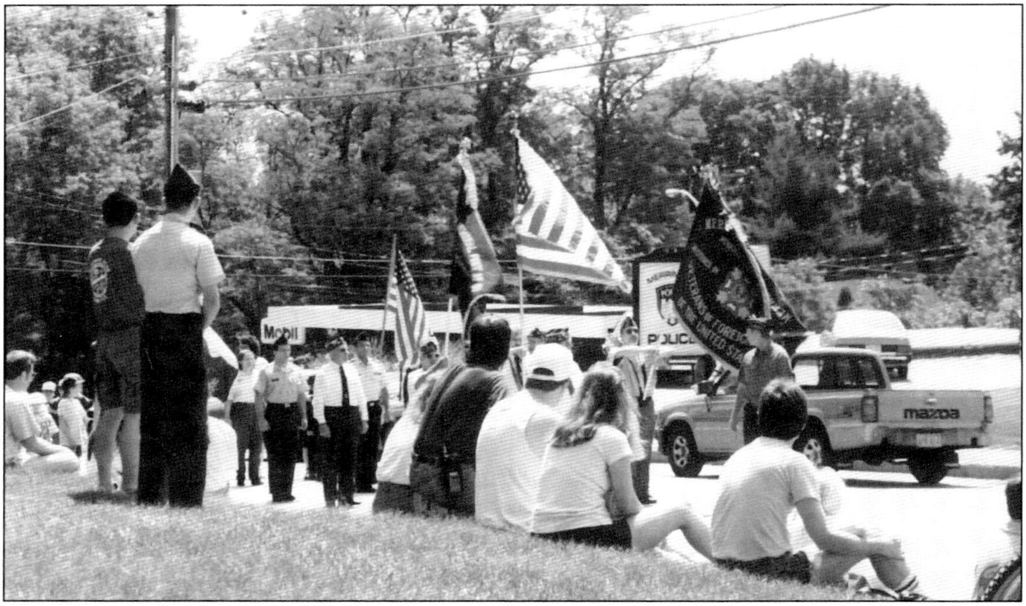

MEMORIAL DAY. Memorial Day is observed by a parade led by the Police Department Honor Guard, and services by the American Legion and the Veterans of Foreign Wars held at the Soldiers and Sailors and the Veterans Monuments on Baboosic Lake Road.

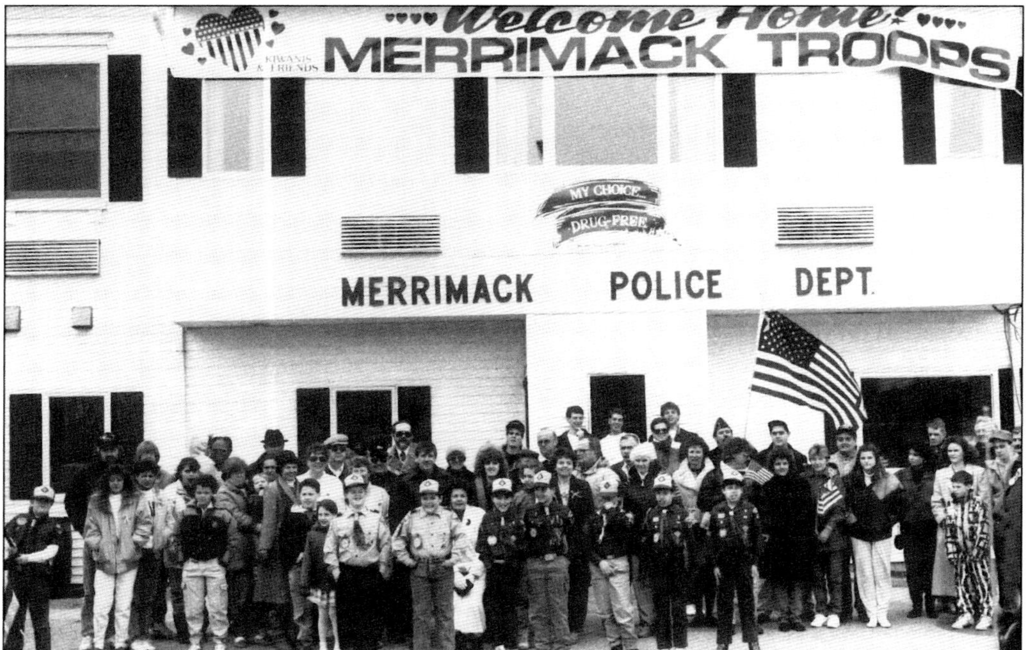

DESERT STORM. Louise Hickey and the Merrimack Kiwanis Club were the forces behind the town's support of Merrimack troops serving in Operation Desert Storm. Christmas cards, packages, and letters written by schoolchildren were collected at the holiday parade, to be mailed to the troops. A Welcome Home celebration was also held, at the police station, for the forty-five who served.

THE HILLSBOROUGH COUNTY FAIR. When Merrimack was more of a farming community, the county fair was a big event. Livestock, produce, and handicrafts were displayed and judged. The Souhegan Grange, a family-oriented farming organization active from 1874 to 1960, placed many entries at the fair.

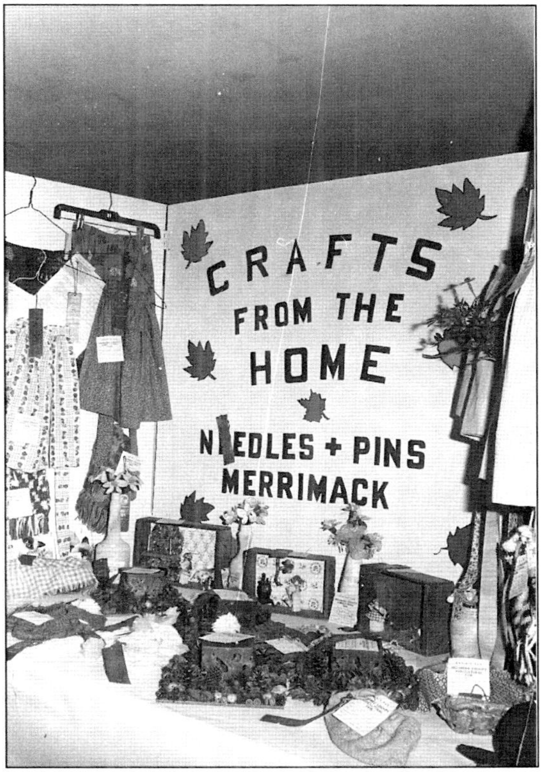

HOLIDAY FAIRS. The livestock and produce are gone, but Merrimack residents still flock to the fairs. The fairs of today are craft fairs held for the purpose of selling handmade goods. Many buy their holiday gifts at these events.

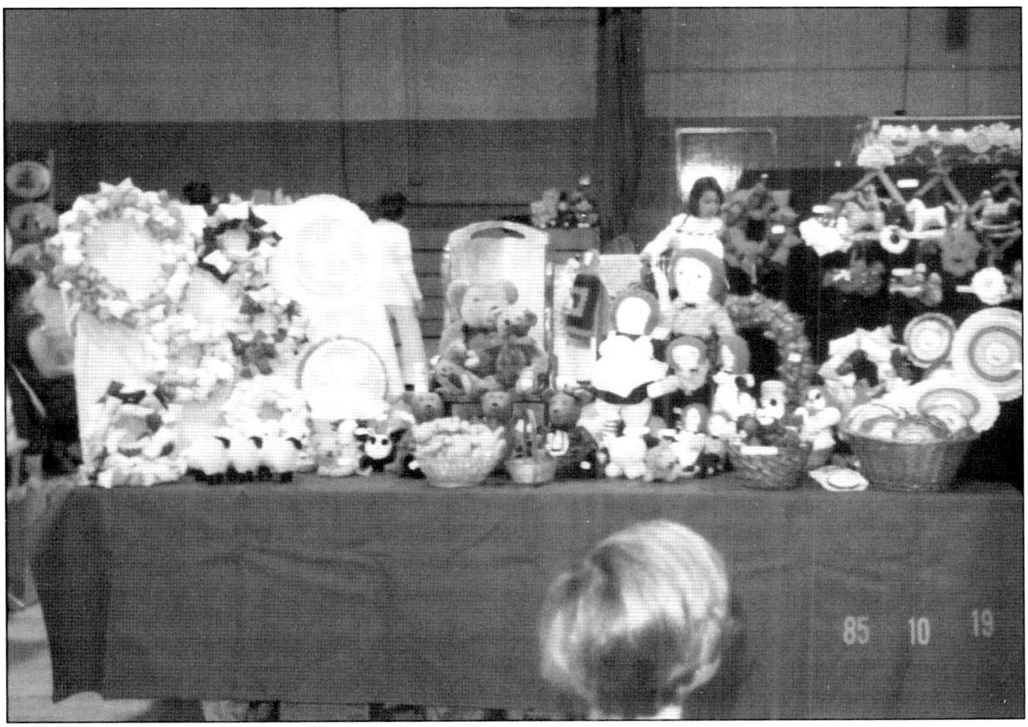

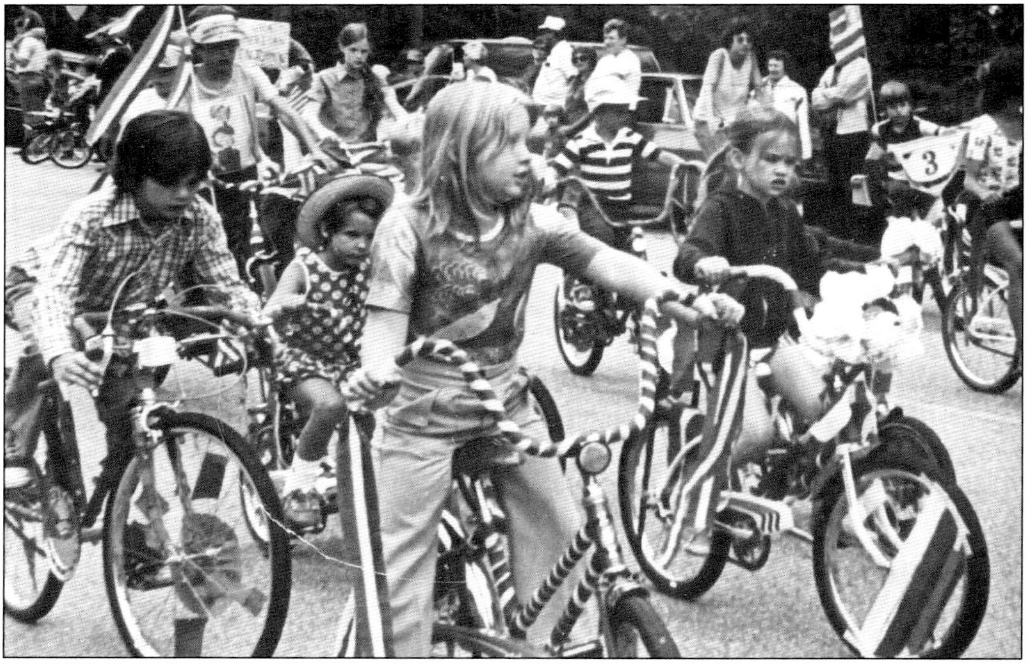

THE JULY FOURTH PARADE. The streets are closed to traffic and lined with townspeople and visitors from near and far for Merrimack's annual July Fourth parade. Beginning at Zyla's on Route 3, the parade proceeds down McGaw Bridge Road, Wire Road, and Route 3 to Baboosic Lake Road. It continues up Baboosic Lake Road to O'Gara Drive and on to the high school, where it disperses.

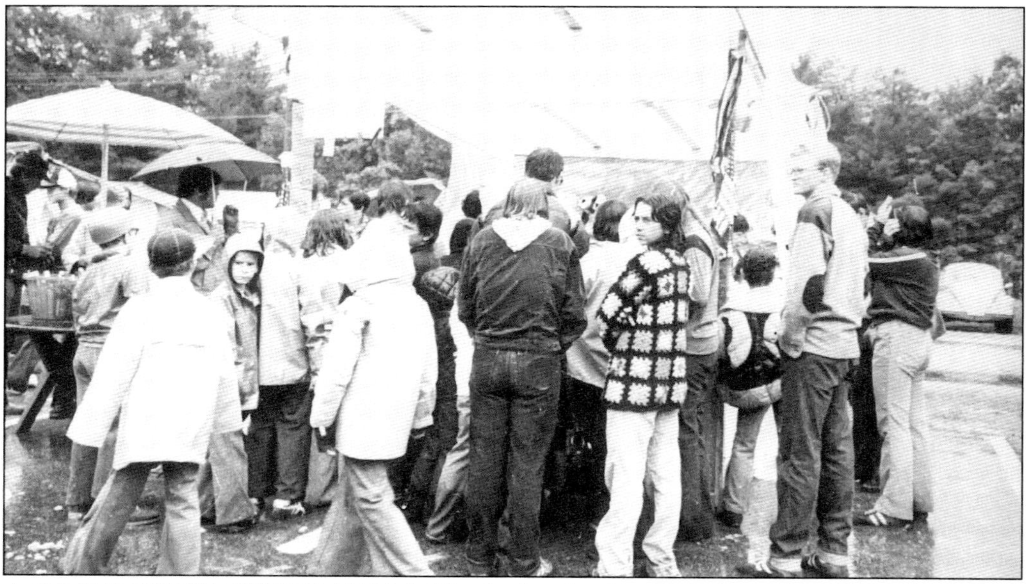

A JULY FOURTH CELEBRATION. The high school parking lot is lined with booths for refreshments, games, exhibits, and rides, as Merrimack celebrates the Fourth of July. The parade, shows, and a street dance are featured during the afternoon with a fireworks display on the athletic field at dusk.

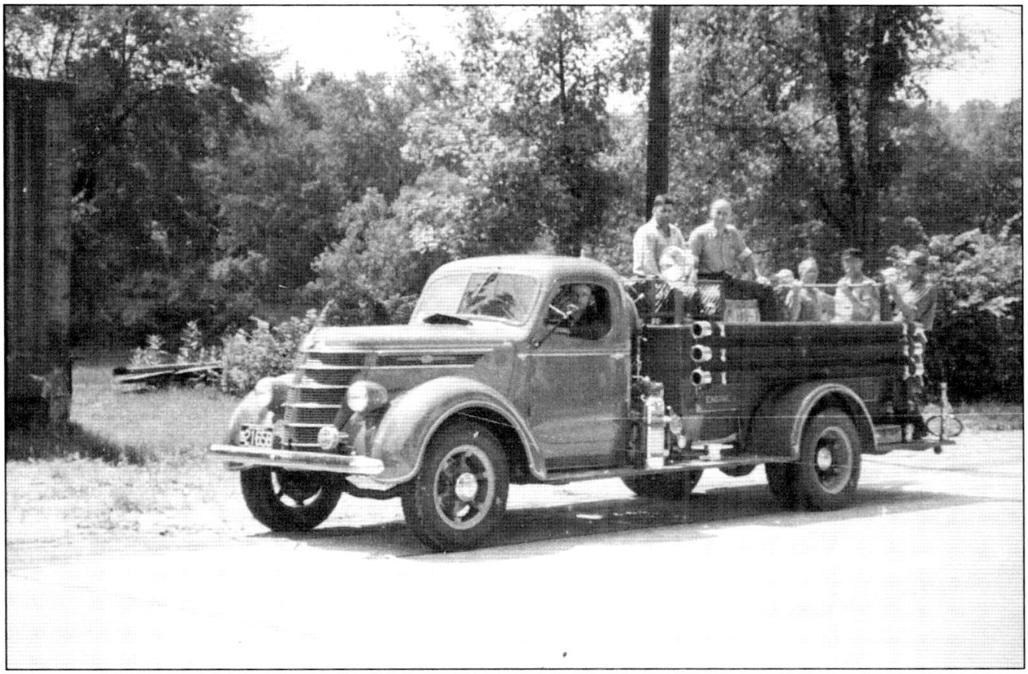

A 1937 FIRE TRUCK. What do you do with a retired fire truck? You give rides on July Fourth. Fire truck rides have long been a favorite attraction at Merrimack's annual July Fourth celebration.

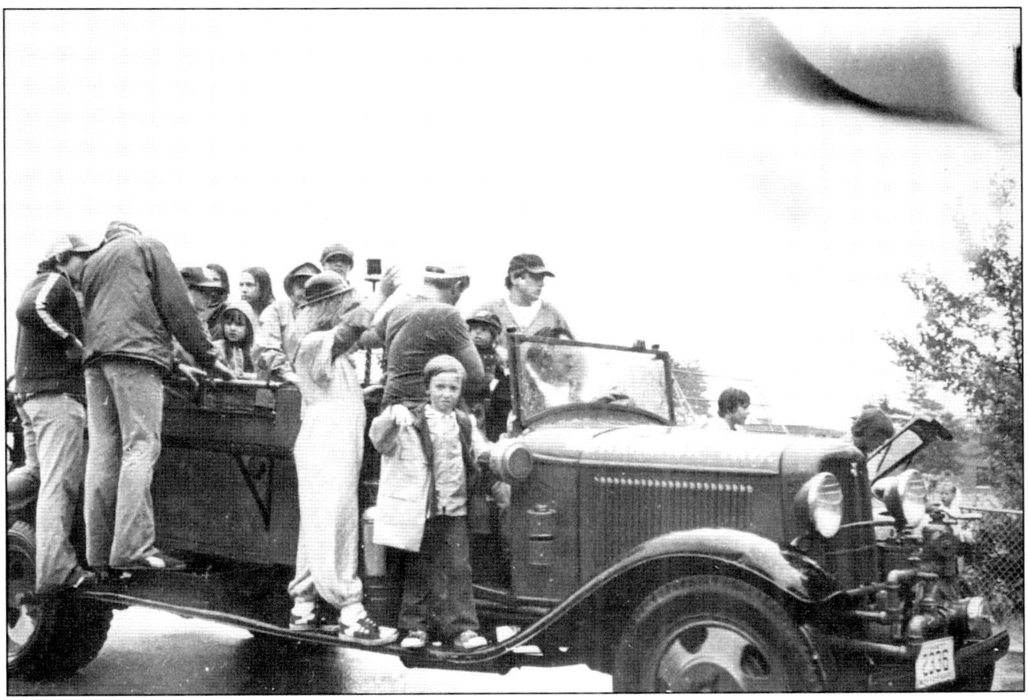

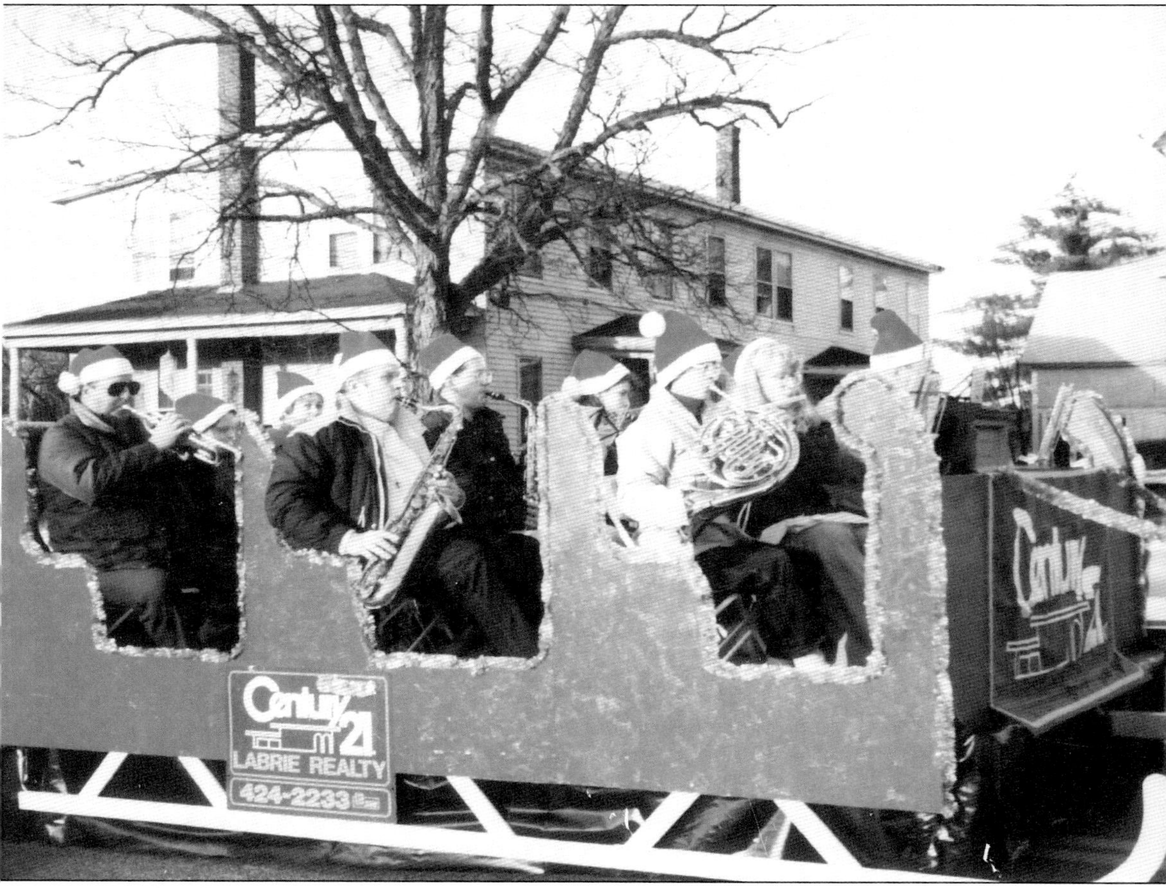

THE MERRIMACK COMMUNITY BAND. The Merrimack Community Band, formed in 1990, has grown from a twenty-eight member concert band with members from many towns to include a jazz ensemble and a chorus. They perform at indoor and outdoor concerts and parades in Merrimack and surrounding towns. The expenses of concert productions are partly-subsidized by corporate and individual sponsors.

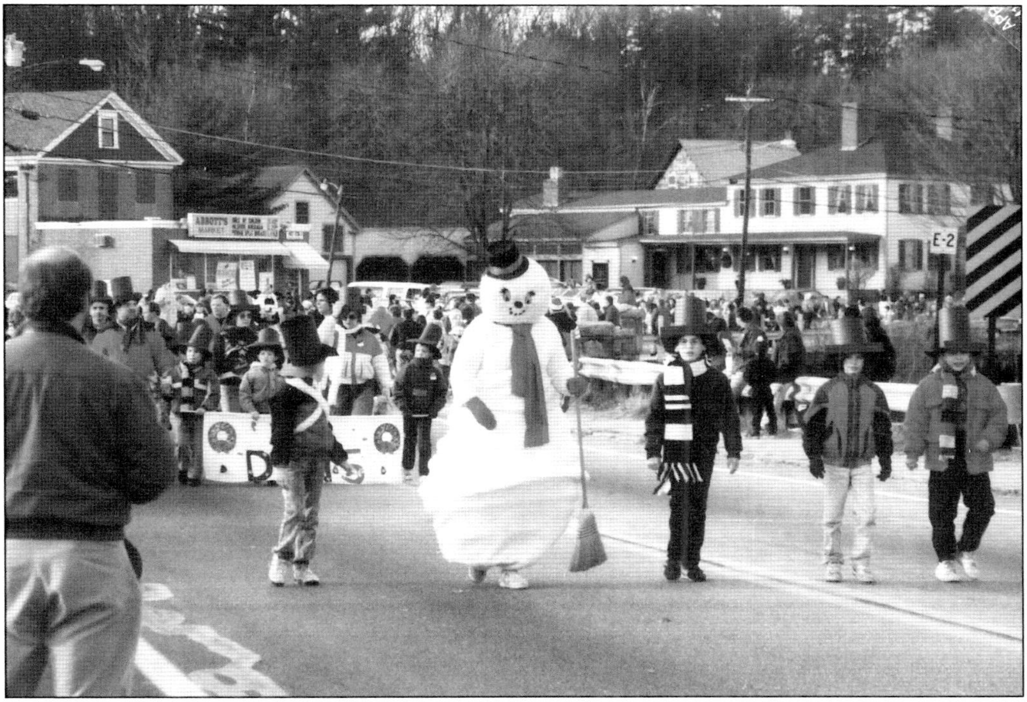

A HOLIDAY PARADE. Merrimack kicks off the Christmas season with an annual holiday parade. Organizations, businesses, and scout troops provide decorated floats and marching groups. The parade ends at Fraser Square where the tree lighting ceremony is held and carols are sung. Much to the delight of the children, Santa Claus is featured in the parade and is on hand at the square to talk with them.

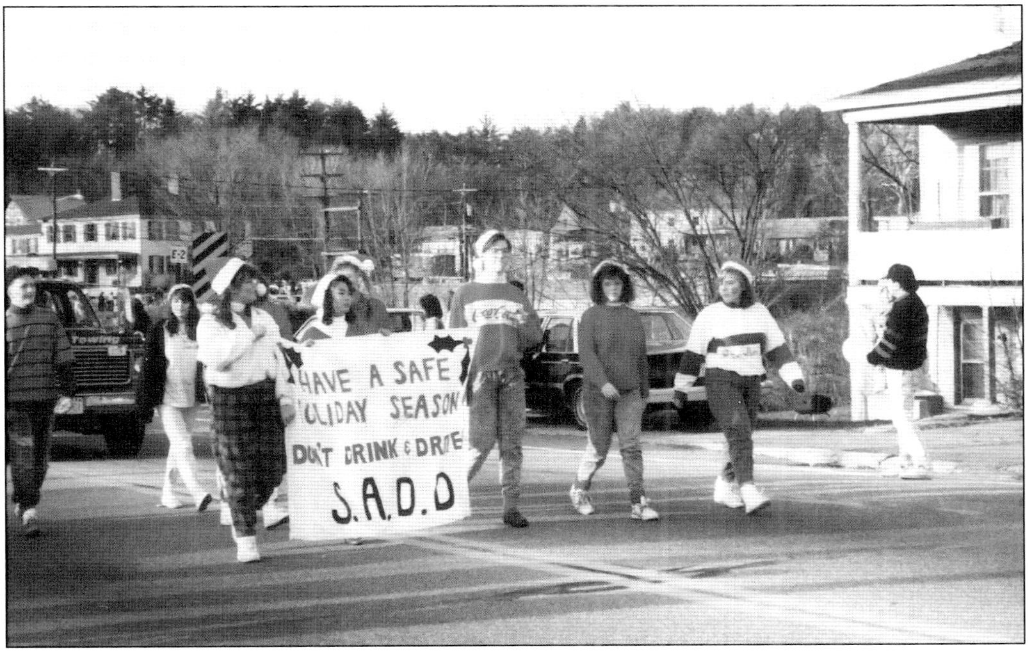

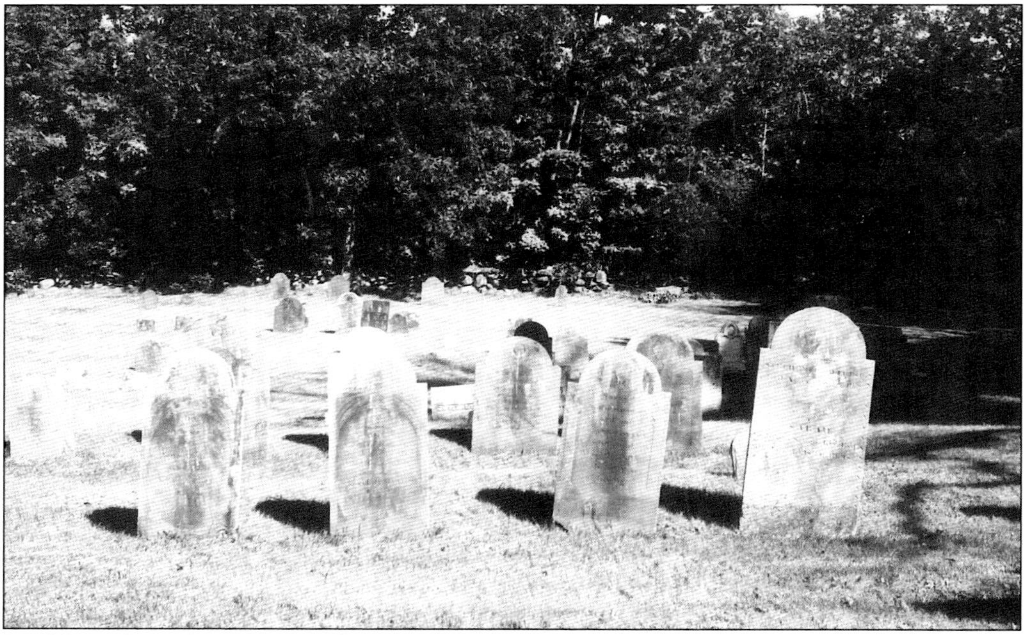

THORNTON CEMETERY. The cemetery on Meetinghouse Road is the first one mentioned in town records, but Thornton Cemetery on Route 3 has the oldest grave stone. Matthew Thornton, a signer of the Declaration of Independence, is buried here. His grave is marked by a simple stone that reads: "An Honest Man."

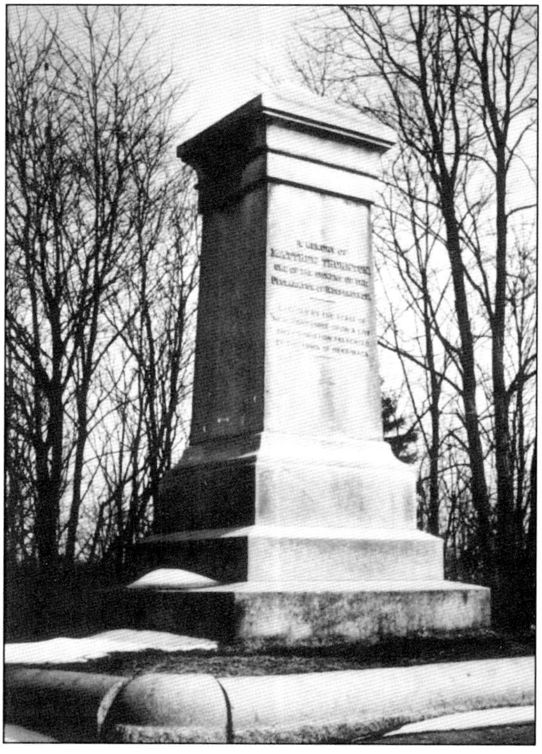

THE THORNTON MONUMENT. In 1892, the State of New Hampshire erected a monument honoring Matthew Thornton. The town of Merrimack provided land, next to the cemetery on Route 3, and the foundation. New England Granite Works of Concord was contracted, and nearly ninety years after his death, the Revolutionary War patriot was honored with a monument.

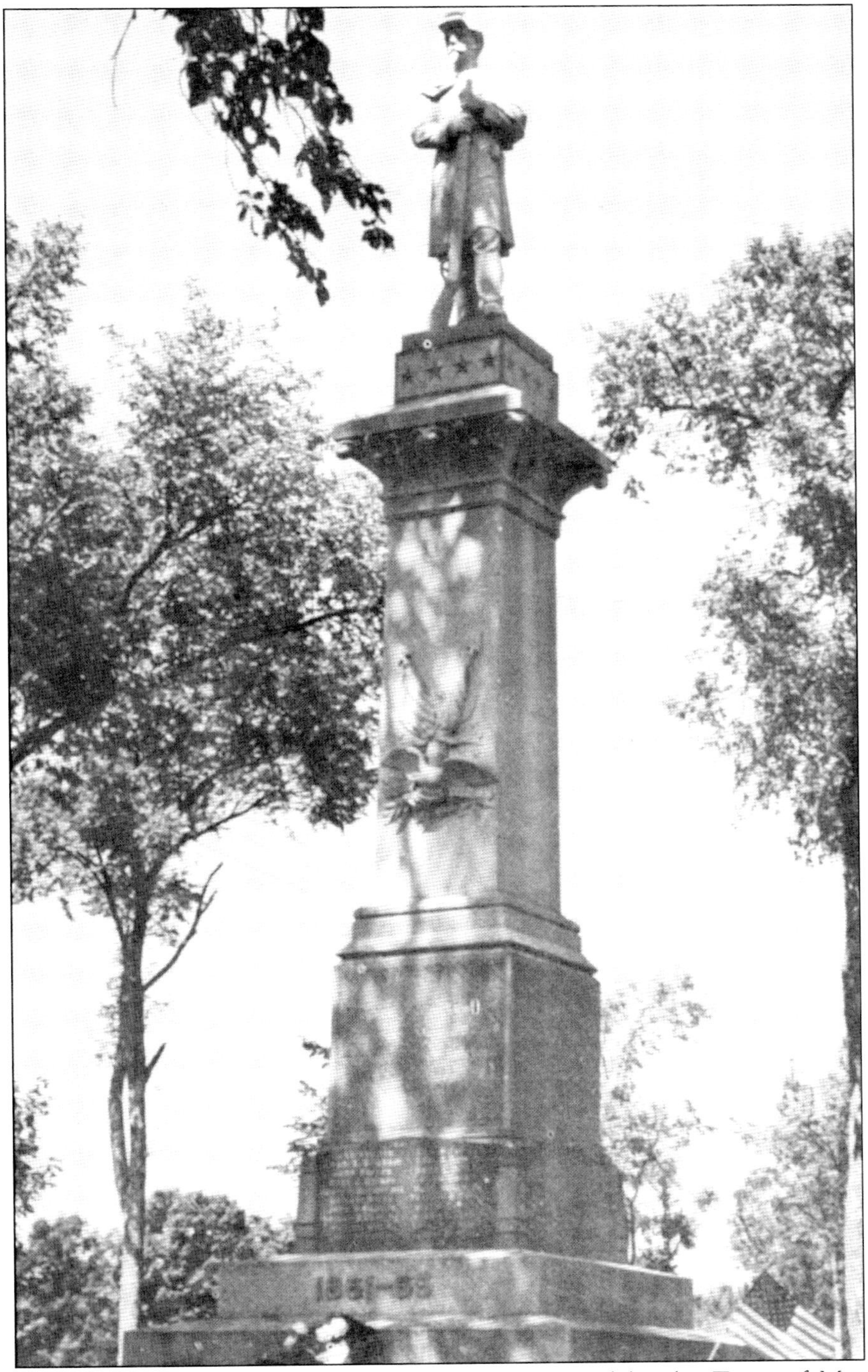

THE SOLDIERS' AND SAILORS' MONUMENT. "Erected by the Town of Merrimack, May 1892, in memory of her soldiers and sailors," reads the inscription on the Soldiers' and Sailors' Monument. Located on Baboosic Lake Road, it is made of a perfect piece of granite atop which stands an infantry soldier. John E. Read, son of John G. Read, unveiled the monument.

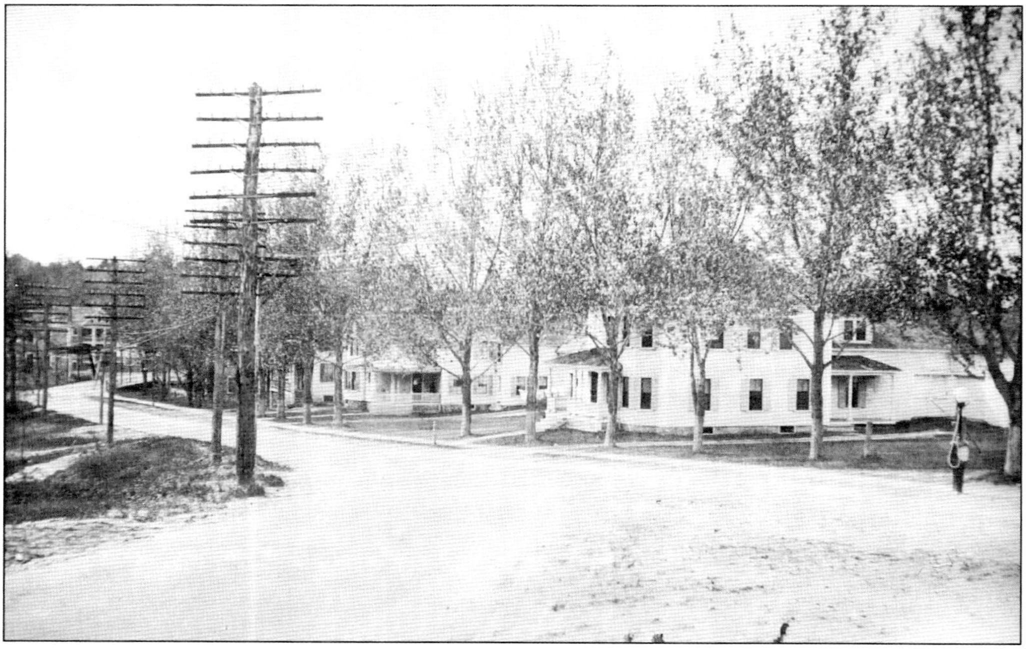

MEMORY LANE. Native Americans roamed the Pennicook Trail here, and stagecoaches traveled here on the road to Concord. It was first named Daniel Webster Highway, and then Route 3. To Merrimack residents it is Main Street.

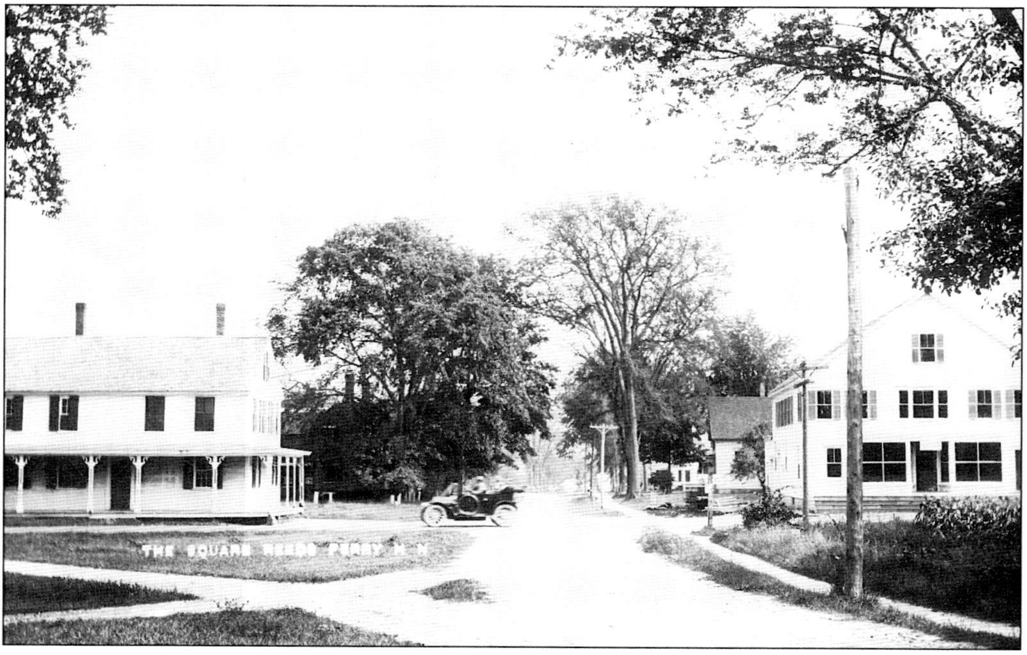